90 0768094 0

*Migration, Minorities and Citizenship*

General Editors: **Zig Layton-Henry**, Professor of Politics, University of Warwick
and **Danièle Joly**, Professor, Director, Centre for Research in Ethnic Relations,
University of Warwick

*Titles include*:

Muhammad Anwar, Patrick Roach and Ranjit Sondhi (*editors*)
FROM LEGISLATION TO INTEGRATION?
Race Relations in Britain

Sophie Body-Gendrot and Marco Martiniello (*editors*)
MINORITIES IN EUROPEAN CITIES
The Dynamics of Social Integration and Social Exclusion at the
Neighbourhood Level

Naomi Carmon (*editor*)
IMMIGRATION AND INTEGRATION IN POST-INDUSTRIAL SOCIETIES
Theoretical Analysis and Policy-Related Research

Malcolm Cross and Robert Moore (*editors*)
GLOBALIZATION AND THE NEW CITY
Migrants, Minorities and Urban Transformations in Comparative Perspective

Adrian Favell
PHILOSOPHIES OF INTEGRATION
Immigration and the Idea of Citizenship in France and Britain

Agata Górny and Paulo Ruspini (*editors*)
MIGRATION IN THE NEW EUROPE
East–West Revisited

James Hampshire
CITIZENSHIP AND BELONGING
Immigration and the Politics of Democratic Governance in Postwar Britain

Simon Holdaway and Anne-Marie Barron
RESIGNERS? THE EXPERIENCE OF BLACK AND ASIAN POLICE OFFICERS

Danièle Joly
GLOBAL CHANGES IN ASYLUM REGIMES (*editor*)
Closing Doors

HAVEN OR HELL?
Asylum Policies and Refugees in Europe

SCAPEGOATS AND SOCIAL ACTORS
The Exclusion and Integration of Minorities in Western and Eastern Europe

Christian Joppke and Ewa Morawska
TOWARD ASSIMILATION AND CITIZENSHIP
Immigrants in Liberal Nation-States

Atsushi Kondo (*editor*)
CITIZENSHIP IN A GLOBAL WORLD
Comparing Citizenship Rights for Aliens

Zig Layton-Henry and Czarina Wilpert (*editors*)
CHALLENGING RACISM IN BRITAIN AND GERMANY

Jørgen S. Nielsen
TOWARDS A EUROPEAN ISLAM

Pontus Odmalm
MIGRATION POLICIES AND POLITICAL PARTICIPATION
Inclusion or Intrusion in Western Europe?

Jan Rath (*editor*)
IMMIGRANT BUSINESSES
The Economic, Political and Social Environment

Peter Ratcliffe (*editor*)
THE POLITICS OF SOCIAL SCIENCE RESEARCH
'Race', Ethnicity and Social Change

Carl-Ulrik Schierup (*editor*)
SCRAMBLE FOR THE BALKANS
Nationalism, Globalism and the Political Economy of Reconstruction

Steven Vertovec and Ceri Peach (*editors*)
ISLAM IN EUROPE
The Politics of Religion and Community

Maarten Vink
LIMITS OF EUROPEAN CITIZENSHIP
European Integration and Domestic Immigration Policies

Östen Wahlbeck
KURDISH DIASPORAS
A Comparative Study of Kurdish Refugee Communities

John Wrench, Andrea Rea and Nouria Ouali (*editors*)
MIGRANTS, ETHNIC MINORITIES AND THE LABOUR MARKET
Integration and Exclusion in Europe

**Migration, Minorities and Citizenship**
**Series Standing Order ISBN 0–333–71047–9**
(*outside North America only*)

You can receive future titles in this series as they are published by placing a standing order. Please contact your bookseller or, in case of difficulty, write to us at the address below with your name and address, the title of the series and the ISBN quoted above.

Customer Services Department, Macmillan Distribution Ltd, Houndmills, Basingstoke, Hampshire RG21 6XS, England

# Migration Policies and Political Participation

## Inclusion or Intrusion in Western Europe?

Pontus Odmalm
*University of Sussex, UK*

First published in 2005 by
PALGRAVE MACMILLAN
Houndmills, Basingstoke, Hampshire RG21 6XS and
175 Fifth Avenue, New York, N.Y. 10010
Companies and representatives throughout the world.

PALGRAVE MACMILLAN is the global academic imprint of the Palgrave Macmillan division of St. Martin's Press, LLC and of Palgrave Macmillan Ltd. Macmillan® is a registered trademark in the United States, United Kingdom and other countries. Palgrave is a registered trademark in the European Union and other countries.

ISBN-13: 978-1-4039-9268-0 hardback
ISBN-10: 1-4039-9268-1     hardback

This book is printed on paper suitable for recycling and made from fully managed and sustained forest sources.

A catalogue record for this book is available from the British Library.

Library of Congress Cataloging-in-Publication Data
Odmalm, Pontus, 1974–
    Migration policies and political participation : inclusion or intrusion in Western Europe? / Pontus Odmalm.
        p. cm.—(Migration, minorities, and citizenship)
    Includes bibliographical references and index.
    ISBN 1-4039-9268-1 (cloth)
        1. Immigrants – Europe, Western – Political activity – Cross-cultural studies. 2. Europe, Western – Emigration and immigration – Government policy – Cross-cultural studies. 3. Citizenship – Europe, Western – Cross-cultural studies. I. Title. II. Series.
JV7590.O36 2005
305.9′06912′094—dc22                                                    2005048471

10  9  8  7  6  5  4  3  2  1
14  13  12  11  10  09  08  07  06  05

Printed and bound in Great Britain by
Antony Rowe Ltd, Chippenham and Eastbourne

# Contents

# List of Tables

# List of Figures

# Acknowledgements

The completion of this book would not have been possible without the help and support from a number of people. First of all, Prof. Russell King and Dr Charles Lees, whom I would like to thank especially for their encouragement, expertise and support as well as for their comments and constructive criticism on the number of drafts they have engaged in over the years. Their unselfish and kind spirit has proved priceless during this work. A special thanks goes to Dr Adrian Favell and Prof. Paul Taggart, who helped and encouraged me during the initial stages. Moreover, special thanks to James Hampshire, Panos Hatziprokopiou, David Lain, Will Leggett, Ivan Manokha, Enric Ruiz-Gelices, Nick Walmsley and Aaron Winter, who alongside my friends, Andreas, Anna, Annika, Didem, Elisabet, Jo, Magnus, Mattias, Mia and Sara made this experience so enjoyable. I would also like to express my gratitude to the researchers and staff at the Institute for Ethnic and Migration Studies at the University of Amsterdam and to Prof. Philip Muus at the School of International Migration and Ethnic Relations at the University of Malmö for their invaluable help during my fieldwork. Special thanks goes to Dr Anja van Heelsum for her very kind assistance and support during my two months in Amsterdam as well as to Dr Floris Vermeulen and Boris Slijper for letting me take part of their research in similar areas. This research also owes a lot to the numerous officials, party and organisation representatives in Malmö and Rotterdam who so generously gave up their time to speak to me during my fieldwork. Finally, my biggest debt of gratitude goes to my parents and my sister for their encouragement, support and belief in this project. It is to them that this book is dedicated.

# 1
# Introduction

This book investigates the opportunities and constraints for migrant groups to participate in the political sphere of the host society. It has two main aims. First, to address the question: what factors influence relative levels of political participation amongst migrant groups? In order to more fully explore this question, the book concentrates on three types of actors: political parties, migrant organisations and individual participants. These actors operate in a given political environment which is formalised by and through the various institutional arrangements set up by the state.[1] The presence of a framework-establishing state sets out the parameters for political action. Second, the book aims to examine what type of opportunities and constraints such arrangements provide by paying closer attention to how specific institutional arrangements give rise to particular political opportunity structures (POS). It will be argued that institutions do matter in that they not only affect actors' options but also that institutions to some extent affect the role of the state, or rather, determine the extent of state involvement.

In order to establish and identify these opportunities and constraints, I will initially focus on the origins of these markers. It will therefore be relevant to bring the concept of the state into the analysis, given that the state is simultaneously the provider, opponent and guarantor of the rights to participate politically in a new environment (Jenkins and Klandermans, 1995). The state will be a key point of reference, or the main contender that influences and sets the parameters for political involvement. In addition, the scope of the analysis will be on two levels. First, at a political-institutional level, where components of the political environment influence the forms of claims-making that take place and how they are made. Second, at a cultural-institutional level which has an impact on the content of the claims. While the former provide settings that make mobilisation easier or more difficult to achieve, the latter provides challengers with cultural resources that enables them to emphasise some claims rather than others (Guigni and Passy, 2004). It will be argued that the way in which a certain political system is organised strongly influences and determines the types of participation and mobilisation that take place, favouring certain types, groups and actors over others.

Having established the appearance, properties and tasks of the state, further attention will be paid to the relationship between a particular state system and policies directed at immigrant groups. It will be argued that migrant policies are independent from the party or parties in power and should rather be viewed as stemming from:

1. prevailing political institutions, norms and attitudes that have been historically established and grounded in a particular type of state system;
2. and as a means by which the host society directly and indirectly sets the boundaries and steers its 'new population' in a certain direction.

Consequently, these features will have an impact on the migrant populations residing within a given nation-state. In terms of policies, migrants differ from the native population in that the state might implement certain measures that are aimed at these groups due to their non-national or immigrant status. The state and its institutions do thus play a crucial role in the process of integrating the new population which can, depending on the attitude of the state, be either extensive or limited. Notions, understandings and perceptions of citizenship and the state's attitudes on majority–minority relations will most likely affect the sense of belonging. Therefore, closer attention will be paid to how these previous settings influence the degree of identification or belonging experienced by the migrant communities and its potential impact on political participation. The much-explored issue of identity and its various ways of construction will be used as a starting point for the discussion on identification. Previous work in the field has tended to ignore the extent to which migrants are able (or not able) to see themselves as legitimate citizens of the new society and, more importantly, the way in which this identification process can be either facilitated or constrained. The concept of identification will be used here as a complement to previous socio-economic interpretations of political integration of migrants.

There are two main reasons for this particular approach. First, literature on POS (Kitschelt, 1986; McAdam, 1996; Tarrow, 1994, 1998; Tilly, 1978) provides useful insight into how these structures influence the choice of strategy adopted by, primarily, social movement actors and the subsequent impact they have on their environment. In Tarrow's (1994) understanding, prevailing POS can serve as incentives for individuals to undertake collective action by affecting their expectations of success or failure. Most scholars of POS have highlighted the important role that institutions play for the development and presence of particular opportunities and constraints. Changes in opportunities come about through shifts in the configuration of institutional power and can be grasped by different types of actors (Lees, 2002). Even though an emphasis is placed on the importance of institutions, the

POS literature has to lesser extent attempted to explain the underpinning factors to why certain institutions are in place and how these give rise to different opportunities or constraints.[2] This book operationalises the POS concept within a historical institutionalist framework and the link between institutions and POS is made more explicit.

Political opportunity structures has also become an increasingly popular concept within the study of migrant political participation (Berger *et al.*, 2002; Ireland, 2000; Koopmans and Statham, 2000). This literature places greater importance on the institutional environment and in particular the role of citizenship and integration policies, but again pays less attention to the context-specific development of these concepts. In contrast, this book discusses the development and rationale behind these developments, which can either constrain or facilitate the political mobilisation of organised migrant interests and determine the role and impact of migrant associations in the political process.

Second, with regard to levels of political participation amongst migrant groups, this book aims to bridge the gap between two types of literature that have previously only had an implicit relationship. Here it will be argued that identification needs to be used as an additional tool since this concept constitutes a 'missing link' between, on the one hand, literature on migration and identity, and on the other, migration and political participation.

The former has been mainly concerned with establishing the nature of identity, the emergence of specific identity types and the importance of recognition by receiving states (Kymlicka, 1995; Mouffe, 1995; Rath *et al.*, 2001; Taylor, 1994). However, the main area of concern is of a normative nature: that is, why states should give recognition to minority identities, and the different ways of achieving this. Less attention has been paid to the interaction and co-existence between different types of sub-collective identities and the relation these have with the host society's overarching national identity. In addition, there seems to be an underlying assumption that different types of identities are mutually exclusive, which this research challenges. In contrast to the more vertical understanding of identity, this research suggests a more horizontal understanding of identity. It will be argued that movement between identities can be either facilitated or constrained according to types of responses and prevailing understandings of inclusion that the receiving state has put in effect.

The vast body of literature concerning migration and political participation deals primarily with socio-economic explanations for relative levels of political participation (Bäck and Soininen, 1993; Bennulf and Hedberg, 1999; Bobo and Gilliam, 1990; Fennema and Tillie, 1999; Olsen, 1970; Petersson *et al.*, 1989; Verba and Nie, 1972) and omits or downplays reference to the potential role of identification. However, given the importance that is placed on identity elsewhere, it seems relevant to test the significance of this variable to enhance our understanding of migrants' involvement in the political process.

The book will exemplify these opportunities and constraints by two types of comparisons. The main emphasis of this book will be on two case-studies: Malmö, Sweden and Rotterdam, the Netherlands given the primary data collected on these two cities. The rationale for adopting a case-study approach is that it will enable several comparative elements to be elucidated. In the first round, two countries that have experienced a large influx of migrants over the past few decades, Sweden and the Netherlands, have been identified as being suitable for this type of comparison. Initially, then, the comparison will focus on the macro-level, examining state appearance. The rationale behind the choice of countries relates to the many similarities found between the two. Not only do Sweden and the Netherlands have a similar type of institutional set-up and political system, but they also exhibit striking similarities in terms of the state's attitude towards its new population. Moreover, both make claims to be 'multicultural societies', and within Europe they are the two countries which have made most progress towards multicultural ideals.

In order to broaden the discussion of what impacts institutions have and how POS affects migrants' political behaviour a second comparative angle involves a five-country study in three areas. First, in Chapter 2, the history of migration, immigration and citizenship policies in France, Germany and Britain will be discussed in addition to the two case-studies. Second, in Chapter 3, the role of institutions as shaping the opportunities and constraints of actors' behaviour will be better understood if contrasted with countries that display difference in terms of their institutional set-up. These settings will also provide different outcomes in terms of how migrants organise along ethnic or national lines within civil society in terms of voluntary organisations and will also point to a different relationship with political parties. Therefore, in Chapter 5, understanding the extent to which migrants organise in formal associations and their potential as channels for claims-making will be as a consequence of the opportunities available from prevailing institutions.

As pointed out above, the main comparative thrust will be on Sweden and the Netherlands with France, Germany and Britain serving as contrasting examples. The reasons for this lie in the empirical restrictions for more systematic comparisons given that the book has been developed after the Dutch and Swedish data had been collected.

However, case-studies have some appealing aspects in that they can provide a richly detailed 'portrait' of a particular social phenomenon (see e.g. Lacey, 1970; McGovern, 1982). Hakim (2000) suggests that case-studies can be a descriptive account of a certain topic, as well as explanatory if little previous research has been done; or they may be illustrative portraits of social entities or patterns thought to be typical, representative or average. This is particularly true with the Swedish and Dutch cases. Both countries have been studied extensively by migration and political science scholars, but few attempts have been made at a more extensive comparative study invoking the migrant–political perspective and relating this to the two countries. Similarly, multi-country comparisons utilising a similar theoretical framework seem to be scarce (although Koopmans *et al.*, 2005 and Soysal, 1994 should be pointed out as exceptions).

Furthermore, the book adopts a city-level approach, focusing on three partially overlapping migrant groups in Malmö and Rotterdam. The focus on the city level has several advantages. Apart from being a local-scale, functional unit, it allows us to more explicitly see the outcomes of both integration and immigration policies in practice. The city level will provide examples of how national-level policies have been implemented further down the steering chain and will also provide the researcher with more focused examples of how multiculturalism works or does not work. In addition, it will act as an example and possibly as a sample of overall trends in the Swedish and Dutch political system in terms of relative participation of migrant communities. This is especially true if one considers the Swedish system with its relatively tight structure of local-regional-national government relationships; but perhaps it is less valid for the Dutch case since local municipalities have less formal ties with the central government and a higher degree of independence. Finally, the city-level comparison will also add to the existing migration/political participation literature in the sense that relatively less attention has been given to this type of comparison and previous research has rather concentrated on cross-national comparisons or single case-studies on a city level.

## Outline of book chapters

In terms of scale, then, the book is divided into two main sections – starting from a national, state-orientated level and then moving down to the local, city level. The first section consists of a historical overview of immigration, immigration policies, status of migrants and citizenship policies followed by a theoretical framework from which these historical developments will be analysed. This encompasses Chapters 2 and 3. These chapters are both descriptive and explanatory in the sense that the theoretical model provides an ideal-type framework to which the cases are compared. This is structured according to a literature review of contemporary theories about the state in which state properties, traits and appearances are examined and evaluated.

First, the main theoretical component brings in writings from the neo-institutionalist school of thought which are applied to the particular institutional arrangements found in Sweden and the Netherlands with the three additional countries used as contrasting examples. By invoking primarily the historical-institutionalist approach, the book argues that the development of certain types of institutions, formal and substantial understandings of citizenship as well as 'rules of the game' create a certain type of political environment with a number of opportunities and constraints for political actors and organised migrant interests.

This premise leads into the second theoretical component which suggests that the prevailing institutions give the political arena a particular appearance. This can be weighted either towards a more pluralist, competitive environment, or towards a more limited – corporatist – arrangement which privileges recognised groups as negotiation partners and thus suggests a bias towards groups based around certain cleavage lines. The findings provide explanatory material as to why we can find variance in the levels of ethnic minority and migrant-based claims between states and why the content of these claims differ.

Chapter 3 then discusses the political systems of the five countries which are outlined and compared to the ideal type. This in turn generates the opportunities and constraints available for actors within this particular system. I analyse these according to the POS approach, operationalised within a historical institutionalist framework (see also Lees, 2002). As suggested by, amongst others, Tarrow (1994) and Kitschelt (1986), POS consists of studying those significant dimensions of the political environment that provide incentives for, primarily, social movements, to undertake collective action by affecting their expectations for success or failure. State structures and institutional configuration set the scope for these opportunities as well as association-providing opportunities to come about when change occurs in these structures. However, seeing that the POS strategy assumes that a certain institutional make-up provides certain sets of openings, it consequently pays less attention to why and how country-specific opportunity structures have come into place. Therefore, the discussion on institutions and their importance serve as background to explain why certain opportunities exist and others are absent in the context of the five countries. In addition, this chapter exemplifies these opportunities by invoking primary data in the form of qualitative interviews conducted with representatives from migrant organisations and political parties in Malmö and Rotterdam.

The second section of the book deals with two issues related to political participation and civic engagement. First, Chapter 4 concentrates on the concept of identity. Here relevant literature will be examined and close attention will be paid to the process of identity construction and its potential relevance as a constraint on political participation. This chapter also embraces a more descriptive section on political participation and on previous explanations for the relatively lower political involvement and turn-out of migrant groups in the two countries. This is followed by a critique and evaluation of these studies in which I argue that they fail to properly incorporate the notion of state system and particular structural settings for the explanation of why many migrants choose not to get involved in political life.

Building on the arguments of the previous two chapters, this chapter posits, first, that identity should not be seen as a movement along a horizontal axis in which competing identities eventually tend to be mutually exclusive, but should rather be perceived as being in a constant state of flux. Second, the construction of identity and its subsequent expression can thus be constrained or facilitated by, predominantly, external settings in the political environment. This argument is complemented both by findings from quantitative data stemming from a questionnaire survey and by more qualitative material. The latter compromises a set of non-elite interviews that were conducted during my fieldwork trips to Malmö and Rotterdam. These interviews are of two types. The first type comprises interviews with respondents who are or have been actively involved in their respective ethnic associations, either on the board or as a representative. The second comprises interviews conducted with members of the association who are not active in the same way as the interviewees in the first category. The aim is here to establish, on the one hand, how the specific association deals with notions of identity within the framework of voluntary organisations and, second, how individual members relate to the host society. This chapter is limited to the Swedish and Dutch case due to the unique nature of the empirical material (described in more detail below).

Second, Chapter 5 exemplifies how prevailing institutional settings affect the role of ethnic associations within a civil society framework in terms of their potential as channels for ethnic claims-making. These suggestions will be illustrated with interview material, both from political party representatives as well as from migrant association representatives from Malmö and Rotterdam but will also involve data from secondary sources relating to France, Germany and Britain.

The sixth and final chapter concludes the book by presenting and summarising the main arguments, and relating the theoretical components to the empirical data. Conclusions from the previous chapters are outlined, compared and reviewed. This chapter also includes an evaluation of how the theoretical and empirical elements have managed to answer the original research questions.

## Data retrieval

### Statistical material

Quantitative material is derived from three sources. Apart from general compilations of migration statistics for the five countries and the two case-study cities of Rotterdam and Malmö, the quantitative part of the research consists of a small-scale questionnaire survey aimed at selected migrant groups: three in each city. The targeted groups where chosen according to two criteria – reason for migrating and geographical origin. Two of the groups are common to both Malmö and Rotterdam (Turks and Iranians), whereas the third (Chileans in Malmö and Surinamese in Rotterdam) are location-specific. However, even the common groups are by no means homogenous: there are a number of differences in terms of regional origin, individual reason for migrating, education, and so forth. The Turkish communities in the Netherlands are by and large labour migrants. They constitute a significant proportion of the Rotterdam population (around 10 per cent) as well as being a major ethnic group in the Netherlands as a whole. The Turkish-speaking community in Malmö is not directly comparable to the Dutch Turks in the sense that they differ in size and are further fractionalised into Turkish-speaking Bulgarian, Macedonian, Turkish and Kurdish groups. In addition, the Turkish community in Malmö is also built up of a mixture of labour migrants and political refugees. The situation for the Iranian community in the two cities is the opposite. The Iranians in Malmö are the sixth largest migrant group and predominantly came for refugee reasons during a ten-year period between 1980 and 1990. However, the Iranians in Rotterdam are a relatively new group, and are consequently smaller and relatively less well established than the Malmö Iranians. The other two groups involved in the study, Chileans and Surinamese, have been chosen according to other criteria. The Chileans are refugees stemming from another global geographical location and having a different length of stay, whilst the Surinamese (as the Turks) constitute an ethnic minority within Dutch society as a consequence of being colonial migrants.

In terms of how migrants figure as part of the total population, Sweden has 1,149,198 (12.7 per cent) persons who are either born abroad or foreign nationals. However, given that naturalisation rates are high and accessible, the number of foreign nationals (if counted separately) comes down to 404,953 (4.4 per cent). Swedish statistics have an additional category for second generation migrants, 'born in Sweden with both parents born abroad', if this group is added then the total number of people of migrant origin goes up to 1,393,248 (15.4 per cent). Naturalisation rates have however gone down since 2000, from 43,474 to 33,222 in 2003 whereas net migration increased slightly in the same period from 24,568 to 28,772 (SCB, 2005). In the Netherlands, persons with a foreign background amounted to 3,112,431 (19.1 per cent) which includes both first and second generation migrants as well as naturalised migrants. Net migration has however dropped dramatically in recent years, from 53,873 in 2000 to a negative –317 in 2003. Naturalisation rates in the Netherlands show a similar decline as in Sweden, from 50,000 in 2000 to 45,300 in 2002 (Migration Information, 2005a).

The three contrasting cases display similar large-scale immigration history but with different ethnic compositions and patterns of migration. France, Germany and Britain all sponsored foreign immigration due to labour shortages from the 1950s up until the mid-1970s when restrictive migration controls were introduced.

France has nevertheless had a positive rate of net migration, rising from 95,000 in 2002 to 105,000 in 2004. In 1999, the total number of immigrants (i.e. foreign born) in relation to the total population was 7.4 per cent or just over 4 million. Naturalisation rates have gone up from the mid-1990s with 109,800 persons acquiring French citizenship in 1996 compared to 150,000 in 2000 (but average around 2 per cent). Its illegal to register the previous nationality of naturalised foreigners or classify them according to ethnic group which makes it difficult to separate statistics on migrants. The 1999 census provides the additional category of 'foreigners by nationality or origin', thus including persons born in France with migrant parents, which gives a perhaps more accurate figure of the population with a migrant heritage. Put together with the group of 'foreign born' (4,310,000 or 7.4 per cent), the total level of migrants rise to 9,930,000 or 17 per cent, on par with Sweden and the Netherlands (Migration Information, 2005b; OECD, 2005). Even though official statistics are not available on specific migrant groups it is still possible to determine the dominant migrant and ethnic groups. Judging by the historical patterns of migration to France one can identify the main migrant groups, as defined by country of birth, to be Portuguese and Algerians (both around 614,207 or 8 per cent) followed by Moroccans, Italians and Spanish but with an increase in migrants from sub-Saharan Africa and South-East Asia (Schnapper *et al.*, 2003).

Germany displays a rise in the level of foreigners until 2003 despite conditions of a negative net migration in recent years; out of a population of around 75 million, just over 7 million (9.7 per cent) were foreign nationals in 2003. The main migrant group, by far, are the Turks (25 per cent) followed by Italians (8 per cent), ex-Yugoslavs (7 per cent), Greeks (5 per cent) and Poles (4 per cent) (Federal Statistical Office Germany, 2005; Koopmans and Statham, 1999). After the change in citizenship legislation in 2000 which made nationality acquisition relatively easier, naturalisation rates went up in 1999 from 120,000 to a 'record' high of 180,000 but has since gone down and are well below the levels found in Sweden and the Netherlands (2–2.5 per cent compared to 6–7 per cent).

Britain has had steady positive net migration rates since the mid-1990s and especially so since 1998 when rates went up from 46,800 to 138,000. Compared to previous years, net migration has been varied with periods of negative rates contrasted with years of relatively high rates. The number of foreign nationals have increased and did in 1999 account for almost 4 per cent of the total population (2,208,000 out of 58,298,000). However, as Koopmans and Statham (1999) point out, this figure underestimates the size of the minority populations since naturalisation legislation is relatively liberal and a large proportion are second and even third generation born in the UK. Therefore, taking into account the number of people identifying themselves as belonging either to 'Mixed'; 'Asian British'; Black British; 'Chinese' or 'Other' rises to 7.8 per cent, a similar figure to Germany (British Census, 2001). Further specifics for each country are discussed in more detail in Chapter 2.

## Questionnaire

The purpose of the four-page questionnaire (see Appendix) is three-fold. First, the aim was to establish the demographic and socio-economic positions of the respective migrant groups in Sweden and in the Netherlands in terms of age, gender, place of birth of respondents and their parents, marital status, education, area of residence, accommodation type and ownership, current and former occupation. Second, an identification scale was constructed. It is important to stress that this term is not used as an equivalent to the concept of integration. Elsewhere, the latter has been adopted for its suitability in that it encompasses a variety of similar, more precise, partial or politically unfashionable terms such as incorporation, absorption, accommodation, toleration or inclusion[3] (Grillo, 1998).

Given that this book aims to explore varying levels of political participation, the purpose of introducing the identification term is to test or apply its relevance for providing a more extensive explanation as to why or why not certain migrant groups choose to participate politically.

This part of the questionnaire consists of questions that attempt to measure this degree of identification with the host society. The identification scale has been divided into two sections – internal and external identification. The respondents were asked to grade a series of seven statements according to their preferences. The four questions dealing with internal identification aimed at establishing a sense of how attached the respondents perceived themselves to be with the host society, options ranging from 'agree strongly' to 'disagree strongly'. The second component of the identification scale concerned external identification. Here, the aim was to establish a sense of how the respondents believed members of the majority population perceived the respondents. Naturally, there is a problem involved with defining who is part of the 'majority population' and who is not. In official Swedish and Dutch statistics, a number of definitions are used – for example, 'foreign nationals', 'persons with a foreign background' or simply 'immigrants'. Depending on which definition one chooses, the number, composition and target groups expand or contract. In the Dutch case this is particularly confusing since there are a number of migrants from former Dutch colonies who up until independence (and in some cases for a probation period afterwards) were Dutch citizens (and born on Dutch territory) and were thus entitled to travel freely within the Kingdom. The most common definition applied within Swedish and Dutch statistics defines the population with a foreign heritage as born abroad or having at least one parent (the Netherlands) or both parents (Sweden) born abroad.[4] If these factors are taken into account, the definition of 'the majority population' is given as referring to 'those individuals who are not affected by immigration and integration policies and do not face socio-economic difficulties depending on language, cultural and social heritage, religious belonging or physical attributes'. In everyday language, they would be labelled 'ethnic Swedes/ white Dutch'.

The answers to the seven statements were given a score between 1 and 5, which gives an identification index ranging from 7 (lowest level of identification) to 35 (highest level of identification).

The line of thought is – the higher the score of internal and external identification, that is, the more the respondents feels (1) strongly attached to the new community and (2) believes that the majority population perceives the respondents to be a legitimate member of the new society, the more likely he or she will be able to take part in various forms of political participation.

Third, the questionnaire posed a series of more encompassing questions regarding the degree and types of political participation. These included questions relating to the satisfaction that the surveyed groups had with the performance of their local municipality in terms of policies that are directly aimed at them as a minority or migrant group (Fennema and Tillie, 1999). In addition to the traditional questions of voting levels and voting preference, the purpose was to map out how the migrant respondents made use of a variety of channels in order to obtain information on local and national issues. It was therefore of importance to pose questions relating to interest in local and national politics, and to what extent, and what type of, organised, political activities the respondents took part in. Previous surveys done in Sweden and the Netherlands have tended to focus primarily on voting levels and party preference and to ignore, as far as the author is aware of, the concept of identification in relation to these concepts.

It should be highlighted that the reader should view these figures cautiously since the questionnaire material did not generate sufficient returns in order to be fully representative and statistically reliable, therefore they should be viewed as indicative rather than conclusive pointing to a possible relationship between the two concepts. Consequently, the research will use these findings to initially map out a sense of the level of identification and also to cross-check voting levels with national surveys. Previous studies have pointed out a general declining trend in the levels of political participation but fail, in a sense, to address the definition problems prevailing in that naturalised migrants, especially in Sweden, fall out of the category of 'non-national voting rates'. The figures available show a remarkable downward trend especially in local voting levels – available for all legally resident non-nationals after three years (Sweden) and five years of residence (the Netherlands) – but do not take into account the individuals who would belong to the particular group due to national origin. Therefore, my questionnaire survey does not distinguish between the naturalised and the non-naturalised migrants belonging to each group. The questionnaire distribution and return ratios are summarised in Table 1.1.

*Table 1.1*   Questionnaire distribution and return rate

|  | Malmö | | | Rotterdam | | |
| --- | --- | --- | --- | --- | --- | --- |
|  | Distributed | Returned | % | Distributed | Returned | % |
| Iranians | 150 | 65 | 43 | 80 | 32 | 40 |
| Turks | 50 | 15 | 30 | 81 | 39 | 48 |
| Chileans | 150 | 39 | 26 | NA | NA | NA |
| Surinamese | NA | NA | NA | 115 | 46 | 40 |

## Interviews

In addition to the quantitative data, a considerable amount of qualitative research was undertaken. For linguistic reasons, more in-depth interviews were conducted in Sweden – a total of 52 – compared to 34 in the Dutch case. The interviews were set up according to a semi-structured technique with identical thematic questions prepared for each group.

The first category of respondents were elite in character, that is, individuals or groups of individuals with the ability to exercise some sort of power or influence over decision-making. In the Swedish case, at least two representatives were interviewed from each of the major parties. One party was left out of the interview process, the Agrarian Party (Centerpartiet), since they failed to gain any seats in the local municipality since 1998. The number of interviews with each party, and their ethnic and gender distribution, are set out in Table 1.2. In addition, I interviewed a selection of representatives from trade unions and civil servants working with migrant issues and/or organisations.

In the Dutch case, representatives from all the major parties[5] were contacted. Since the Dutch political system displays a much larger number of political parties, the main effort was geared towards the six largest parties in order to get a similar party spread as in Malmö. The number of interviewees was less compared to the Swedish case as well as displaying an overrepresentation of male politicians (13 male and 3 female). The choice of interviewees in Rotterdam was furthermore dependent on the interviewees' ability to communicate in English. In combination with a higher frequency of male councillors and the dominance of white Dutch in the city council, this provides the setting for the gender and ethnicity division (see Table 1.3).

In six cases (Green Party, Groen Links, Christian Democrats, CDA, D66 and VVD) the party leader was interviewed. The remaining respondents were as follows:

1. Respondents, either ethnic Swedes or ethnic Dutch, whose main political interest lay in immigration-related topics or who worked specifically with

*Table 1.2* Gender and ethnicity distribution of political party interviewees: Malmö

| Party | Male | Female | Ethnic councillor |
|---|---|---|---|
| Conservatives | 2 | 2 | 1 Male |
| Christian Democrats | 2 | 0 | 2 Male |
| Liberals | 1 | 1 | 1 Male, 1 Female |
| Socialdemocrats | 3 | 2 | 1 Male, 2 Female |
| Green Party | 3 | 1 | 2 Male |
| Left Party | 1 | 3 | 1 Male, 1 Female |
| Total | 12 | 9 | 8 Male, 4 Female |

*Table 1.3* Gender and ethnicity distribution of political party interviewees: Rotterdam

| Party | Male | Female | Ethnic councilor |
|---|---|---|---|
| VVD | 2 | 0 | N/A |
| CDA | 2 | 0 | N/A |
| D66 | 2 | 1 | 1 Male, 1 Female |
| PvdA | 4 | 1 | 2 Male |
| Groen Links | 1 | 1 | 1 Male |
| SP | 2 | 0 | N/A |
| Total | 13 | 3 | 4 Male, 1 Female |

those issues (Malmö: Conservatives, Socialdemocrats, Left Party, Green Party; Rotterdam: Groen Links, PvdA, VVD, SP, CDA)
2. Respondents who had a foreign heritage

A set of questions or themes was prepared beforehand which were identical for all respondents in the respective category, and structured around the following four themes:

1. How do the parties differ from each other in terms of their understanding of the term integration and the current immigration policy?
2. In what way has the party tried to target the migrant population?
3. To what extent are ethnic-specific claims possible to make within the party structure and/or within the overall political structure?
4. Why are immigrants less likely to participate politically?

The second category of interviewees consisted of active members in the different ethnic associations.

In Malmö, the on-line association register lists ten Iranian, three Chilean and seven Turkish-speaking associations.[6] There are however a number of Latin- and South American associations with several Chilean members along with a substantial number of Kurdish associations which could also include Turkish-speaking members. The research did try to limit the sample to the predominantly mono-ethnic associations but in the case of the Chilean and Turkish groups contacts had to be made with multicultural associations. The situation in Rotterdam is quite the opposite. According to a database made by researchers from the Institute for Migration and Ethnic Studies at the University of Amsterdam, the total number of Surinamese and Turkish associations amount to 135 and 80 respectively. However, only two Iranian associations existed and these dealt primarily with intermediary work between the Iranian refugees and the local authorities.

Judging by the names of the Rotterdam associations, 10 per cent of the Turkish ones were foundations and 10 per cent were explicitly religious, whereas those remaining were secular, voluntary organisations. This compared to almost 50 per cent of the Surinamese associations which had a foundation status. An association with a foundation tag has a different status compared to non-foundation organisations in that they serve as an umbrella organisation for a number of individual associations as well as having a certain degree of influence when it comes to ethnic minority policy-making. In Table 1.4, I set out a list of the associations dealt with in the two cities.

A total of 16 interviews were conducted in Malmö with predominantly male representatives (15 male; 1 female): six Iranian, four Chilean and six Turkish speaking. This compared to nine in Rotterdam (7 male; 2 female): two Iranian, three Surinamese and four Turkish (see Table 1.5). The over-representation of males in the interviews is both interesting and problematic for the research.[7] The problem is related to representativity and to some degree also to validity. The answers obtained were exclusively those stemming from a male perspective and would most likely differ if a similar quota of females were interviewed. Attempts were repeatedly made by the researcher to contact female representatives, but these approaches were turned down by the subjects. In the Turkish cases, the researcher was told that women do not frequent the associations, apart from attending certain organised social events.

The interview settings were identical to those conducted with the elite interviewees where pre-arranged themes had been formulated in advance although the interview as such was conducted in a semi-structured way. The following themes were covered:

1. What is the main purpose of the association?
2. What type of relationship exists between the association and (a) other associations with the same ethnic background, (b) with other ethnic associations, (c) local authorities and (d) local parties?

*Table 1.4*   Migrant associations covered in the qualitative survey

*Malmö*
  Iranian associations
    Iranska Kulturföreningen (The Iranian Culture Association)
    Iranska Solidaritetsföreningen (The Iranian Solidarity Association)
    Centrum för Demokratifrämjande i Iran (Centre for Democracy in Iran)
    Iransk-Svenska Föreningen (The Iranian-Swedish Association)
  Chilean Associations
    Victor-Jara föreningen (The Victor-Jara Association)
    Föreningen Inter-America (The Inter-America Association)
  Turkish Associations
    Turkiska Föreningen (The Turkish Association)
    Ataturk Sport och Kultur Förening (Ataturks Sport and Culture Association)
    Turk Anadolu FF (Turkish Football Association)
*Rotterdam*
  Iranian associations
    Iranian Refugee Council
  Turkish associations
    SAHNE (Turkish Arts Association)
    HADD (Turkish Culture Association)
    MOSAIC (Turkish Student Association)
  Surinamese Associations
    Wimasanga 1st July (Creole, Culture Association)
    Prabhakar-Arya Samaadj (Hindustani, Culture/Religious Association)
    Stichting Krosbe (Hindustani Advisory Organisation)

*Table 1.5*   Gender division of association representatives

| Malmö | | | Rotterdam | | |
|---|---|---|---|---|---|
| | **Male** | **Female** | | **Male** | **Female** |
| Iranians | 5 | 1 | Iranians | 1 | 1 |
| Chileans | 4 | 0 | Surinamese | 3 | 0 |
| Turkish | 6 | 0 | Turkish | 3 | 1 |
| *Total* | 15 | 1 | | 7 | 2 |

3. Has the association tried to campaign for issues concerning their own ethnic group?
4. What are the main types of problem that face these associations?
5. What type of reaction has the association received from the majority population?

The third category of interviewees consisted of members of associations. The question settings and pre-interview information for the association members were identical to the elites and association representatives and the number of association member interviews amounted to a total of fourteen with the

*Table 1.6*   Gender division among association members interviewed

| Malmö | | | Rotterdam | | |
| --- | --- | --- | --- | --- | --- |
| | Male | Female | | Male | Female |
| Iranians | 4 | 3 | Iranians | 1 | 3 |
| Chileans | 2 | 1 | Surinamese | 0 | 0 |
| Turkish | 0 | 0 | Turkish | 0 | 0 |
| *Total* | 6 | 4 | | 1 | 3 |

ethnic and gender division shown in Table 1.6. The relative or absolute absence of Chilean, Surinamese and Turkish respondents, especially in the female category, gives more weight in the research to elite and association representatives than was initially intended. On balance, I do feel that the range of interviewees covered a fairly representative section of the studied groups, but I cannot, of course, claim true representativity on the basis of a small sample. The findings from these particular interviews must be viewed with due caution – but are worth including in the overall analysis.

## Conclusion

This chapter has presented the key research questions for this book and outlined the chapter sequencing. Furthermore, this chapter has covered the research methodology, addressed the quantitative and qualitative data collected in Malmö and Rotterdam as well as discussed some of the research problems related to this data. In addition, the main theoretical component has been introduced – the historical institutionalist approach – which serves as a heuristic framework to explain levels of identification in relation to political participation. This approach also facilitates our understanding of the space available for ethnic organisations to act both as partners in the political process and their opportunities to put forward claims relating to their particular ethnic or national group. The presence of various kinds of formal – as well as informal – institutions provides the socio-political sphere with a set of POS which can either facilitate or hinder certain types of actions and/or claims. This approach constitutes the original part of the research, given that my work aims to link neo-institutional theory with the presence of societal-specific opportunity structures which in turn will affect levels of political participation. Furthermore, the choice of case-studies and the way in which the comparative angle is utilised will offer new insights into both the effects of country-specific institutional make-up on the receiving societies' new population and provide an evaluation of the adopted integration policies. Hence, the set of hypotheses I seek to examine in this book can be summarised as:

1. Formal institutions (political system, societal regulations) determine the appearance of the POS available.

2. Over time, institutions develop routines and certain *modus operandi* which influence actors' behaviour and create opportunities and constraints.
3. Receiving societies' policy (in terms of integration and citizenship) and choice of incorporation, influences the level of identification that migrants have with the host society.
4. Higher levels of identification will yield higher levels of political participation (as opposed to higher levels of social, political and economical integration).

# 2
# Historical Overview: Patterns of Immigration, Immigration and Citizenship Policies

## Introduction

This chapter provides a historical overview of France, Germany, the Netherlands, Sweden and Britain. It is structured around three themes in order to provide a consistent country by country overview of the development within these areas. First, the chapter discusses migrant composition, types of migration and describes the main migrant groups residing in the five countries. Here, it is made clear that different migration histories have prompted different types of responses to large-scale migration in the postwar era. Second, the chapter covers developments in immigration and integration policy and how these have affected the status of migrants. Third, the chapter discusses developments and changes with regard to formal citizenship criteria. Despite having a number of differences among the five countries, they all share a similar feature: immigration and citizenship appear to be working in tandem. That is, restrictive measures introduced in one area (e.g. making immigration more difficult for non-EU nationals) is reflected in similar changes in the other (e.g. more exclusive citizenship legislation and notions of belonging) and vice versa. All five cases display similar developments even though they have different interpretations of citizenship, principles for naturalisation and different patterns of immigration.

## France

### Composition of immigrant population

France has had a lengthy history of immigration. Becoming a reality in the 1850s, France experienced several waves of immigration up until the First World War. In 1851, the first official census states that the number of foreigners residing on French territory amounted to around 300,000. Fifty years later, the figure was almost one million. During this period, migration to France was primarily intra-European stemming from Italy, Spain, Portugal, Belgium and Poland by those who were attracted to France by the ample employment opportunities in manufacturing, construction and agriculture. This process continued and to some extent also increased, making France one of the few countries of immigration in the mid-nineteenth century due to a period of economic expansion and industrial growth. In contrast to other Western European countries, France had an early start in terms of recruiting foreigners for labour purposes. In 1916 active recruitment began in the colonies, especially from the Maghreb and Asian territories (Withol de Wenden, 1994). This particular approach, by and large, remained unchanged until the 1980s. Castles and Miller (2003) point out that France was one of the few Western European countries to experience inter-war migration due to the demographic deficit. Government and employers began refining the labour recruitment system already in place and agreements were set up between Poland, Italy and Czechoslovakia. The recruitment was largely handled by the Société générale d'immigration (SGI), a private body set up by farm and mining interests. Foreign labour were monitored and controlled through a system of identity cards and work contracts and then channelled into sectors where work was needed. From 1920 to 1930 around two million workers entered France and by 1931, 6.6 per cent of the population were foreigners. Following the depression of the 1930s, xenophobic sentiments gave way to a more restrictive immigration policy (compared to the previous attitude of laissez-faire), which linked residence to employment and introduced a hierarchy of residency permits. During the post-war period, France began to recruit labour migrants more heavily, initially from the European periphery and later from the former or existing colonies. In 1945 the National Office for Immigration (ONI) was set up in order to solve the problem of post-war labour shortages and demographic deficits. Even though the ONI was heavily involved in co-ordinating the inflow of migrant workers, many did in fact enter illegally and then attempted to regularise their position. However, in contrast to the United Kingdom, France was not concerned with trying to make it more difficult for colonial subjects to enter France and subsequently colonial migration was large and spontaneous. By 1970, there were over 600,000 Algerians; 140,000 Moroccans and 90,000 Tunisians in addition to a substantial amount of migrants from the French West African colonies of Senegal, Mali and Mauritania who came as French citizens pre-independence. The dominance of Algerians was a consequence of the bilateral agreements which regulated Algerian immigration and thus put these migrants in a special status as opposed to the Moroccan and Tunisian migrants who were admitted through the ONI. In addition, a large number of migrants stemming from French overseas territories such as Guadeloupe, Martinique and Réunion arrived at the same time. Since these migrants were French citizens they had the right to travel freely and thus few accurate statistics exist regarding their numbers but an early 1970s estimate puts their number at around 300,000 (Castles and Miller, 2003). During the period 1945–74, the public authorities operated according to a policy aimed at selecting migrants and their families with the aim of permanent settlement and possible naturalisation. The pattern of recruitment of labour migrants followed that of many other recruiting countries during this period, starting with Southern Europeans (Italians and Spanish in the 1950s, Portuguese in the 1960s), followed by the Balkans (Yugoslavs in the 1960s and 1970s) and then from North Africa in the 1970s (Morocco and Tunisia). Despite immigration being under the co-ordination of the ONI, migration to France was by and large occurring independently of the public authorities and managed primarily by the recruiting companies. In 1968, the ONI recruited only 18 per cent of all entries whereas the remaining 82 per cent entered illegally and where eventually legalised (Withol de Wenden, 1994).

As in other countries at the same time, France halted the entry of labour migration in the wake of the oil crisis and subsequently the nature of immigration changed. Efforts were made to reduce the numbers of family reunifications but by 1978 the Council of State had overturned the suspension of family migration since it went against the constitutional right to family life. Furthermore, the suspension did not apply to EU nationals who could enter freely; asylum seekers (who were covered by different laws) and skilled migrants who could still access the French labour market. The previous law can thus be said to have had specific migrants in mind and especially non-European migrants who were considered to be difficult to assimilate into the French republican model of citizenship; a similar feature shared with the British restrictive changes to citizenship in the same era (Schain, 1999). However, the suspension had a number of 'unintended' consequences for France in that it encouraged long-term settlement and an increase of women migrants while also substantially changing the demographic make-up when more younger and older people joined their relatives. Since the 1980s, the main sources of migrants stem from areas with a colonial link to France (South-East Asia and French speaking parts of Africa). Immigration originating from the main source countries (Spain, Portugal, Algeria and Morocco) also show a dominance of women and children. European migrants are still the main group, accounting for about 40 per cent of the average foreign population with Algerians and Moroccans in second and third place. French statistics are, however, somewhat misleading in that they tend to omit foreign born people who eventually naturalise when they produce figures on foreigners. In addition, the economic effects meant an overall reduction in labour market participation and an increased engagement with the French welfare state, particularly with regard to education and housing. The nature of the labour market was also affected in that more migrants were unemployed and more migrants participated in the service sector and small business employment (Geddes, 2003).

A failed policy of repatriation was introduced in 1977 but, as in Germany, only the migrants who were already planning to return took on this offer.

Immigration as such did also not appear to diminish despite lack of job opportunities and reached a peak in 1982 but dropped dramatically during the rest of the 1980s. A new feature for France was the shift towards refugee migration in the late-1980s and 1990s (with entry levels between 18,800 to 50,000 in the mid-1990s) but has since then decreased due to both changes in statistical calculations and a political shift aiming at reducing the number of asylum seekers. Thus, in 1999 France had 3.3 million foreign residents in addition to the approximately one million immigrants who had naturalised.

## Immigration policy and status of migrants

Since the post-war period, the ordinance of 2 November 1945 has regulated the entry of foreigners and their residence in France. Even though modified on a number of occasions and supplemented by bi-lateral agreements, this text is key to all legislation governing the status of aliens in France. Prior to that it is difficult to talk about any specific regulations concerning aliens apart from the sovereign state's right to deport non-nationals (although a law dating back to 1893 covers aliens' residency and as such constitutes an early form of immigration control). A number of additional early measures were introduced in order to regulate, primarily, foreign labour. A law from August 1926 proposed further regulation of migrant labourers in that the word 'worker' had to be printed on their identity card and they were also not allowed to take up employment outside of approved economic sectors (Barats-Malbrel, 1999). Immigration prior to 1945 was driven by three types of ideas: political values (granting asylum to political refugees and guaranteeing residence to foreigners); remedies to demographic shortages (favouring the immigration of families deemed as 'naturalisable') and, finally, economic concerns (the need for an able workforce, primarily single males). The 1945 ordinance thus reflected these ideas and outlined different types of administrative status that applied to resident aliens. Three types of residency permits were established: temporary residents (e.g. students, seasonal workers); ordinary residents (valid for three years and renewable, e.g. labour) and privileged residents (valid for ten years and renewable). The latter two were in a more favourable position compared to the temporary residents in that only they were allowed to apply for work permits from the Ministry of Labour.

French immigration policy at the time can thus be said to be primarily driven by fulfilling economic objectives based on a cost/benefit analysis with less emphasis on guaranteeing rights and enforcing administrative procedures. As a result, France adopted a comparatively relaxed approach to clandestine migration with the possibility of becoming regularised after a period of time. Immigration declined somewhat in the mid-1970s but restrictive policies were, as Barats-Malbrel (1999) points out symbolic and the working and residency permits that were issued were still dependent on economic parameters.

The 1980s were characterised by a number of changes in French immigration policy and it is during this decade that one can see the discourse on immigration changing. Whereas migrants had previously not been considered a problem, the effects of long-term settlement and the growing up of second and third generation migrants where now perceived as a 'threat' to the nation (Wieviorka, 1992). The relation between immigration, nationality and citizenship was now at the forefront. Following the 1981 election, the Socialist government emphasised the importance of social integration in an effort to come to terms with illegal immigration. The new policy extended the rights of foreigners and initiated a generous amnesty for undocumented migrants; expansion of the rights for migrants' associations and suppressed the expulsion act (the so-called Bonnet law). In addition, France became more prone to deal effectively with further illegal migration. By the mid-1980s, the Conservative Chirac government took a U-turn regarding the status of immigrants and a regulation from 1986 (the loi Pasqua) made entry of non-EU foreigners more difficult and their expulsion easier. Practically, this meant that additional entry requirements were introduced such as providing proof of financial subsistence during the stay in France (Bouchard and Chandler, 2005). Limits were also imposed on the categories of aliens readily able to obtain resident cards such as spouses of French nationals who now had to wait a year before applying as well as provide proof of his/her marital living arrangement. The law seemed to aim specifically at non-EU migrants which went in line with Pasqua's discourse of 'zero immigration'.

This law was later revoked when the Socialist government returned to power in 1988 and introduced an immigration policy with three main aims: labour market regulation; restrictions on undocumented migrants and integration of settled migrants. In 1989, tougher immigration controls were introduced although these were counterbalanced by extended anti-discrimination legislation with severe sanctions but with a high burden of proof level. While the British race relations act took inspiration from civil rights and anti-discrimination acts from the United States, the main reference point for France, as Geddes (2003) notes, was the racist Vichy regime. As a means to counter the increasing popularity of the Front National, the Right's victory in the legislative elections in 1993 prompted further tightening of immigration controls and amending the rights of foreigners. Family reunification was extended to two years for students and foreign workers and welfare benefits for illegal migrants were denied. In addition, regularisation of undocumented migrants who married French citizens was suspended; increased powers were given to mayors to annul suspected marriages of convenience and re-entry of expellees was prohibited for a year after deportation. The evolution of French immigration policy can again be said to focus almost exclusively on non-EU migrants. This suspicion of non-EU nationals as being 'welfare spongers' has led to a significant growth of laws based on the postulate of fraud. This postulate allowed for systematic controls of foreigners as well as lengthy and complex administrative procedures designed to weaken the status of aliens in France. These tougher laws led to a substantial reduction of non-EU nationals, especially with regard to family reunification with levels decreasing from 35,000 in 1990 to around 21,000 in 1994 as well as in terms of asylum applications (e.g. 26,000 applications were filed in 1994 and 7025 were granted compared to 19,000 applications and 2825 granted in 1995) (Barats-Malbrel, 1999). The status for third country nationals in France has thus developed into a precarious one since application procedures are complex and resident cards increasingly harder to obtain leading to a clandestine situation.

Efforts to restrict immigration continued with the proposition of the Debré law in 1997 which specifically targeted the so-called *sans papiers* migrants who had been in France for several years and because of stricter laws had not been able to regularise. The new law specified that to renew a residence permit individuals had to prove that they were not a threat to public order; that children under the age of 16 would need to prove ten years of residence before they could become naturalised and that French citizens should notify the authorities if they received a non-EU national as a guest. With a list exempting nationals from around 30 countries, the law specifically targeted 'unwanted' immigrants from African countries. Due to its controversial nature, the proposed law was met with strong opposition and the final version was left with the obligation of non-EU foreigners to report their movements. The problems with passing the original proposal relates to what Hollifield (2000) describes as the nation-state's dilemma of not being able to legitimise internal controls on the population since it infringes on civil liberties. With the Socialists back in power in 1997, Prime Minister Jospin resurrected earlier republican values in order to reform immigration and nationality laws. The republican model would strive to welcome legal immigrants and respect their rights while simultaneously clamp down on illegal migration and informal employment. The end result were two new bills presented for the national assembly in late 1997, the so-called Guigou law (on nationality) and the Chevénement law (on immigration). The latter's full name became the Act of Entry and Residence of Foreigners and the Right to Seek Asylum (RESEDA) and was passed on 11 May 1998 and aimed to simplify immigration in four areas: entry procedures; expanding and individualising the right to residency status; better guarantees to exercise the right to asylum and controlling entry of foreigners more effectively (i.e. illegal migrants) (Samers, 2003; Official Website of the Office of the French Prime Minister and Government, 2005).

In contrast to the United Kingdom and the Netherlands, France does not recognise migrants as being distinct ethnic groups but instead favours an approach which aims at transforming them into citizens without consideration for their national or ethnic origin (Schnapper *et al.*, 2003). This approach is reflected in the French way of incorporating migrants which is characterised by an individual and centralised approach. Similarly to

Sweden and the Netherlands, the French state is actively involved and bears more responsibility towards migrants in terms of welfare provisions given that these are already centralised and organised by the state. The historical relationship between the state and its citizens are key components for the understanding of migrant incorporation in France and as such, the main concern for French authorities is citizenship and 'creating' new French citizens. Hence, the concept of integration suggests that individual migrants should access the regular institutions and services since ethnic-specific provisions run a possibility of clashing with the overarching goal of equality as in Sweden. Consequently, ethnic and religious minorities are not officially or legally recognised categories. The individual nature of migrants in France shows the secular and republican understanding of French membership and clearly distinguishes it from the corporatist nature of Sweden and the Netherlands. Instead France displays similarities with the United Kingdom in terms of having the market and educational system as the main instruments for integration but without direct state intervention (Soysal, 1994). The religiously, regionally and ethnically neutral educational system is particularly interesting and has also been the subject of much integration debate (see e.g. Moloktos Liederman, 2000; Wieviorka, 2000). Although mother tongue classes are allowed, these are usually sponsored by the governments of the sending country and taught by foreigners with French certificates.

Migrant organisations have traditionally been a dilemma for the French government since voluntary associations have been organised within a system that promotes more general types of associations aimed at both migrants and non-migrants in combination with restrictive regulation policies on the founding of explicit ethnic organisations. However, since 1981 these regulations have become more relaxed and an increasing number of migrants organisations have been set up and are also becoming increasingly more acknowledged as representatives of migrants' interests.

Despite the emphasis on the individual, France nevertheless displays certain policy instruments that deal with migrant integration. These instruments are however geared towards providing the newcomers with the necessary skills to gain access to these institutions rather than the collective organisation of migrants. The well-established Social Action Fund for Immigrant Workers and their Families (FAS) provides assistance for migrants in the areas of housing, education, training as well as social and cultural activities. The main aim is to expose migrants to the French way of life and FAS increasingly supports initiatives stemming from migrants themselves such as cultural preservation which seemingly contradicts traditional French views on citizenship but also signals the new emphasis in policy stemming from the mid-1980s. However, as Soysal (1994) notes, this evolvement towards multiculturalism still remains within a republican framework that emphasises individual membership.

## Citizenship policy

Integration and citizenship are closely connected terms in the French context. Becoming formally French means that immigrants acquire the same rights as any other French citizen. In contrast to other European countries, France lacks an explicit integration policy due to the particular republican model of citizenship which has been in place since the third republic (1871). This model forbids any differentiation between French nationals regardless of their origin and can help to explain why measures aimed at improving the situation for immigrants are part of the general welfare provisions with a majority of the budget spent on revitalising urban and suburban neighbourhoods, combating crime, reducing employment and improving the quality of education (Dommernik, 1998). Thus the best way to achieve integration is by not having a policy of integration and instead simply consider everyone as French or potential French citizens. Furthermore, the model favours mixing of people and internalising French values in order to create a harmonious society.

However, Schnapper *et al.* (2003) notes that even if no integration policy exists for adult migrants, France has always been concerned with the successful integration of migrants' children. Therefore, great importance is placed on the educational system which is supposed to teach pupils the French language and the rights and duties of citizenship. Since schools are secular and free of charge, this institution, it is believed, is the best arena to ensure equal opportunities and produce a cohesive French nation regardless of social, religious or ethnic background.

The foundations of the French understanding of nationhood and belonging is constituted by political unity and is centrally expressed in the striving for cultural unity (Brubaker, 1992; Favell, 1998). Political inclusion within the French nation-state has thus come to require socio-cultural assimilation of both indigenous groups as well as migrants. This particular republican model of national integration with a strong assimilatory emphasis rests on ideas tracing back to the French revolution and as Geddes (2003) summarises, on four main points: universalism (as guaranteed by the Rights of Man of 1789); unitarism (the indivisible republic); secularism (separation of church and state) and a norm of assimilation to become 'French' through French institutions. In other words, everyone can and should become French but at the price of giving up ones cultural baggage.

Converting foreigners into Frenchmen became a political issue during the era of nation-state building in the late nineteenth century. In 1889, the nationality law automatically gave French citizenship to all children born to foreign parents in France without any act of affirmation such as swearing allegiance. The law was passed during a period when France had a large presence of resident foreigners in contrast to, say, Germany. Even though naturalisation was granted for children of migrants, there was nevertheless a distinction between foreigners and nationals. The main principle of citizenship acquisition was through descent from a French father (or in the case of an illegitimate child, a French mother). Simultaneously, however, this was reinforced by a principle of birth. Stolcke (1999) interprets this as a liberal, inclusive solution or compromise struck for military and ideological purposes in the context of increased tension with Germany. At this time France also adopted a separatist stance towards its colonies since the 1889 code did not apply to the inhabitants of French colonies and remained so until after the Second World War. The legislation was relaxed in terms of first generation migrants to naturalise in 1927 and in 1945 the implicit law of naturalisation through birth and residence was reaffirmed resulting in an inclusive system of combining birth and descent. As Weil (1996) points out, acquisition of French citizenship is thus almost automatic for a child born in France by foreign parents but the acceptance of French nationality only becomes binding once the child has declared a voluntary desire to become French at some point between the ages of 16 and 21. For persons without any birth ties to France, a formal connection must be created through either marriage or residency. This form of naturalisation, Weil continues, provides the French state with two sets of checks. The first being a posteriori and weaker, that is, a request is made by the applicant for French nationality by declaring a wish to become French which constitutes, for those who meet the criteria laid out in the law, a right. In other words, all that is needed here is a formally expressed desire to become a French national. The second check, being slightly more powerful and a priori, involves a naturalisation request (which is usually met but with a waiting period of around 18 months) and relatively strict naturalisation criteria (such as a minimum period of five years of residency, knowledge of the French language, stable financial position and having one's current place of residence in France). Although some of these criteria are fairly common (e.g. residency) the others appear to be a part of an overall European trend of imposing some form of citizenship test (e.g. language and regular income) in order for the state to distinguish who the 'proper' citizens are.

The French conceptualisation of citizenship consists of two unique components; socialisation and passive citizenship through the *jus soli* principle. But instead of a contract-based (as in the United States) or an ethnic origin-based citizenship, the French understanding of nationality indicates acquisition of certain codes of sociability through an expression of one's will, one's origin or birthplace. This, as Weil suggests, poses problems for individual national identity in the sense that it is difficult to place this upon, for example, ancestry. Instead, the republican ideals and values are the common factors – you are French because you adhere to republican values. Hence, there is no differentiation between identity, citizenship, nationality or between local and national citizenship. In other words, French citizenship and belonging is expressed in such a way that it permits incorporation of all foreigners who can subject themselves to these values but is simultaneously emphasising cultural assimilation in order for this to work.

# Germany

## Composition of immigrant population

Similar to Sweden, Germany was for a long time a country of emigration with the main shift towards net immigration only becoming a factor in the post-war era. Of the almost 50 million immigrants who arrived in the United States between 1820 and 1960 about 7 million were from Germany. Once the German economy shifted its emphasis from agriculture to industry in the late nineteenth century, internal migration became more important than its transatlantic counterpart. Most of the migration at this time was from east to west, from East Prussia to the central German cities of Berlin, Leipzig and Dresden, with the eastern settlers being replaced by Polish migrants. The number of foreigners in Germany during this period was quite significant. The population census of 1900 recorded almost 800,000 resident aliens whereas in 1910 the figure had grown to 1.3 million making them 2 per cent of the population. The main nationalities in both periods were Austrians (50 per cent); Dutch (10 per cent) and Italians (9 per cent) with a majority being employed in agriculture. In 1926 the census reported around 1 million foreigners including 25 per cent from Poland and the then Austrian-controlled Czechoslovakia (Martin, 1994). Despite the quite long experience of immigration, Germany resisted to admit being a country of immigration for a substantially longer period than many other European countries which had important consequences for both the status of immigrants as well as to the citizenship policy pursued and the German interpretation of belonging.

The main shift towards immigration came in the post-war period. Following the restructuring of the German state and economy more or less immediately after the Second World War, Germany became one of key destination countries in Europe and was also one of the main recruiters of foreign labour. The numbers of foreign residents rose from half a million in 1950 to four million in 1975, thus being one of the fastest growing countries of immigration in Europe (Castles and Miller, 2003). Marshall (2000) points to German immigration as being characterised by different categories of migrants (all having a different legal status) and one therefore needs to differentiate between them. First, the group of German refugees and expellees who were German nationals having lived in areas intermitted by German jurisdiction prior to 1945 and who fled or were expelled from these ex-German areas. Between 1945 and 1949, these so called Aussiedlers amounted to around 12–15 million refugees and expellees who made the migratory journey back. Despite being part of the same *volk*, these refugees were presented with several problems concerning accommodation, food and employment and tension between the expellees and the receiving population rose once it became clear that the process of migration was permanent. A number of measures were introduced by the Allied and German authorities in order to ease the process of integration and to prevent social decline, for example, the Refugee Law of 1946 stating that refugees were not allowed to be employed in work that they were over-qualified for. Despite encountering problems in the labour market and being hit severely by the Currency Reform of 1948 which penalised savers, the integration of this group of migrants was considered to be a relatively smooth affair since they were already German nationals with similar cultural and social compositions to the receiving population and their point of migration coincided with a larger and internal German migration. Within this category were also the ethnic Germans in Eastern Europe who were either unable to or refused to migrate due to advancing Soviet troops. The ethnic Germans were of concern for the German state and its understanding of citizenship in the sense that the members of the national community were defined by descent and thus affected by German nationality law. Article 116 of the 1949 basic Law gave automatic German citizenship to those who were German nationals; a refugee or expellee of German descent or as their spouse or descendent who had resided within German territories as of December 1937. The Aussiedlers were thus considered to belong to the German community even if they were geographically distant (Geddes, 2003). Even though the main source of migrants shifted in the 1950s towards Guestworkers, the flow of ethnic Germans continued in several waves. This process was problematic for the German authorities since it coincided with a period of economic decline and several negative views were expressed about the ethnic Germans, something that would have been unthinkable in previous decades. The debate regarding Aussiedlers culminated in imposed restrictions in 1989 which limited the potential as well as actual flow of ethnic Germans from Eastern and Central Europe and limiting the access to migrate under this banner to migrants from the former Soviet Union (Levy, 1999). This limitation came about as a consequence of the increasing numbers of ethnic Germans immigrating, as well as due to the controversy regarding the law passed by the German government authorising DM 2.2 billion for the construction of cheap housing for these migrants. Critics pointed to the unfairness of the special treatment that the ethnic Germans received through the legal framework compared to the difficulties that resident foreigners faced in terms of integration as well as asylum-seekers, whose need for access seemed greater (Marshall, 2000).

Despite the initial large influx of refugees and ethnic Germans in the early post-war period, the German labour market suffered severe labour shortages in some sectors of the economy as early as 1953. Guestworkers were at first requested in agriculture but then increasingly more within the industry. The first formal agreement was set up with Italy (1955) followed by Spain and Greece (1960); Turkey (1961); Portugal (1964) and ex-Yugoslavia (1968). By July 1960, Germany had recruited around a quarter of a million Guestworkers, primarily from Italy and following the construction of the Berlin Wall, which halted labour migration from Eastern Germany, the recruitment scheme became much more large scale. The recruitment of foreign labour was subjected to the economic interests of Germany and residency permits were issued as long as the recruited migrant did not harm the interests of the FRG (Geddes, 2003). The Federal Labour Office (Bundesanstalt fur Arbeit, BfA) recruited directly in the Mediterranean countries through local offices. Employers who were in need of foreign labour went through the BfA which selected workers, tested vocational skills, conducted medical examinations and screened police records. Workers, if approved, were then brought to Germany in groups where the employer provided accommodation facilities whereas recruitment procedures, working conditions and social security was established through bi-lateral agreements between the sending countries and the FRG. The number of Guestworkers in Germany peaked in the mid-1960s (1.3 million in 1966) but dropped dramatically in the short period of recession in 1967 (to 0.9 million) but picked up again when the economy recovered between 1967 and 1973. However, by this time the ethnic composition of the Guestworkers had changed with fewer southern Europeans and with more Turks (Geddes, 2003). German labour recruitment can be viewed as the prime example of the rotation approach. This was a convenient tactic for policy makers, employers and migrants to believe that after a shorter period – one to two years – most of the Guestworkers would leave with their savings and be replaced by fresh recruits. However, the reality was that this was not feasible for either the migrants or the recruiters in that migrants had to stay for a longer period of time in order to achieve their goals since living costs were a lot higher than expected and most workers eventually sent for their families to migrate over. Family reunification was not discouraged by employers but the German state had a more ambivalent attitude. Thus, instead of enforcing rotation strictly, the German state relaxed regulations regarding unification after pressure from German unions and migrant assistance groups.

The oil crisis in 1973 acted as a justification for a stop to labour recruitment and the official German stance was to encourage and expect a permanent return of the Guestworkers. However, it had become clear that many of the temporary guests had become permanent settlers and also that many Germans were opposed to further settlement of primarily Turkish and Yugoslav migrants. The German government had previously responded by restricting immigration and introducing an increase of the employer-paid recruitment fee in February 1973 in order to discourage the recruitment of foreign labour. The policy of halted recruitment was counter measured by new policies to improve the status of migrants in Germany. New measures introduced were that no migrant could be forced to leave Germany due to unemployment, although migrants affected by unemployment were encouraged to return. Family reunification could continue given that the migrant in question had valid work and residence permits and proof of suitable housing (Martin, 1994).

But immigration as such did not stop, it only changed appearance. Germany therefore continued to be one of the main countries of destination. Economic interests and favourable economic conditions had underpinned the policy of large scale recruitment but post-1973, as Geddes (2003) suggests, Germany displayed a moral responsibility to the migrants and as such tolerated, but did not encourage family reunification.

Another major source of immigration were the refugees and asylum-seekers. Although a late starter as a receiving country, the FRG became the main destination for most migrants claiming asylum in Europe post-1989. Faist (1994) points to two factors that have contributed to make Germany such an attractive destination. First, Article 16 in the Basic Law enshrined the right of the politically persecuted to enjoy the right to asylum with the important difference that asylum-seekers where allowed to make an application rather than, as is more common in other European countries, for the state to consider a claim. In practice, this meant that asylum-seekers were empowered at the expense of the state. In addition, Article 19 of the Basic Law enabled rejected claimants to pursue a lengthy legal battle to redress the legal outcome often resulting in the process taking up to eight years after which deportation would be ruled out on humanitarian grounds. In addition, Germany has – in contrast to other EU countries – since 1991 allowed asylum seekers to seek employment while waiting for a decision. In the peak year of 1992, Germany received almost half a million claims which amounted to 80 per cent of all asylum claims in Western Europe. In addition, almost a million ethnic Germans moved to Germany between 1989 and 1992. In a larger time frame, this can be compared to the almost two million claims received between 1987 and 1995 (Thränhardt, 1999).

The general trend in the composition of Germany's migrants is that it is changing. In 1995 the number of foreign workers amounted to around 2.5 million (a figure which is 27 per cent higher than in 1980) but the number of resident foreigners as a whole increased by almost two-thirds during the same period. This is due to a higher fertility rate in addition to increased immigration amongst especially the Turks. However, migration in Germany is also characterised by a high degree of mobility which despite very high levels of immigration gives relatively manageable levels of net migration (e.g. in 1994 and 1995, inflows of almost 800,000 can be compared to an outflow of nearly 650,000). Marshall (2000) points out that the exact measurement of migration into Germany is problematic since one consequence of Germany's claim not to be a country of immigration means that German statistics does not include the category of 'migrant' with German authorities only registering arrivals and departures and not intention to stay or anticipated duration. In addition, the number of resident foreigners may also create either an underestimation of actual numbers (migrants actually registering their arrival/departure) or exaggerate the figures (foreigners registering several times a year and thus counted more than once). Similarly to Sweden,

Germany also practices an ethnically based way of determining who is considered an immigrant by also counting second and third generation migrants as part of the 'foreigner' stock. This results in a slightly paradoxical situation in that ethnic Germans with a foreign passport and with little connection to Germany are counted as 'German' upon naturalisation whereas a third generation Turk born and raised in Germany with little connection to the parents' or grandparents' country of origin is counted as a 'migrant'.

## Immigration policy and status of migrants

Due to Germany's geographical position and many borders, immigration has by and large been considered to be problematic for the German state. In addition, Germany has been affected by strong anti-immigration sentiments, especially so since the early 1990s and directed primarily at asylum-seekers (Marshall, 2000). Germany has also been pushing for increased 'burden-sharing' and tighter external border controls (Thielemann, 2003). Despite lacking an explicit immigration policy as such, Germany has developed an elaborate system of controls for entry and internal monitoring of foreigners with legal entry restricted to ports, airports and along the eastern green border (the land border is part of the Schengen system and as such an internal border). Legal entry is dependent on a valid visa or for reasons of preferential treatment. An interesting feature in terms of entry on a tourist visa is that German authorities do not date-stamp passports which makes the determination of entry at a later stage difficult. Similar to the long and difficult-to-control US border, German border controls have been difficult to monitor although a safety net has been introduced along its Schengen neighbours which means that German officials can pursue suspected illegals up to 30 kilometres into German territory without formalities. Despite facing problems with controlling entry, the most effective way of monitoring and controlling immigration is through labour market and social security means. In contrast to the more liberated British labour market in which illegal migrants can virtually disappear, the German labour market is tightly regulated in terms of both employment and social benefits which makes long-term survival of illegal migrants difficult. The Ministry of Labour's method of cutting down the size of the informal market has been to develop a social welfare card, an extensive database and enforce a requirement that this card should be shown when a worker is hired and that it be carried by employees in sectors where abuses are common such as construction (Martin, 1994).

As a consequence of Germany's reluctance to label itself as a country of immigration, it is difficult to talk about the existence of an immigration policy as such. Geddes (2003) suggests that Germany lacked an explicit system of immigration regulation and integration of migrant newcomers up until 1998. Initiated during the early 1990s, a manifesto produced by leading academics (Manifest der 60: Deutschland und die Einwandrung) explored concepts that could serve as an underpinning for an immigration policy with humanitarian obligations and economic interests as important foundations. Having established a system of short-term rotation migration in the labour market, labour shortages in specific sectors such as IT had now been identified and something had to be done about the previous immigration regime. German immigration policy was thus subsequently reviewed in the summer of 2001 by the SPD/Green coalition. The report had taken the Dutch experience into account and stated that Germany needed migrants and that a successful integration of these was a priority. The Dutch experience suggested that German language education was crucial and raised the possibility of 'integration contracts' which would offer a fast lane to unlimited residence or work permits given that they passed a German language test and that penalties such as delayed family reunification would be given if this test was failed. Thus, in August 2001 Interior Minister Otto Schilly declared the symbolically important fact that Germany was now a country of immigration as well as proposing a bill that would give Germany its first ever regulated immigration policy. Furthermore, this meant that the German government also reasserted its capabilities to regulate access to German territory via restrictions on ethnic German migration and asylum seeking (Geddes, 2003; see also Bade, 1994). On 1 January 2005 a new immigration law came into effect which served two purposes. First, to facilitate the entry of highly skilled migrants by merging residency and work permit applications to one that is a residence permit application to the responsible foreigner's authority will suffice. Another key element of the Immigration Act is its provisions on integration. The Act places an emphasis on integration from a new perspectice. Now all new immigrants, regardless of origin, will be entitled to basic integration support measures. However, this entitlement also indicates an obligation to attend language classes (failure to do so will result in reduced social benefits) (Federal Ministry of the Interior, www.bmi.bund.de). Germany's previously relaxed approach regarding the integration of immigrants was partly due to the belief that migrants, especially Guestworkers, would return at some point. Despite lacking immigration as well as integration policies this did not mean that there was no concern about the incorporation of the foreign population. Since full membership via citizenship was of an exclusive nature (which will be explored in more detail later), migrants were restricted from political membership but had nevertheless access to social and economic rights. This situation put them in the category of 'denizens' (Hammar, 1985) which indicated partial inclusion into the German polity.

This situation is reflected in terms of the status that migrants have in Germany. As Soysal (1994) points out, Germany displays both corporatist and statist characteristics. However, in contrast to corporatist countries such as Sweden and the Netherlands, Germany displays a similar type of structure mainly in the area of social services for migrants and does overall not refer to ethnic minorities or make special provisions for migrants as collectives. The welfare state of Germany is in contrast a highly centralised affair and welfare provision is the responsibility of trade unions or the major social service organisations which in turn are closely connected to the state both financially and organisationally. Migrants are then assigned to these agencies according to their religious and national orientations. There is, however, a great deal of variance in terms of migrant policy and implementation due to the degree of decentralisation and self-governance amongst the German states (Länder). This gives the local states room for ample interpretation opportunities since national level policies are formulated according to general principles serving as guidelines.

The presence of different cultures are acknowledged but not actively supported and are not given an institutional status through which migrants can organise and exercise influence as corporate bodies. Similar to the British approach to integration, German integration policy focuses on the labour market and language acquisition. This is considered especially important for the second generation where vocational training is seen as the gateway for entering German society. Although Germany does not officially support migrant groups, the autonomy of the states and the concentration of migrant groups have generated different types of incorporation structures with, for example, Berlin having a more group-orientated approach compared to other states. In Germany, semi-public institutions as part of the state bureaucracy organise and manage social and educational activities for migrant groups. In the former, three major welfare organisations (two religious – the Catholic and the Protestant church – and one political – the Social Democratic Party) handle migrants welfare according to their religious affiliation. In addition, a number of publicly funded projects target the concerns of specific migrant groups with an emphasis on language training. Although the German state – either federal or local – is the main sponsor of migrant related measures and programmes, no federal agencies have specific responsibility to administer and deal with migrant-related issues. Furthermore, no representatives from migrant groups are present on the committee within the Ministry of Labour and Social Affairs which is designed to co-ordinate integration measures taken by states, local and semi-public authorities.

The German welfare state plays a crucial role in the incorporation of non-national migrants. In accordance with the post-national argument put forward by Soysal (1994), foreign workers were given virtually the same access to citizenship privileges. Article 21(1) of the Basic Law commits Germany to the social inclusion of all citizens and in 1964 the federal government introduced measures covering accommodation and social provisions for Guestworkers, but these were specifically in place with their eventual return in mind (Esser and Korte, 1985).

## Citizenship policy

Any academic text on immigration to Germany eventually acknowledges the almost unique understanding and interpretation of citizenship in Germany (see e.g. Brubaker, 1992; Fulbrook, 1996) as being based on a remarkably ethnic concept of citizenship and belonging.

The Basic Law (Grundgesetz) of 1949 refused to recognise the legitimacy of the post-war division of Germany and the loss of former Germany territories and the West German constitution maintained a virtual blood-right notion of German citizenship. Article 116 of the Basic Law thus states that automatic citizenship and residence should be granted to those who were spouses or descendents of German citizens who resided within territories belonging to the Germany of 1937. This situation is applied to individuals and their descendents who had been deprived of citizenship on political, racial or religious grounds between 1933 and 1945. The principle of ancestry – *jus sanguinis* – was clearly prioritised over principles of birth and residence. The implicit assumption was that an ethnic German nation could be clearly defined and that it should be gathered together in a homogenous area under a common political framework and this view remained a fixture for most of the post-war period (Fulbrook, 1996). Naturalisation has consequently been notoriously difficult for immigrants without an ethnic link to Germany. Up to 1990 naturalisation was possible according to Section 8 of the RStG (Reiche und Staatsangehörigkeitgesetz) of 1913. This allowed naturalisation of aliens living in West Germany on fulfilment of certain requirements – a fixed place of residence, the means of supporting themselves and their dependents as well as leading an impeccable life. In addition, applicants had to demonstrate ability to write and speak German; knowledge of the German political system; display a commitment to the democratic order and, finally, have been resident for at least ten years. However, if these conditions were fulfilled, the formal process had ultimately to be approved by German officials and immigrants were granted naturalisation if they were perceived to serve the public interest, not according to personal circumstances (Marshall, 2000). This legislation thus put several obstacles for non-Germans since becoming German was simply not a question of naturalisation similar to the French understanding of the term but rather, as Brubaker (1992) puts it, that it involved a social transubstantiation that was both difficult to imagine let alone desirable. This national feeling of particularity traces back to a development that took place in Germany prior to the creation of the nation-state. During this period, the German nation was perceived as an organic cultural community, a *volksgemeinschaft*, in which belonging was based on ethnocultural rather than political principles as in France. The 1977 Naturalisation Guidelines express this clearly when stating that '[t]he Federal Republic of Germany is not a country of immigration, it does not seek to deliberately increase the number of German citizens through naturalisation' (quoted in Geddes, 2003: 94). Consequently, naturalisation in Germany during the

1980s was less than 0.5 per cent of the foreign population and dual nationality was described as an 'evil' by a 1976 Constitutional Court ruling but in practice dual nationality became increasingly more common especially for the Aussiedler migrants.

German nationality legislation became heavily criticised by the Left during the 1980s and it took three attempts before a new citizenship legislation was passed in 1990, entering into effect in 1991. The new Ausländergesetz completed the legal institutionalisation of the de facto residence framework for non-nationals that had been in place in the late 1970s. In addition to providing clear entitlements to secure residence permits and the main elements of family reunification, the law also made a clear break from the 1977 guidelines in that the previous legislation had failed to incorporate the foreign population legally by means of citizenship. This new and 'simple' procedure intended to address the problems facing two particular groups of foreigners: migrants with over 15 years' residence and foreigners aged between 16 and 23 with over eight years' residence and six years' attendance of German education. However, naturalising was subject to giving up one's former nationality but the application fee went down significantly (from DM 5000 to DM 100). The effect in policy change came almost immediately with a trebling of naturalisations from 0.4 per cent in 1990 to 1.2 in 1996 and 2 per cent in 2000. Although these figures are comparatively small in a wider European context, they are still quite remarkable and display the significance that prevailing formal opportunity structures may play. Green (2004) points out that much of this increase can be attributed to the high level of naturalisations amongst Germany's Turkish population when, at its peak, five per cent received German citizenship. However, as Green continues, the figures were not dramatically high and failed to accomplish the governmental target of reducing the overall numbers of foreigners since net immigration levels continued to be high throughout the 1990s.

More importantly, however, the change in legislation was an important step towards a more inclusive political German society. Even though most civil and social aspects of citizenship were available to legal resident non-nationals, lacking citizenship – especially for non-EU nationals – still meant exclusion from German society. In addition to security of residence and full political rights, being a national is in many instances a prerequisite for a number of middle- and senior-ranking positions in the public sector which includes judges, civil servants, university professors and teachers. Since full political rights had been denied in a decision made by the Constitutional Court in 1990, becoming a German citizen was the only means by which to bring Germany's migrant population into the political community.

As an additional headache, the issue of dual nationality took several rounds of negotiation and did not come into effect until 2000. Germany's uneasiness with this concept as well as lack of a coherent policy also contributed to the low levels of naturalisation. Apart from the emotional loss of giving up one's nationality there were also some practical monetary considerations involved. Until 1995, Turkish citizens, for instance, lost their inheritance rights if they gave up their nationality and Turkish youth were required to pay a high fee in order to be released from military service. In addition, home country administration could prolong the process by either being technically unable or unwilling to release their nationals. It was thus ultimately down to the individual Land to decide whether dual nationality should be allowed after it had been proven that the release procedure was going on in absurdum. The federal structure in combination with a lack of secondary legislation for the Ausländergesetz for most of the 1990s meant that the Länder were free to interpret as they wished leading in turn to a great variety between states with regard to both levels of naturalisation and tolerance of dual nationality. The effect of these complexities was that many foreigners would find the costs outweighing the benefits and would simply not bother to apply. In terms of actually reducing the numbers of non-nationals in Germany, Green (2004) further suggests that a more general acceptance of dual nationality in combination with a *jus soli* principle would have been a much more effective policy instrument.

Even though the new law primarily gave increased legal security, gaining access to German nationality still remained very difficult.[8] The new legislation in a sense saw an 'end' to the classic juxtaposition between the French republican and German ethno-cultural citizenship in that Germany moved towards a combination of *jus sanguinis* and *jus soli*, which to some extent acknowledged that Germany was now a country of immigration.

## The Netherlands

### Composition of immigrant population

As a former colonial power, the main post-war migrants stemmed from overseas territories. The earliest group to arrive were the Moluccans, who were former employees of the Dutch army. On their arrival in the Netherlands, these were considered as a special case in that they were dismissed from the army and had also become stateless in the wake of independence. In addition, a number of repatriates of mixed Indonesian-Dutch descent were entitled to settle in the Netherlands on the grounds of citizenship. These differed from the Moluccans in that they held government and business jobs at higher levels in colonial society and were thus greeted differently – perhaps more favourably – than the military personnel. Both the Moluccans and the Dutch government considered the soldiers' stay as temporary and therefore few efforts were made to accommodate these migrants (for further discussion on the Moluccan experience, see Smeets and Veenman, 2000).

In terms of numbers, the largest group of post-colonial migrants are the Surinamese. These became Dutch citizens in 1954 as the Dutch government started to dismantle its colonial territories, and this change was used as a window of opportunity to migrate before proper independence was introduced in 1975[9] (Thränhardt, 2000). Having been subjected to Dutch rule for centuries, the Surinamese were accustomed to the Dutch way of life and some strata of the population had migrated prior to independence to attend Dutch universities. Two major waves of Surinamese migration occurred, the first shortly before independence in the early 1970s and the second following independence, when a five-year transitional agreement was put into effect to regulate migration to the Netherlands until 1980. During this period, Surinamese who settled in the Netherlands could still elect to become Dutch citizens. After 1980, a visa requirement was introduced for Surinamese citizens who wanted to migrate and settle in the Netherlands. This meant that an additional 30,000 opted to move during 1979 and 1980 since it was anticipated that the ending of this period of transition would hinder entrance (van Niekerk, 2000). However, Dutch officials did not calculate on the continuation of growth of Surinamese migrants in the form of family reunification or formation. Also, the unfavourable post-independence economic conditions in Surinam meant that there has been a steady, but relatively small, flow of immigration since the early 1980s.

The third main group of migrants come from the Dutch Antilles. These are still Dutch citizens and can therefore travel freely to the Netherlands. Like the ethnic composition of Surinam, the Dutch Antilleans are highly heterogeneous and constitute a variety of sub-ethnic groups[10] (van Hulst, 2000). Their large-scale migration to the Netherlands is relatively recent and consisted initially of the children of white colonists. Following the end of colonial rule in 1954 and the closing down of the main employer – the oil sector – this led to a severe economic crisis which resulted in an emigration boom. This increased the Antillean and Aruban population in the Netherlands from 34,000 in 1984 to over 90,000 in 1992 (Imhoff *et al.*, 1994).

The Netherlands was, like Sweden, quite late in recruiting labour migrants. The consequence of this late start has been fewer foreign residents overall, but with an over-representation of non-European labour migrants, with Turks and Moroccans as the two main labour groups (Ireland, 2000). As with the labour market conditions elsewhere in Western Europe in the post-war period, the Netherlands experienced a shortage of labour primarily at the lower levels of the labour market. This prompted Dutch industry, together with active encouragement from the authorities, to systematically recruit labour, mainly from Mediterranean countries. In contrast to Sweden, these labourers were considered to solve temporary labour shortages and were expected to return after their contract expired. Following a short recession in the late 1950s, the economy once again picked up rapidly and the Dutch government followed these developments by regulating recruitment procedures through a number of bilateral agreements which were put into effect between 1960 and 1970. By 1967, around 75,000 persons from the recruiting source countries were residing in the Netherlands, amounting to one-third of the total foreign population. Labour migration was halted in the early 1970s and a number of restrictive measures were introduced to regulate these flows. Despite these efforts, immigration continued to increase throughout the decade, primarily amongst the Turkish and Moroccan communities, since family reunification was still a legal point of entry. By 1999, the number of residents from the recruitment countries were around 380,000 (a slight decrease from figures in 1990, primarily as a consequence of naturalisation rather than by country of birth) (Muus and Gerritsma, 2000; Penninx *et al.*, 1994).

In addition to these main groups, a number of smaller immigrant groups complete the Dutch migration stock. Following the end of the Second World War, the Netherlands admitted around 30,000 political refugees, initially from Eastern Europe but later from a variety of non-European countries such as Uganda, Chile and Vietnam. However, compared to the Swedish case, the numbers of refugees have been rather low (Entzinger, 1985). Between 1945 and 1969 around 13,000 were admitted, of whom half had returned by 1969. The number of refugees admitted since 1970 has been estimated at around 15,000 a year, but the number of asylum applicants from developing countries has increased since the early 1980s: from around 1000 in 1982 to almost 14,000 in 1987. In the late 1980s, a stricter reception policy was put into effect which caused a temporary decline, but figures were back at the 1987 levels following the political events in former Yugoslavia in the early 1990s. Refugees from primarily Hungary (1956) and Czechoslovakia (1968) arrived up until the mid-1970s, followed by refugees from countries with right-wing authoritarian regimes in South America. However, Dutch policy with respect to refugees and asylum-seekers has been significantly stricter compared to the more liberal Swedish policy. Although less harsh and restrictive than in other mainland European countries, Dutch policy has undergone some major changes, especially in the wake of the sharp growth in applications, as well as asylum policy becoming an increasingly sensitive political issue.

In addition, migrants from other countries have continued to settle in the Netherlands. The total number of EU citizens was almost 200,000 in 1994 and has increased steadily during the 1990s, although a majority of these migrants tend to be temporary (Nicolaas and Sprangers, 2001). The number of migrants from other industrialised countries such as the United States (13,000 in 1994) and Japan (5000 in 1994) has increased too. The size of the immigrant population from developing countries – not part of the main refugee flow – primarily from China, has increased as well, especially in the last 15 years, to around 50,000 in 1988 (Penninx, 1996).

## Immigration policy and status of migrants

Despite official resistance to acknowledging the Netherlands as a country of immigration, the number of migrants who settled in the kingdom has in fact been large.

In the period between 1960 and 1970, the population with a foreign nationality approximately doubled, and doubled once again by the early 1980s. By 1999, the foreign-born population was 1,556,337 (Muus and Gerritsma, 2000). The increase is mainly due to the Turkish and Moroccan migrants' heavy family-related migration, low levels of return migration and a relatively high level of fertility (Vermeulen and Penninx, 2000). The foreign population as such has however decreased, from almost 800,000 in 1994 to 650,000 in 2000, due to an increase in the number of naturalisations and the facilitation of dual nationality (although, dual nationality acquisition has become increasingly more difficult).

Up until the 1970s, few immigration regulations were in effect since all the categories of immigrants entering the country since the Second World War were supposed to have done so on a temporary basis (Entzinger, 1985). This meant that the gap between the norm – the Netherlands not being a country of immigration – and the fact that it had started to be, increased.

The admission and settlement of all immigrants of foreign nationality is governed by the 2000 Aliens Act (in effect from 2001) and the General Administrative Orders based on the Act. However, some migrants enjoy certain forms of preferential treatment, such as EU nationals or foreigners married to Dutch nationals. These rules were meant to regulate rather than to prevent immigration. Since the early 1980s, Dutch immigration policy states that migrants entering the country legally can acquire a permanent residency after five years of continuous stay in the country. Individuals entering the country as family members of legally resident migrants may acquire a permanent settlement permit after three years.

It was not until the early 1980s that Surinamese, Moluccan, Antillean and Mediterranean migrants were considered to be permanent. This idea of temporariness was deeply rooted in admission policies, laws and regulations governing the legal position of non-national migrants. Mother-tongue education, introduced in 1974, was not so much a display of acknowledging a more plural society but was rather aimed at facilitating the reintegration of these children in their country of origin.

A number of incidents in the late 1970s changed the political discussion on immigrants and their status (see further Bartels, 1986; Dalstra, 1983), above all a shift in the official view on the duration of stay of these resident migrants. The Moluccan train-hijacking incident in 1978 sparked the drafting of a new policy document which in 1979 became the report on 'Ethnic Minorities' by the Scientific Council for Government Policy. This proposal was subsequently expanded and this line of thought was also applied to other immigrant groups. This led to the introduction of a new overall ethnic minorities policy which later became a Minorities Bill in 1983. Here, four components were suggested: stability of residency after five years; enlarged participation including easier naturalisation and voting rights for legally resident foreigners in local elections; special programmes for underprivileged minorities such as assistance for self-organisation and representation for various groups; and the fight against racism and discrimination (Thränhardt, 2000).

The term 'ethnic minority' was primarily implemented as a practical policy term and refers to an ethnic group with a relatively lower socio-economic position compared to the majority population. This position is also calculated over a number of generations. The target groups were first defined in 1980 and later introduced in the 'minority memorandum'. The discussion centred around which groups should be included and which should be left out (for a more thorough discussion on this issue, see Kruyt and Niessen, 1997).

The Dutch understanding of the term indicates that minority policies should be understood as primarily being directed against combating deprivation and not as supporting social categories. The authorities thus attempt to relieve the inferior socio-economic position of the designated minorities by providing target-group measures in terms of special budgets for labour market, educational, housing and health care remedies. The aim is to bring about equal participation in the crucial areas of labour, education and housing. Similar to the equality goal practised in Sweden, Dutch migrant management has attempted to create a society in which the disadvantaged position of ethnic groups is to be raised to the same level as the indigenous population. This would in turn generate a more normative type of multicultural society where difference would not only be tolerated but also seen as enriching the country (Vermeulen and Penninx, 2000). When unemployment amongst minorities started to increase drastically in the late 1980s, emphasis shifted towards education and labour market areas.

In terms of the cultural status of migrants and minorities, this still seems to be considered as a private or independent area in Dutch society. In the 1980s, this was phrased as integration with preservation of cultural identity, which became a common understanding for the Dutch type of multicultural practice. This was underscored by a number of measures aimed at facilitating these processes, such as governmental subsidies for mosque building, provisions for mother-tongue education and self-organisation (Broeder and Extra, 1997).

As a consequence of this new direction, migrant organisations emerged as important players in this field and were given the task of preserving and developing the particular group's culture and identity. The role played by organisations and their representatives in the Dutch multicultural process was further institutionalised by the establishing of participatory and consultative structures for recognised minorities. The Memorandum on Minorities (1983) suggested a participatory body for all groups recognised as ethnic minorities. The legal basis for this consultative structure lies in the Minority Consultation Act (Wet Overleg Minderheden). At present, the emphasis lies more on exchanging views than on giving advice, with the latter more present at the local level. The Municipalities Act of 1993 suggests that municipal administrators where minorities live are obliged to create conditions that provide minorities with real opportunities for participation in policy areas that affect them (Vermeulen and Penninx, 2000). This situation thus makes the Dutch view on what political role migrants should have in society remarkably different compared to the other four countries.

In terms of admissions, Dutch policy distinguishes between different nationalities and their access to entry. Similar to the Scandinavian labour movement agreement, nationals from the Benelux countries can settle freely in the Netherlands as well as other EU nationals. Current policies state that foreigners arriving from outside these areas – unless from the refugee or asylum-seeker category – can only qualify for temporary residency if this can be justified according to fundamental Dutch interests or humanitarian conditions. The latter refers primarily to family reunification for foreigners with a residency history of at least 24 months and who have the intention of staying at least an additional 12 months. The Netherlands, like many other Western European countries, has also experienced the presence of illegal or undocumented migrants, but has not yet enforced expatriation laws in any stricter way, provided that no legal violations have been committed although this has now become a hot political issue.

Refugees and asylum-seekers are naturally subjected to different forms of legal control compared to foreign workers and their families resulting from a number of ad-hoc changes that have taken place. Several international agreements, primarily the 1951 Geneva Convention, the 1967 Refugee Status Protocol and the Aliens Act, govern the granting of refugee status. The Netherlands has adopted two categories of asylum-seekers. The first encompasses individuals who fulfil the conditions ascribed by the international agreements, and the second relates to those who do not fit the first category but who nevertheless are eligible for asylum if the political situation in the sending country makes it impossible for them to return.

## Citizenship policy

The Dutch experience, practice and understanding of citizenship displays a number of similarities with the Swedish case, but is based on a completely different rationale. The Dutch idea of citizenship is in many ways the outcome of a historical development as well as a political sociology of 'who is Dutch'. Initially, official Dutch policy for many years resisted the idea that the Netherlands was a country of immigration. Instead, due to the density of the population and the small size of the country, Dutch policy encouraged emigration – a policy that was in effect up until the mid-1960s. In contrast to Sweden, the Netherlands experienced a large outflow of people from the motherland to the former colonies. Following the Second World War, a substantial amount also left for traditional immigration countries like the United States, Canada and Australia.

Given the long experience of movement, both to and from the country, immigration as such does not appear to be as clear-cut compared to the Swedish case. Immigration to the Netherlands has been a constant procedure very much rooted in the country's colonial past. This historical context is also a prime explanatory factor for the direction of citizenship policy and the development of the Dutch model of integration policy. Prior to the labour migrants of the post-war era, migration to the Netherlands was dominated by several waves of colonial migration and was also characterised by its heterogeneity. Since some colonial inhabitants (Surinamese, Dutch Antilleans) were already Dutch citizens, they were also free to move to the Netherlands as they wished. The Dutch colonies were geographically dispersed, which contributed to the diversity of Dutch society from an early stage. Dutch policy resisted labelling its new inhabitants as 'immigrants', and opted for the term 'ethnic minorities'. This term relates to the Dutch government's wish to monitor the socio-economic progress of the migrants, based on a conception that certain migrant groups were in a disadvantaged socio-economic position in Dutch society and that the Dutch government had a special responsibility towards these groups (Entzinger, 2003; Vermeulen and Penninx, 2000).

Therefore, immigrants' position on the social ladder has been the major justification of Dutch ethnic minority policy. Immigrant groups whose position in society is not considered to be 'difficult' either by themselves or by Dutch society, are not subject to this policy. This definition is in effect set up in order to improve the living conditions for the groups in question, primarily along the lines of ethnically 'different' groups, sometimes in a rather arbitrary fashion. The target groups included Guestworkers from the Mediterranean region (primarily Turks and Moroccans), the Surinamese, the Antilleans, the Moluccans and refugees with the four main 'ethnic minority' groups being – Turks, Moroccans, Surinamese and Antilleans. Previously, the 'Southern Europeans' formed a separate ethnic minority but they have fallen out of that category since they are no longer perceived as being a 'problem' for Dutch society (Entzinger, 1985; Penninx *et al.*, 1994; for further discussion relating to the evolution of Dutch ethnic minority policy see Amersfoort, 1982; Vermeulen and Penninx, 2000).

The preference for using the 'ethnic minorities' definition rather than 'immigrants' has two main reasons.[11] First, it enables Dutch policy to include the increasing numbers of children born in or brought to the Netherlands at an early age by parents of migrant origin. Second, Dutch society has a long tradition of indigenous minorities, although primarily of a religious rather than of an ethnic character. This division traces back to the so-called pillarisation of Dutch society which I describe in more detail in Chapter 3. Following this political philosophy, migrant groups were considered to be yet another pillar of society, similar to the Swedish concept of migrants as a 'social group'. Paradoxically, when the influx of migrants increased, the pillar system came under pressure and underwent a dismantling process, partly due to a growing secularisation and partly due to the uncertainty as to where the new religious affiliations should be directed. Therefore, in contrast to Swedish policy, with its preference for the 'immigrant' category, using similar terms was deemed inappropriate since most non-white inhabitants in the Netherlands were already in possession of Dutch citizenship.

When the post-war decolonisation process was underway, citizenship regulations were subjected to change. However, this process experienced a certain degree of inconsistency. When the Dutch East Indies (Indonesia) became independent in 1949, no 'commonwealth' privileges applied to the Indonesians apart from the Moluccans. This group, who served in the Dutch East Indian Army, were given an option to be transferred to the Netherlands.[12] Their stay was considered as a temporary measure until it was safe for these soldiers to return. Even though they were now officially Indonesian citizens, they had been socialised into thinking of themselves as Dutch and did not feel Indonesian in any way (Vermeulen and Penninx, 2000). The Moluccan situation is remarkably different from that experienced by other colonial groups, such as the Surinamese. The decolonisation of the Dutch West Indies started several decades later. The inhabitants of Surinam and the Dutch Antilles were also already Dutch citizens since 1954. When Surinam became independent in 1975, a transition period of five years remained where Surinamese were still officially Dutch and free to migrate to the Netherlands. Furthermore, the Surinamese had the advantage of having Dutch as their official language, but they were more heterogeneous in terms of their ethnic composition. However, the Surinamese were less well accepted by the native population compared to the Moluccans, which was naturally a matter of frustration since the Surinamese also considered themselves to be 'legitimate' Dutch (Penninx *et al.*, 1994).

The Dutch government was at this time hesitant as to how to go forward with the notion of citizenship, fearing more spontaneous mass migration from primarily Surinam which had been the case on two previous occasions in 1974 and 1980. Despite increasing migration, the official Dutch perception resisted acknowledging that the Netherlands was a country of immigration. Most migrants were expected to return home, unless they had established a connection with the country in the form of marriage or gone through a process of naturalisation. Also, the labour migrants, especially the Turks and Moroccans, were not returning on the scale anticipated by the Dutch government. During the 1970s, the increasing divide between policy and reality started to be recognised by scholars as well as policy-makers, but a formal political recognition was not on the agenda until the 1980s.

The experiences of colonial migration, the pillar system and the change in migration flows have all contributed to the particular understanding of citizenship and naturalisation laws practised in the Netherlands. As in Sweden, the Netherlands considers citizenship to be a matter of residence. The formal requirements differ in terms of age (21 compared to 18) but are the same with regard to duration of stay (five years, although a shorter time span concerns Nordic migrants to Sweden) before the application procedure can be initiated. The conditions for applying are stricter than in the Swedish case but are left purposely vague – the conditions state that there should be no objection to the applicant's unlimited stay in the Netherlands and that he or she has been 'sufficiently acclimatised' to Dutch society. This condition has been applied to two areas – sufficient language skills and no previous criminal record (Enzinger, 1985). However, the laws have been changed in order to improve the legal position of foreigners and their children with regard to naturalisation and citizen benefits. A law dating from January 1985 suggests a number of new changes as regards who is eligible for Dutch citizenship. This proposal not only suggests that children of male Dutch citizens, but also the children of female Dutch citizens should be made Dutch citizens by birth. In addition, both male and female non-Dutch marriage partners of a Dutch national have special rights to apply for Dutch citizenship and third-generation children would automatically become Dutch citizens.

The Dutch government has never encouraged the new population to naturalise to the same extent as the Swedish government. Instead, citizenship has been perceived as a symbolic act towards further integration rather than as an end in itself. Also, Dutch policy with regard to social and economic rights has been constructed in such a way that they also apply to non-nationals, guaranteed by the constitution which declares that fundamental rights do not differ according to nationality, thus giving foreigners equal access to basic constitutional rights.

Given the rather laissez-faire attitude towards naturalisation, one might find the high level of state involvement and encouragement in minority affairs quite surprising. Upon realising that a majority of the migrants intended to stay, Dutch policy shifted from a stance which could be described as exclusionary to become more inclusive. Drawing on the previous pillar society, migrants were now to be perceived as distinct, minority groups which were to enjoy specific rights vis-à-vis the state and also be in a position to hold certain entitlements. Similar to the Swedish way of organising migrants, minority groups in the Netherlands were now categorised in the same way as Dutch society had dealt with the religious groups – by means of corporatist consultation. As mentioned previously, the recognition of certain ethnic groups as distinct minorities enabled the Dutch government to monitor socio-economic development amongst the targeted groups as well as inviting the groups to policy-formulating negotiations. Although distinct from a traditional understanding of what citizenship implies, the way in which these consulting structures have developed displays an obvious connection between this emancipatory, civic understanding of citizenship and the way in which Dutch migrant policy has proceeded. Similar to the Swedish handling of the term, the Netherlands emphasises the interdependence between the state and the citizen, although the countries differ quite significantly in terms of how far different groups are considered to have reached the status of single-group advisory/consultancy status.

Closely linked to these preconditions is the corporatist organisation of both policy and implementation, structured from a top-down and highly centralised perspective. Migrant-related policy is primarily determined at the national level in co-operation with the Council for Scientific Policy (WRR).[13] While lacking a unitary centralised state agency devoted to migrant matters as such, a wide range of ministerial bodies and autonomous, but fully funded, intermediary institutions can be found in its place which are in charge of different aspects of incorporation. The key word here is co-ordination, which is carried out on a national level by several groups of ministerial committees working under the Ministry of Home Affairs and the Interministerial Co-ordinating Committee on Minorities Policy. These intermediary bodies act as a structural relationship between the national government and the migrant groups in general but, more importantly, with the recognised ethnic minorities. Furthermore, there are direct links down to the municipalities which in turn are responsible for implementing, co-ordinating and administrating policy at the local level.

Organisation-wise, the Netherlands more clearly reflects the corporatist mode of incorporation than the Swedish model. The central state subsidises quasi-public institutions that handle different nationalities. The overarching body is the Dutch Center for Foreigners (NCB), primarily handling the 'old' labour migrant groups, predominantly the Turks and Morroccans.[14] Other organs of assistance for foreign workers also exist but are mainly engineered by private institutions. Although included under the national umbrella, the NCB, lacks any formal ties with these units. The NCB is closely linked to the state, and can also potentially influence decision-making, since it is involved as a consultant when policy is formulated regarding the minorities.

The emphasis on emancipating the state's new population led to an expansion of these umbrella consulting units and by the mid-1980s, two similar organisations were set up dealing specifically with Surinamese and Antilleans. At this time, the Dutch welfare system underwent restructuring and consequently reorganised its support for migrants leading to a shift away from group-specific organisation towards institutions serving the general population, giving greater responsibility to the organisations and consultant bodies at the local level (Soysal, 1994). Therefore, the remains of the consultant bodies on the national level serve as aggregates for the different advisory bodies found at the local level. These sub-councils serve as federations for the officially recognised groups, whereas other nationalities are directed to the more general advisory board. Soysal's disposition highlights how these formal arrangements are set up in order to enable disadvantaged groups to become part of the policy-making chain and influence its outcome. In both cases, migrants are incorporated as societal collectives into the state's organisational and legal framework, contributing to a highly uniform and institutionalised understanding at all levels of what policy is (or even should be) by providing a common language and legitimate categories.

This guiding principle for the Dutch pluralistic society suggests that migrants and ethnic minorities should have the same rights and opportunities to develop their cultural and religious identity (Doomernik, 1998). In this vein, Dutch authorities sought to promote the acceptance of principles of multiculturalism by encouraging self-organisation within the communities. This meant that Dutch society was to make extensive efforts towards the target groups since they were deemed to be in a disadvantaged position. New religious beliefs such as Islam, Hinduism and Buddhism were given a legitimate social position in the new environment. The presence of these groups led to the emphasis of three common principles: freedom of religion, equality between religious groups and a division between church and state. In this new scenario, migrant organisations started to play an increasingly important role in terms of challenging claims vis-à-vis the state (De Graaf *et al.*, 1988). When the first migrant associations were set up in the 1960s, they were primarily directed towards the country of origin but became increasingly orientated towards the situation in the host society. However, as Östergaard-Nielsen (2000) observes, this has been a direct consequence of the steering put upon the associations by the authorities.

In the 1990s, Dutch funding policy towards migrant associations tightened and funding was redirected towards activities rather than organisations. This meant that homeland political issues became excluded from state funding in favour of immigrant political activities. Organisations were further encouraged to co-operate with other migrant organisations on points of common interest such as issues of integration. However, the Dutch policy of integrating migrants through the typology of pillarisation has been criticised for creating what Rath (1991) describes as a social construction of ethnic minorities in which the difference between the minorities and the majority is stressed in every aspect of life. Similar to Miles's (1996) discussion on the racialisation process in Britain, Rath argues that in the process of planned social engineering, the socio-cultural signifiers and the dividing lines of ethnic groups are stressed and brought to the attention of the general public.

In the Netherlands, the existence and symbolic arrangement of migrant and ethnic organisations created an incorporation of ethnic leaders into the political system in which they functioned as a buffer between their own ethnic group and the administration. The latter is furthermore in a privileged position in that they have a strong influence on the process and can recognise and select the right representatives and organisations. Rath continues by noting that this has created an 'ethnic minorities industry' – a term which parallels the British race relations industry – that by means of institutionalisation shows the underlying existence of dividing lines which shape the minds of people and their way of acceptance. Through these mechanisms group-specific political institutions become products of 'minorisation' and express the idea that ethnic minorities are not full members of the Dutch 'imagined community'. Thränhardt (2000) suggests further that if ethnic minorities are not perceived as full members of a society, they will tend to be tolerated but not accepted into key positions or as equals. This notion conflicts with the idea of pillarisation, on which ethnic minority management was modelled. The old verzuiling concept comprised various pillars that were kept largely separated but nevertheless enjoyed real power and influence in the parliament, whereas the new minorities were by and large dependent on the goodwill of the indigenous population. In addition, ethnic minorities, as the Dutch definition goes, are only acknowledged when they are perceived to be performing at a below-average socio-economic standard. This clearly shows the influence that the receiving state has on the new population in terms of recognising difference and allowing it into the public sphere. Or, as Abell *et al.* (1997: 136) frame it, 'nation-states play a crucial role in the rise of ethnicity through their definitions and treating various groups differently'.

## Rotterdam

As in other receiving countries of Western Europe, immigrants in the Netherlands have tended to settle in the bigger cities and over 40 per cent of the Netherlands' minorities are found in the four largest urban centres – Amsterdam, Rotterdam, The Hague and Utrecht (Rogers *et al.*, 2001). Rotterdam has a sizeable migrant population which corresponds to the ethnic composition of the country in general (although the Cape Verdians are by and large Rotterdam specific). The five largest groups in Rotterdam are Surinamese (52,092), Turks (42,661), Moroccans (31,144), Antilleans (19,373) and Cape Verdians (14,827) (COS, all figures are from January 2002). Refugee groups form the sixth ethnic category and are composed of a number of nationalities (as opposed to the socio-economic categorisation of the previous five). As for this study, the latest figures on the Iranian population amounted to 1105 (January 1999).

Early migrants to Rotterdam originated from Flanders, followed by Huguenots from France, Jewish refugees from Spain and Eastern Europe and recruited labour from Germany and Belgium. However, as with the country in general, large-scale migration to Rotterdam started in the post-war era. Most of the Mediterranean Guestworkers came during the 1950s and up to the end of official recruitment in 1973. These Guestworkers were mostly single men or males with their families in the country of origin. Often these workers were poorly educated, and did menial work for which there were few indigenous volunteers, for instance in the metal industry and the cleaning sector. When labour recruitment came to an end following the oil crisis of the early 1970s, migration continued since many resident migrants decided to bring their families to Rotterdam. Following the events in Surinam in the 1970s and 1980s, a large number of Surinamese migrants settled in the city. Since the 1980s, the number of refugees and asylum seekers taken in by Rotterdam has increased considerably as a result of political developments in the international arena.

The Guestworker migration took place against the backdrop of a favourable economic conjuncture. After an initial period of post-war reconstruction in the city, the 1960s and 1970s were characterised by steady economic growth, the promotion of social equality and the final implementation of the welfare state. A policy of urban renewal was put into effect during the mid-1970s, with large-scale investments in the inner-city neighbourhoods in which older buildings and housing stock were refurbished in order to be affordable to buyers at the lower end of the economic scale.

At the end of the decade, as economic recession set in, social segregation and deprivation became concentrated in certain sections of the city. These areas are to some extent still characterised by high levels of long-term unemployment and criminal activities in combination with a relatively large percentage of ethnic minority inhabitants. Therefore, by the end of the 1970s, the Migrants Office was set up and in 1978 the Memorandum on Immigrants in Rotterdam (*Nota Migranten in Rotterdam*, 1978) was published. This report was followed by a Minorities Policy in a Changed Situation in 1985 (*Minderhedenbeleid in een gewijzige situatie*, 1985).

The ethnic minorities were to be incorporated within the national and local framework by means of certain consultation bodies referred to as platforms. All minorities were to have separate platforms, organised according to country of origin or combinations of them. A Surinamese and Antillean platform was set up in 1981 alongside a general co-ordinating body (Platform Buitenlanders Rijnmond, PBR), whereas a Turkish consultation body came two years later. In terms of platforms aimed at the Moroccans, less official effort was made and the main goal was to get these groups involved in the general Muslim (although primarily Turkish) platform. This related to Rotterdam's official policy, strongly focused on integration, if not assimilation, in which special provisions towards minorities were discouraged (Rath *et al.*, 2001).

In the mid-1990s, a new governmental policy (as opposed to the local initiatives described above) was initiated in order to develop the four major cities (Amsterdam, Rotterdam, The Hague and Utrecht). This social renewal programme was based on the following principles:

1. customisation – towards the specific situation and the needs of the people in the given situation;
2. co-operation – mutual co-ordination of the efforts of various bodies;
3. activation – linking up with self-motivation of the target groups involved;
4. prevention – measures introduced to prevent undesirable developments instead of sweeping them aside.

Local authorities expressed concerns about certain areas of the city becoming deprived, which meant that efforts had to be made to strengthen the economic structure of these areas, improve facilities for the local economy and encourage commercial activity. This new approach suggested that economic and social thinking were now to be intertwined – deprivation was no longer merely a social phenomenon corrected through the redistribution of wealth or considered as a consequence of individual failure.

## Sweden

### Composition of immigrant population

The conception of Sweden as a country of immigration is relatively new. Between 1851 and 1930, Sweden was a net population exporter when a total of nearly 1.5 million Swedes emigrated, primarily to North America. In the 1930s, the flows began to reverse with the return of the Swedish-Americans (Petersson, 1994). This did not mean that immigration started to increase significantly, rather that emigration levels started to decline. The small scale of both immigration and emigration meant that net migration to Sweden continued to be limited with around 10,000 per year during the 1940s.

Immigration started to increase more notably in connection with the Second World War. Although remaining a neutral actor during the war, Sweden still considered it had a moral obligation towards its neighbouring countries and kept the borders open for refugees. These stemmed primarily from Finland (70,000), the Baltic countries (around 30,000), alongside an estimated 60,000 Danes and Norwegians (Regeringskansliet, 2000). The early post-war period reinforced this shift to net influxes with immigration of individuals without any previous link to the country. Already by 1945 there were almost 200,000 foreign nationals living in Sweden (SIP, 1983). The post-war years were characterised by a continuation of refugee flows with two main peaks – 8000 Hungarian migrants after the 1956 Soviet invasion and around 2000 asylum-seekers who left Czechoslovakia following the events in 1968. However, most of the migrants coming to Sweden up until the early 1970s were labour migrants rather than refugees. The demand for labour was considerable, due to a low birth rate and an increasing average age. In contrast to other receiving countries in Western Europe, Sweden could not draw its manpower from a colonial heritage. A treaty was signed in 1947 with Italy, Hungary and Austria in which labour recruitment was the main objective. The effects of this agreement were modest in terms of the numbers of people actually taking advantage of the opportunities. A second agreement was signed in 1954 between the Nordic countries regarding free movement and employment which resulted in a large influx of primarily Finnish labour migrants. Alongside the Finnish-speaking minority of Tornedal-Finns, the Finnish-speaking community today amounts to almost 300,000, making them the largest migrant group.

Much like other countries in north-west Europe, Sweden initiated a number of bi-lateral agreements to recruit workers from Mediterranean countries, primarily from ex-Yugoslavia (around 40,000) and Greece (20,000) and to a lesser extent from Turkey (around 12,000). However, in contrast to other recruitment countries such as Germany and Switzerland, Sweden never employed a Guestworker system. Although direct recruitment for specific labour purposes was in place, labour migration was not planned on a large scale or explicitly aimed at remedying short- or long-term economic problems. Instead, these migrants were considered to be permanent residents and as such were accepted as individuals rather than as commodities (Hammar, 1985). Following this view, a definition change was introduced in 1966 in which the Swedish government proclaimed that newcomers were to be called 'immigrants' (invandrare) rather than 'foreigners' (utlänningar).

Labour migration reached a peak in 1970 when a total of 75,000 persons immigrated to Sweden. From that year on, labour migration decreased dramatically following the deteriorating economic climate and some harsh labour migration policies. From 1972, most non-Nordic economic migration was terminated, which meant that the only legal ways to settle in Sweden were joining family members or as asylum-seekers.

Previous experience of refugees had been limited to a few, small-scale groups. During the 1930s attempts were made to receive Jewish refugees from Germany. However, at this time, the term refugee primarily referred to individuals who were subjected to political persecution. To seek political asylum due to racial claims was not seen as reason enough, which meant that a considerable number of Jewish refugees were denied entrance. The restrictive policy changed in 1941 when practically anyone who claimed status as a political refugee was granted access to asylum in Sweden (Widgren, 1982). Between 1950 and 1989, 176,000 refugees obtained permanent residency in Sweden. A majority of these came from Iran, Chile, Hungary and Poland. However, refugee immigration during 1950–67 was relatively small with an average of 1300 per year. These migrants were selected from international refugee camps organised by the UNHCR and others. In addition to these more organised flows, Sweden granted asylum to between 2000–3000 asylum-seekers per year. In comparison to other European countries, Sweden has followed a policy of generous examination of asylum claims – which has meant that around 80 per cent of all claims have tended to be accepted – combined with a rather strict deportation policy of those whose claims have been refused. The major change in numbers came during the 1980s when the rate of asylum applicants rose from 4000 in 1983 to 20,000 in 1988. Asylum applicants reached an all-time high the following year with 30,000 applicants (Hohensinner *et al.*, 1993). This policy changed in 1989 and by 1991 less than half of all applicants were granted permission to stay, while deportation was implemented as strictly as before. This meant that the previous 'generous' Swedish model was now becoming more similar to that of the rest of Europe (Hammar, 1990).

During the 1990s, an average of 53,000 foreign nationals immigrated annually. However, these figures tend to be exaggerated since they include the exceptional year of 1994 when around 85,000 persons were registered as immigrants having waited for residency permit for more than two years. This was the effect of the very large number of refugees from Bosnia-Herzegovina that arrived in 1992. If these are not included, the average falls to around 50,000.

In addition, there has been a considerable amount of intra-Nordic migration during the 1990s. Around one-third of the migration during this decade consisted of Nordic citizens. The numbers of EU citizens have been increasing; between 1995 and 1999 the average amounted to almost 4000 per year compared to the 2500 during the first half of the decade.

### Immigration policy and status of migrants

As mentioned earlier, Sweden did not experience any colonial migration, nor were the labour migrants subjected to repatriation after the end of their work contracts. Instead, as Hammar (1991) notes, Sweden had invented its own model based on an efficient regulation and permanent settlement for immigrants once these had been admitted. Furthermore, Swedish immigration regulation and control was exercised according to two traditions. First, there was a well-developed legal tradition that ensured the civil rights of non-nationals and offered a guarantee to appeal their cases to the highest administrative authority. This tradition dates back to the 1950s when the general consensus regarding migrant management was that they should be incorporated into the general welfare state and become 'Swedish' as quickly as possible (SOU 1996:55). In practical terms this meant that few distinctions existed between Swedish and non-Swedish citizens with regard to positive rights. Policies and measures were in broad terms identical to anyone legally resident. Second, there was a tradition of placing Swedish interests first when deciding the scope of immigration. The numbers of admissions could vary but the system of regulation should be the same. Laws regulating immigration date back to the beginning of the twentieth century. Prior to this period, almost no regulations were in effect. In 1914, the introduction of the Deportation Act (Utvisningslagen) enabled the government to impose thresholds to entry in emergency situations. This was followed in 1917 with a passport and visa requirement in order to enter the country in combination with work and residency permits for resident foreigners.

Immigration control gradually developed into a more permanent character when the relevant executive authority was incorporated into a single central, administrative body. However, as Hammar notes (1985), the aims of Swedish immigration policy have been expressed in vague and even somewhat contradictory terms. The content of policy and its application to particular situations have been subject to a number of interpretations. The aim of immigration regulation could be considered long-term rather than short-term in the sense that the principles on which they were based have remained part of official policy up until now. However, since the interpretation has varied according to Swedish needs at different times and towards different national groups, the regulations have subsequently been altered to fit different situations, and primarily directed at protecting the domestic labour market.

Up until the mid-1960s, issues of integration, in so far as this concept existed, were handled through the general welfare mechanisms. This proved somewhat inadequate in that language deficiency was identified as a key problem on the labour market. Moreover, without substantial knowledge about Swedish society, migrants would face difficulties to function on an equal level alongside the native population. Therefore, several directives were formulated in 1965 with the specific aim to facilitate the adaptation of the new population. A number of these – public funds for instruction in Swedish, immigrant newsletters, information on migrants' rights and responsibilities – had previously been considered superfluous since it was thought that access to social welfare would make the problem of integrating the new population 'solve itself' (SOU 1996:55).

With the governmental bill of the late 1960s (1968:142), the foundations to what would become the 'Swedish model' were mapped out. It was argued that immigration needed to be regulated in order to provide the same type of living standards for migrants as for the native population. This required controlling the inflow of persons, otherwise the resources would not be sufficient. However, much attention was not given to whether migrants were deemed to have any particular needs that differentiated them from the majority population. It had been recognised that preserving cultural traditions and languages were an important issue, but this was weighted against the societal resources and was given less priority in comparison with learning Swedish and getting accustomed to the new environment.

The idea that immigrants were supposed to assimilate began to be questioned in the early 1970s. This led to a governmental investigation in 1974 (SOU 1974:69) in which the guidelines for immigration and integration policies were outlined. These guidelines expressed an approach to the social, political and cultural rights of immigrants which by international standards were of a generous nature. This new direction put the migrant population in a privileged position in terms of accessing rights and privileges previously only available to citizens of the state. The aim was to minimise differences between native Swedes, naturalised Swedes and denizens in terms of formal rights (Soininen, 1999). Furthermore, language and 'traditional' cultural practices were to be accepted and supported as long as this did not conflict with Swedish law and/or deviated from societal norms and values. More specifically, the government wanted to draw attention to the long-term consequences of immigration for Swedish society and that it was necessary to express more clearly the basic views of Swedish society on a number of issues of principle (Governmental Bill 1985/86:98). Unintentionally, this policy resulted in controversy over the issue of who was to be considered a minority. The presence of an ethnic minority-type discourse in official policy raised expectations amongst certain groups, primarily the Finnish migrants. But recognising certain groups as 'ethnic minorities', it was argued, conflicted with the goal of equality as well as international civil law praxis. The governmental decision concluded that immigrant groups could not be considered minorities in this sense and that only Samis and Tornedal-Finns were indigenous minorities (although this was only formally recognised in the late 1990s).

The new direction of Swedish integration policy also stipulated that the various migrant groups and the native population would benefit from working together. As partners in the development of society, they would be granted access to the civil society arena in the same way as the majority population. In addition they would also receive public support in order to build and maintain their own associations. At the same time, immigrants were encouraged to participate, individually and/or collectively, in labour unions and in political life. As in the Netherlands, migrant voluntary associations were considered to be the key players between the immigrant communities and the receiving society (Hammar, 1985).

### Citizenship policy

In the Swedish case, immigration was until the late 1960s not perceived as anything but a temporary phenomenon. However, by the end of this decade the authorities and public opinion-makers began to define Sweden as a country of immigration as a result of both labour migrants becoming permanent settlers and an ongoing and increasing process of family re-unification. This new situation also led to a rethinking of the prevailing policies. After the National Board of Immigration was set up in 1969, the three prime objectives were to deal with immigration control, citizenship regulations and the new population's adjustment to Swedish society. The main efforts, however, were not dedicated to putting forward a radically different citizenship policy; in fact this was given less attention in relation to the two other objectives. It could be said that changes in citizenship policy were a spin-off from the integration initiatives rather than a separate development.

By the beginning of the 1970s, a large proportion of the labour migrants had decided to become permanent settlers in Sweden and this scenario forced policy-makers and politicians to consider what was to happen next. One of the first measures came with the 1968 governmental bill stating that non-nationals should be given the same opportunities to live under the same conditions as the native population and have an opportunity to naturalise. The Swedish state chose here to emphasise the civic republic side of citizenry, thereby giving greater importance to obligations and participation in order to pursue common interests. This, it was argued, would be enabled by diminishing the social and economic differences between Swedes' and immigrants'. At this stage, citizenship meant equality, rather than community reciprocity, and would be dealt with through the use of general welfare policies. During the labour migration heyday, the main efforts were primarily aimed at achieving equality on the labour market. This can by and large be credited to the extensive influence that the trade unions had on policy-making. The trade unions emphasised the importance of having the same type of working conditions for native as well as foreign workers in order to not create a new class of underprivileged workers. Following the 1968 directives, working and living conditions for migrants become more of a general welfare state concern than purely a labour market problem (Borevi, 2002).

However, Ring (1995) suggests that this policy initially managed to exclude parts of the new population. When social rights are codified in the sense of a formal guarantee of economic security and the possibility to obtain a living standard which ensures material as well as cultural satisfaction, it only applies to naturalised migrants and not to those whose status qualifications in the country are under investigation. The argument that civil and political rights are prerequisites for social rights falls short when one considers individuals without residency permits in that they lack political representation, the right to vote and in most cases do not have any organisations that can represent them in the political process. This is an important objection in terms of the political dimension of citizenship but does not fully apply to the group which Ring refers to – refugees – since this group, at least to a certain extent, benefits from social and economic categories of citizenship in terms of housing and health care. Regardless of this access to certain citizenry privileges, immigrants were considered to be underprivileged in terms of language skills, knowledge about Swedish society and, most importantly, the Swedish 'way of life'. The slogan of equality was not only fundamental for the state's views on newcomers, it also touched upon one of the cornerstones of the Socialdemocrats' beliefs in their quest to restructure and reform the Swedish society making this slogan an unquestioned part of the new integration procedure (Westin, 1996).

With regard to citizenship formalities, one can find several different policies. This is due to the Swedish involvement in different international agreements. This gives rise to a number of different ways of naturalising depending on the applicants' nationality: for instance, applicants from the Nordic countries can apply for Swedish citizenship after two years of residence whereas non-Nordic nationals have to wait five years. In addition to applying for citizenship, persons born in Sweden with parents who are foreign citizens are eligible for a Swedish nationality through a registration process. Persons born with one parent being a Swedish national are given Swedish citizenship by birth.

With regard to dual citizenship, the attitude has been sceptical but not entirely forbidden. Sweden signed the 1963 Strasbourg convention which aimed at reducing the number of dual nationalities in order to avoid conflicts of loyalty when it came to military obligations. This convention was applied to applicants stemming from non-contracting states and worked as an imperative for the applicant to renounce his or her former nationality. This law, however, was not enforced in all areas of citizenship applications, but mostly practised during the application process and not valid in the case of registration (De Rahm, 1990). The ambiguity in terms of when dual nationality should be permitted or not, spawned a governmental investigation aiming to revise the current citizenship regulations. An additional directive was to 'analyse and consider the consequences of a general abandonment of the present principle that dual citizenship should be avoided, and suggest any constitutional and other measures which may result from these considerations' (Govt. Directive 1998:50, p. 328). The commission suggested in their final report that a new citizenship law should fully accept dual citizenship (SOU 1999:34). The outcome was positive and a new law was adopted in February 2001 which stated that foreign nationals who acquire Swedish citizenship through naturalisation would no longer have to renounce their former citizenship.

However, naturalisation is not a formal requirement when it comes to access rights enjoyed by Swedish citizens such as health benefits or education, but rather dependent on holding a valid residency permit. The devaluation of citizenship, in this sense, follows Soysal's (1994) argument of post-national citizenship. The traditional understandings of citizenship – defined as a bounded population, with a specific set of rights and duties, which excludes others on the basis of nationality – now seems to have shifted towards a new situation. Soysal considers citizenship benefits to no longer be characterised by territorial notions but rather to be legitimised on the basis of personhood. The end result of this change can be seen in the decline in applications regarding naturalisation, since no real extra benefits are extracted through the change of nationality. However, this may be true for countries in which naturalisation has been more or less impossible (Germany) or in countries where naturalisation requires the individual to abandon his or her previous national identity in favour of the new society's (France). In the Swedish understanding of citizenship, this does not necessarily apply. Soysal is correct in her observations that the differences in terms of rights and benefits between nationals and non-nationals are minimal, or even virtually non-existent, but naturalisation applications have in fact not declined, but rather increased in the last decades (Swedish Institute, 2001). To adopt a policy that facilitated naturalisation was a conscious choice by the Swedish government following the integration objectives that were set up in the late 1960s. These liberal arrangements were supposed to encourage naturalisation from an equality point of view and had virtually unanimous support from all parties across the political spectre. However, the main area of disagreement lay in the question of whether or not to extend national-level voting rights to include non-nationals. This disagreement fell along a Left–Right division, in which the

Socialist parties seemed to advocate the introduction of these ideas, whereas the Right coalition remained more sceptical.

Swedish citizenship law allows the individual to apply for a nationality change by a simple procedure. If the applicant complies with certain basic criteria (length of legal residency and no criminal record), Swedish citizenship is usually granted. Although, labour migration is nowadays limited to skilled labour or intra-EU migrants, migration from non-EU countries still counts for a significant amount of residency and visa permits each year. Since the early 1970s, Swedish policy was redirected towards refugees and asylum-seekers, which altered the migrant composition over the next twenty years. The 1951 Geneva Convention and the 1967 Protocol on refugee rights have been leading trajectories for Swedish refugee policy. However, individuals who do not correspond to the Geneva Convention, primarily quota refugees, who claim asylum due to humanitarian or political reasons, are in most cases granted residency as well. When this category of migrants became larger than the labour migrant category, a governmental decision was taken which legally binds Sweden to pursue a generous and humane refugee policy which has significantly altered the migration composition towards family reunification migrants (Hohensinner *et al.*, 1993).

A major shift towards a more explicit multicultural stance came in 1975 when the previous objectives were incorporated into official policy. The three goals, equality, freedom of choice and partnership, not only provided new practical imperatives for immigrant management but also provided the state with a radically original view on its new inhabitants. This aim was supported more or less unconditionally by parliament and was constructed in a general fashion, serving as principles for local and regional government to follow. The goal of equality was initiated already in 1967, following the regulations of tighter immigration control and work permit acquisition prior to moving to Sweden. The argument, officially established the following year, stated that the state should have responsibility for all its members and consequently combat social inequalities. The prime task was to minimise socio-economic differences and to provide immigrants with the same living standards as the native population and, more importantly, with equality on the labour market. Here, the solution was to incorporate migrants into the efficient welfare state body that has dealt with labour market problems since the 1930s. Equal participation in this area was one of the most important aims for the Socialdemocratic government since it generated social integration and positive spin-off effects such as independence, solidarity and dignity. A first step in this direction came with the law passed in 1972 which provided immigrants with free Swedish language instruction during paid work hours in addition to incorporating immigrants into the framework of the facilities provided by the National Board of Labour. This body not only supervised available working opportunities but also provided retraining centres all over the country under the same conditions as for Swedes (Hammar, 1985; Westin, 1996).

The goal of freedom of choice is more directly related to the new understanding of Swedish citizenship compared to the previous two directives. Stemming from the Parliamentary Commission on Immigration in 1974, this goal attempted to reflect the ethnic reality in Sweden and sought to provide an opportunity for individuals, rather than entire ethnic groups, collectives or organisations, to determine their personal cultural affiliation and, more importantly, their identity. However, state support should also be provided for those who chose to maintain their cultural and linguistic heritage in terms of having access to literature in the native tongue, language education in schools, radio and television broadcasts, and funding for ethnic organisations (SIP, 1983). This would not be an action initiated by the government, however, but rather set into motion only if approached by a certain immigrant community. Interestingly, the new directives avoided the issue of labelling the new communities as being ethnic minorities. The reasons were that first, Sweden was seen as an ethnically homogenous country,[15] and second, the groups in question were not historically rooted or numerous enough to be recognised as minorities. The debate on indigenous minorities had to a large extent been absent from official policy and much academic literature in Sweden. The influential policy directives (Govt. Bills, 1975:26 and 1997/98:16) omit any reference to the existence of ethnic minorities, most likely due to the conception that these groups did not significantly differ from the majority population culture and practice. The freedom of choice goal was an explicit rejection of the previous policies' implicit demands of assimilation, and an attempt to establish a Swedish understanding of multiculturalism.

Seeing that the Swedish state put a great deal of emphasis on minimising inequalities between the native and the new population by means of group, or corporatist, orientated policies, the level of organisation needed to be highly co-ordinated and very centralised. In contrast to Dutch policy, the Swedish understanding of ethnic management was not a result of a radically new way of thinking but rather the case of adjusting existing policies and established solutions to the new situation. The incorporation of migrants was to be the responsibility of the public authorities, both locally and nationally. A well co-ordinated system had already been established to manage the population, stemming from the creation of the welfare state in the 1930s, where social services, housing, education and health care were provided by the municipal authorities working together with several national, supervising governmental bodies.

When migrant integration became an apparent issue, it was perceived as a natural progression that this would also be dealt with by the welfare state. On the national level, two institutions have the main responsibility for the population – the Swedish Labour Market Board (Arbetsmarknadsstyelsen, AMS) and Swedish Immigration Board (Statens Invandrarverk). Since the abrupt halt to labour migration was imposed by pressure from the trade unions, AMS has been responsible for the implementation of an extensive labour market strategy which aims to train and provide employment projects in order to contribute to the economic integration of the migrant groups. These boards were closely intertwined with the local-level employment agencies as well as being responsible for orientating individuals to adult education programmes combined with Swedish language education. The board operated under the Ministry of Labour and served as the prime authority in terms of organisation and co-ordination of migrant affairs. The immigration board's responsibilities range from issuing visas and conducting research on ethnic relations to granting citizenship and funding national migrant associations.

The Swedish Immigration Board changed its name to the Swedish Migration Board (Migrationsverket) in July 2000. This signalled a change in direction in two ways. First, the change indicates a shift away from the previous conception of migrants as a group and now emphasised the individual; and second, it indicates that the board's responsibilities stretch not only to immigration but also to other areas that resulted as a consequence of migration. Apart from the traditional areas of general refugee and immigration policy, the board now emphasises the importance of co-ordinating integration and return migration policies (Migrationsverket, 2001). Since its formation in 1969, the migration board has expanded organisationally as well as in terms of responsibilities, today encompassing numerous nationwide sections and divisions and with an increasingly large number of employees (300 in 1981 increasing to 1800 in 2001). Although the board stresses its decentralised character, in which the local authorities have a substantial degree of autonomy, the issue of incorporating migrants is still highly centralised.

The migration board redirects the decisions taken by the government down to the local authorities who in turn co-ordinate their efforts, working very closely with the board in replicating the national discourse and modes of organisation. This centralisation is sustained by constant communication and consultation between central and local levels of government in which the migration board offers guidelines and suggestions for the local authorities, characterised by regular meetings between national and local administrative officials (Hammar, 1985). This particular way of structuring policy is complemented by a number of national-level commissions and advisory councils which deal specifically with migrant issues, very much similar to the organisational structure found in other areas of policy-making. Some, but not all, of these commissions have a permanent status and hold a significant position in terms of initiating, formulating and evaluating policy. As Hammar (1985) points out, migrant policy is not so much the product of governmental investigation but rather formulated on the basis of the reports generated by these commissions and advisory councils. These commissions have attempted to persuade the government to take a decision with regard to ethnic and racial discrimination in the labour market, which is the crucial area for integration according to, primarily, the Socialdemocratic understanding of integration and citizenry rights. Two attempts have been made to introduce governmental regulations against ethnic and racial discrimination on the labour market: in 1985 by the Commission on Ethnic Discrimination and in 1988 by the Commission on Racism and Xenophobia. Although these commissions are in a position of considerable power, these propositions were both declined by the government, which took the view that discrimination would best be resolved by the labour market itself. It took until 1994, when the Conservative bloc finally passed a law prohibiting ethnic labour-market discrimination.

The rather diffuse slogan of partnership is more complicated to understand. As its official meaning stands, it was designed to induce a 'mutual and comprehensive process between the immigrant communities and the majority population in matters of common concern' (SIP, 1983: 11). There are two interpretations of this. On the one hand, it suggests that immigrants were to be seen as collaborators in the development of the new society. They were not only granted permission to mobilise in terms of self-organisations but would also receive public support for these activities. By contrast, Widgren (1982) states that partnership was intended to express the need for tolerance and solidarity between immigrant groups and native Swedes. Here, migrants were encouraged, and given greater opportunities, to play an active part in Swedish politics as well as enlarging their opportunities for cultural activities. The goal of partnership would be employed by the use of two important instruments – supporting immigrant associations and extending political rights for non-nationals. As with the general immigration policy, the use of these instruments was to a large extent an extrapolation from the welfare state's pioneering years in combination with an uninterrupted 40-year Socialdemocratic dominance in which the party established its leading role on behalf of the Swedish working class. The ideas and practices developed in working-class incorporation were transferred to the field of immigrant incorporation under the headings of multiculturalism, preservation of mother-tongue language and cultural heritage. This was to be conducted in the same way as the state had provided support for the people's movements earlier.

This specific way of organising the population and its paradoxical results for the migrant part of the population have been examined extensively over the last decade by Swedish scholars (Ålund and Schierup, 1991; Löfgren, 1989; Westin, 1996) who argued that the institutionalisation of 'culture' produced a 'culturalisation of everyday life'. What had previously been part of everyday practice was now transformed into 'immigrant culture' when confronted with Swedish society and, more importantly, with the stronghold which Swedish culture had over the public sphere. An increasing process of exoticising migrant habits led to ready-made matrices of what constituted 'authentic immigrant culture' by means of institutionalisation and standardising the tools available for this practice. At the same time as the ethnic associations served as an arena in which the home country's rituals, interesting gastronomy, language and dances could be maintained, the association also served as a boot-camp for teaching the new population about folk-movement practice in terms of board meeting technique, record keeping and schooling into Swedish democracy.

## Malmö

Up until the late nineteenth century, migration to Malmö was mainly small scale and primarily of German, Polish and Danish origin. In 1890, official statistics began to separate nationals from non-nationals showing that out of Malmö's 48,504 inhabitants, 174 were foreign nationals. At the turn of the century, 1535 were registered as being born abroad. At this time, migration to Malmö can be described as being of a skilled nature consisting mainly of entrepreneurs and businessmen who helped to set the foundation to the forthcoming industrial city. Immigration levels continued to be positive during the early part of the century.

A number of refugees and displaced persons started to arrive in Malmö during the Second World War. This process continued during the late 1940s and early 1950s and included migrants from Russia, Poland and the Baltic states but also a number of Sudeten-Germans. Unlike other countries affected by the war, these migrants did not, by and large, play a significant role in the post-war reconstruction (Järtelius, 1999). The expanding shipbuilding, textile and clothing industries in Malmö were nevertheless in a serious deficit of workers, whereby overseas labour recruiting commenced on a large scale. Most of these skilled to semi-skilled workers originated from nearby countries such as Denmark and Germany, and to some extent from Italy. During the late 1950s up until the early 1970s, demand shifted towards non-skilled labour which changed the composition of the labour force as well as its origins. Swedish industries and the Swedish state began active recruitment campaigns from south-eastern Mediterranean countries such as former Yugoslavia, Greece and Turkey. By the mid-1960s, labour migration was at its peak, which made the national trade union (LO) conscious about its impact on wage levels. With the increasing amount of cheap foreign labour, LO representatives feared that this would bring down overall wage levels and affect the labour force negatively. This prompted the government to restrict entry and regulate labour migration, which came to an abrupt stop in the late 1960s. In the post-oil crisis period, migration to Malmö shifted dramatically to include only asylum and refugee migrants.

Migrant reception in Malmö became institutionalised in the late 1960s with the creation of the 'unit for immigrant service' (Informationstjänst för utländska medborgare, also known as Invandrarbyrån). This unit dealt almost exclusively with all areas in which migrants could experience problems and provided services relating to information and advice, interpretation, language education co-ordination and recreational activities. The local government considered the immigrant service to be a link between the migrant communities and the existing societal institutions. Prior to this, migrant reception and management were by and large not a concern for the public authorities but left to NGOs and migrant voluntary organisations. This new initiative originated from a proposition dating back to 1967 in which it was deemed necessary to set up a body that would facilitate the adjustment of immigrants to Swedish society. The main concerns facing the local authorities related to employment and housing. However, this unit also provided language education for the city's newcomers, in collaboration with the University of Lund, a situation which was later handed over to the study-circle organisation for labourers, ABF (Arbetarnas Bildningsförbund).

Swedner (1973) points out that it was during the 1960s that a clear division of responsibilities emerged. During this decade, employers' associations and voluntary organisations acted as receivers for the employment-seeking migrants. The societal institutions exercised the controlling and steering functions whereas the 'private' institutions acted as supporting and advisory units. When the number of migrants started to increase in the early 1970s, the burden on the 'private' institutions become overwhelming and the societal institutions became more actively engaged in the reception procedure. One of the more immediate issues was to accommodate the new population.

In the 1960s, Malmö had over 30,000 people who had applied for accommodation. Since a very small share of the real estate market was managed through private ownership, a majority of the housing was owned by national or local housing corporations. The potential accommodation scarcity in the three metropolitan cities (Stockholm, Gothenburg and Malmö) had been recognised a few years earlier. The national government had taken a decision to commence building a number of high-rise developments which would accommodate needy families in the outskirts of the cities, the so-called 'Miljonprogrammet'. In Malmö, the Rosengård project was finished by the mid-1970s. Initially, this area was intended to be a step up from the living conditions of downtown Malmö. The new residential buildings sported highly modernised interiors and were made affordable to lower-income households due to rent subsidies. However, during the 15-year period 1970–85, the demographics changed and the population in Malmö started to decrease, by no less than 35,000 over the whole period. This led to a surplus of flats, primarily in these high-rise buildings, and landlords began to offer favourable deals for families who wanted to fill the empty spaces which in turn generated few new constructions. In 1985, the population began to rise again as a consequence of the increasing number of refugees. The new group of arrivals was almost exclusively limited to housing in the Rosengård area. The main reason for this situation can be found in the large number of people moving out of this district of flatted blocks. After completion of the housing project in the 1970s, most inhabitants were working-class, ethnically Swedish families. As these groups advanced socio-economically, they began to move out of the area, heading to neighbouring suburbs. Since there was a need to accommodate the increasing inflow of refugees and asylum seekers, these were directed towards Rosengård (see further Andersson, 2001).

In terms of demographic and ethnic composition, the shift from labour migrants to refugees runs clearly through the statistics. Just prior to the formal halt of labour migration, the five largest non-national, legally resident migrant groups were: ex-Yugoslavs (4348), Danes (2765), Finns (2234), Germans (1192) and Hungarians (644) (Järtelius, 1998). However, these figures only account for foreign nationals and therefore exclude the current definition of a migrant (as being someone born abroad or with both parents born abroad), as well as naturalised migrants. In 2002, however, with the current definition, the largest migrant communities were: ex-Yugoslavs (9337), Poles (5374), Bosnia-Herzegovinans (5146), Iraqis (5067) and Danes (3999) (Malmö Statistics Office, 2002). In addition, another 150 nationalities make up the ethnographic composition in Malmö, ranging from reasonably large (Lebanese, 2802) to very small (Angolans, 10).

Overall, in the Malmö city area, an average of 35 per cent of inhabitants have a foreign origin. However, the differences between the various urban areas are remarkable, from 18 per cent in the middle-class area of Västra Innerstaden and Limhamn to 85 per cent in Rosengård.

## Britain

### Composition of immigrant population

Comparatively, Britain has had a longer experience of immigration tracing back almost 400 years. Banton (1972) estimates that around 2 per cent of the population of London were of black descent as early as the eighteenth century. Although, prior to the post-war waves of immigration from the Indian subcontinent and the West Indies, the major source of migrants came from more closer to home, Ireland.

Irish immigration to Britain can be traced back to the late eighteenth century and to a period of great economic and social change which, as Miles (1982) points out, created a demand for labour as a consequence of economic change, urbanisation and class formation. Land reform in Ireland at the time created dispossession and ejection from the land especially so in the south and west of the country which was predominantly populated by peasants and small tenant producers. The initial migration from Ireland was mainly seasonal, related to the potato farming cycle, and figures from the time estimate that Britain received around 60,000 migrants in 1841. This type of migration was the privilege of farmers who had access to land whereas the growing demand for labour in low- and semi-skilled sectors resulted in semi- to permanent settlement of Irish migrants in Britain. However, the major influx of Irish migrants was not solely due to temporary migration but was rather the direct result of the potato famine of the mid-nineteenth century which saw an increase of the Irish population from 400,000 in 1841 to 800,000 in 1861 (Solomos, 2003; see also Jackson, 1963). Irish migration to Britain, as with the Finns to Sweden, is by far the greatest in numerical terms but in contrast to Jewish or Black immigration, there was little state intervention to regulate Irish migration and the Irish had a unique position compared to other nationalities in that they were free to enter, settle, work and vote in Britain. Solomos (ibid.) points to the Act of Union established in 1800 and the incorporation of Ireland into the United Kingdom which made Irish citizens on par with British citizens. This situation was maintained after the establishment of the Republic of Ireland in 1922 as well as after Ireland left the Commonwealth in 1947, which echoes the Nordic Free Movement agreement. Despite the officially relaxed attitude towards Irish migrants, strong anti-Irish sentiments had been prevailing throughout the nineteenth and twentieth century amongst both the working class and the elite.

Another key migrant group during this period were the Jewish settlers from Eastern Europe who came as refugees following the pogroms between 1875 and 1914 and established themselves in London's East End (Castles and Miller, 2003). The Jewish migration was Britain's first experience of mass migration from beyond the British aisles which also coincided with economic depression and high levels of unemployment. These circumstances, as pointed out in more detail below, sparked early debates on restrictions to immigration and changes in citizenship policy (Cesarani, 1996). Despite strong anti-Jewish sentiments, Castles and Miller (2003) suggest that the Jewish experience of social mobility proved to be quite extraordinary. A large number of the first generation managed to move out of wage employment and into small entrepreneur enterprises in rag trade or retail while placing a strong emphasis on education for the children who, in turn, were able to move into business or white-collar employment[16] (see also Feldman, 1983). Worthy of note is that prior to the Jewish migration of the early twentieth century, the immigration climate was comparatively healthier with many aliens enjoying unrestricted entry although this was primarily related to 'unproblematic' migrants from mainland Europe.

However, the most significant change in terms of the British demographical composition occurred in the decades following the Second World War. As a colonial power, Britain experienced immigration of Blacks and Asians from the overseas territories starting in the late 1940s. As Hampshire (2005) acknowledges, this post-war migration was not so much a movement of aliens towards a sovereign territory but rather a movement of citizens within an imperial polity. This meant that up until the 1962 Commonwealth Immigrants Act, persons born in colonial or Commonwealth countries were formally permitted to travel and enter the United Kingdom freely by virtue of being citizens of the United Kingdom and Colonies. Thus, between 1955 and 1961, net inward migration from India, Pakistan and the Caribbean totalled around 200,000 and given the imminence of tighter immigration control, between 1961 up until July 1962, the figure was 191,060 (Evans, 1971). Many of those arriving during this period came predominantly as labour migrants (although the Ugandan Asian are a special case of being expatriated involuntarily) and were in some cases the result of active recruitment by firms (e.g. London Transport) but a majority emigrated voluntarily, responding to labour market needs. The 1962 Immigrants Act put severe restrictions to further spontaneous movement in combination with the British economy going through a period of stagnation. Although, as one channel for immigration closed, another opened in the form of family reunification which continued up until the implementation of the 1971 Immigration Act. At this point it was clear that the immigrant population was becoming permanent with the population from the New Commonwealth countries increasing from 1.2 million in 1971 to 2.2 million in 1981. Migration from the ex-colonies was further encouraged by the reports sent back by previous migrants in terms of information passed on about job opportunities and by the role of travel agents who made a good living by encouraging migration (Layton-Henry, 1984).

Today, the ethnic minority population, as officially defined, amounts to 8 per cent of the total population (around 4.5 million) with a breakdown into British Asian 4 per cent; Black British 2 per cent; Chinese 0.4 per cent and Other ethnic groups 0.4 (National Statistics, 2004). Similar to other recruiting countries in the post-war era, most Black and Asian workers found unskilled and manual jobs in industry and services, with specific concentrations of ethnic groups around cities such as London and in the northern part of England (e.g. Bradford, Birmingham, Leeds). Although, the ethnic population is relatively small in comparison to the total population, the concentration of this population to certain key areas or regions has on the one hand generated an idea of 'multicultural cities' rather than a multicultural nation and on the other, as argued by Adolini (1998), created a cause for attention given the role that these minorities can play as electors in areas of their concentration. Although, at the same time, the geographical dispersal between the ethnic groups has produced a wide variety of settlement patterns, minority political organisation and lack of national political unity among these communities. In the inner cities there is still a high degree of residential segregation in neighbourhoods and, as such, ethnic minorities have retained certain barriers of cultural mix and political organisation (Jacobs, 1988).

In addition, an increasing proportion of the ethnic minority population is born in the United Kingdom. The 1991 census indicates that 55.7 per cent of the Black British population were born in the United Kingdom, compared to 44.1 per cent of the Asian population. These differences reflect the timing to their immigration with the former group having arrived in the United Kingdom at an earlier stage. This development is of interest for the further discussion on citizenship and belonging since the proportion of 'immigrant' ethnic minorities is constantly decreasing, giving way to native-born British minorities (Adolino, 1998).

### Immigration policy and status of migrants

As mentioned in the previous section, immigration became a political issue in the early twentieth century following the large influx of Jews fleeing the pogroms. The anti-immigrant sentiments or perceptions of immigration being a 'problem' were to some extent a consequence of the anti-Semitic attitudes and thus contributed to produce political debate in order to come up with a legislation that would control immigration. This resulted in the Aliens Order of 1905 which was a radical departure from previous immigration policies and laid the foundation for future legislation, especially for the post-war era. The first decades of the twentieth century were characterised by a number of restrictive policies on migration sparked by racist sentiments towards the Jewish migrants (see further Gainer, 1972). This new policy applied to the entry into Britain of all non-United Kingdom subjects or to those generally perceived as aliens. Solomos (2003: 42) points to two major implications of this new legislation. First, aliens could be refused permission to enter Britain if they did not have, or did not have the means to obtain, the means to subsist in adequate sanitary conditions and, second, that an alien could be expelled from Britain without trial or appeal if he or she was found to be receiving poor relief from within a year of entering Britain, was found guilty of vagrancy or was found to be living in insanitary conditions due to overcrowding. Powers were also extended so that the home secretary would be able to expel migrants deemed to be undesirable but measures were also introduced in order for individuals to appeal to an immigration board if they had been refused entry. Similarly, the law also encompassed a clause that an immigrant could not be refused entry if he or she had been subjected to political or religious persecution. Although the law was in place, successive governments were not implementing it rigorously which meant that Jewish immigration to Britain continued up until 1914 when a new, more forceful, act was adopted – the Aliens Restrictions Act. The justification was national security during wartime and enabled the government to decide who would be prevented from entering, who would be deported and who could be made subject to restrictions in terms of accommodation and mobility.

The first two decades of the twentieth century were busy times with regards to changes and amendments of immigration acts. By the end of the First World War, the Aliens Restrictions (Amendment) Act of 1919 replaced the 1905 law and extended the 1914 Act for one year. In 1920, the Aliens Order was passed which meant that the Acts of 1914 were renewed annually.

The 1920 legislation did further increase the state's power to control entry to Britain in terms of granting immigration officers the right to refuse entry of immigrants who could not support themselves in the country and to deal with immigration evaders. At this time a number of measures were introduced in order to monitor migrants such as aliens being obliged to register their address and change thereof and also some slightly arbitrary measures which allowed the home secretary to deport migrants who were not 'conducive to the public good'. In addition, labour mobility was further restricted by the introduction of work permits issued to a prospective employer by the Ministry of Labour only if it could be shown that there were no British workers available for the position (see further Evans, 1983). This legislation had an important impact on the political and religious refugees throughout the period 1933–39 during which the official British response was to limit these flows due to reasons of overcrowding and high levels of unemployment. Therefore Jewish refugees from Germany and elsewhere in occupied Europe was limited and amounted to about 55,000 (Sherman, 1973).

Even though migration up until the mid-twentieth century had been relatively small scale, the major shift in terms of numerical numbers came with the post-war reconstruction. Therefore, as Hampshire (2005) argues, the British government experienced a dilemma in terms of how to respond to labour shortages but at the same time attempt to keep the racial demography in check without appearing racist. Britain is somewhat unique in terms of ex-colonial migration in that these subjects, although not British citizens as such, had free access to entry. The reasons for this can be found in the 1948 British Nationality Act which stated the rights of citizens of British colonies and Commonwealth countries to enter, work and settle in Britain. This also meant that once in Britain, these 'internal' migrants had access to the same rights as British citizens and were qualified for naturalisation after a period of residence. In contrast to other former colonial powers such as France, who clearly defined citizens from former colonies as foreigners, immigrants to Britain had immediate access to political rights. The aim of this Act was not to facilitate immigration or as an attempt to make British identity more inclusive, instead it was a constitutional exercise and few predicted that any of the ex-colonial subjects would take advantage of their right to free movement.

However, this situation soon became a political issue and both the Labour governments of 1945–51 and the Conservative government in the 1950s considered various ways in which to reduce immigration from the perspective that Black and Asian immigration was, by and large, a 'problem' that needed to be dealt with and controlled. In addition, it was during this time that the political debate on 'coloured' immigration was established and, as Solomos (2003) argues, that the link between race and immigration emerged. However, debates on the need to control immigration had already begun in the mid-1940s especially with reference to coloured immigration. The crux of the matter, which prevented the discussion from becoming a bill until 1961, was that the introduction of controlling Black immigration would most likely cause embarrassment to Britain as head of the Commonwealth and Colonies, divide public opinion and question the legality of such control based on colour in both British and International law (Miles and Phizacklea, 1984). Despite these considerations, debate in parliament on a new immigration legislation was fierce, from both the Left and Right as well as being an issue in the media where housing, social conditions, employment and competition for jobs were all linked, or made in reference, to immigration in general and Black immigration in particular. These events culminated in the 1962 Commonwealth Immigrants Act.

The restrictions introduced by this legislation to reduce certain Commonwealth immigration was justified with reference to the perceived difficulties Britain experienced in terms of assimilating Black immigrants. Despite being criticised for being a covert racist policy as Solomos (2003) notes, the collective pressure on controlling Black immigration was so strong that the bill eventually became a law and as such goes against common historical views that migration was at first welcome and then opposed when it became unmanageable (Spencer, 1997). The main difference with previous acts is that the 1962 legislation put forward a more firm distinction between British citizens and its colonies and those who held passports from independent Commonwealth countries. This meant that immigration control was now imposed on all Commonwealth migrants except if they had been born in Britain; held British passports issued by the British government or were included in the passport of a person allowed entry under the previous two (MacDonald and Blake, 1995). In addition, the Act also introduced important restrictions on labour mobility in that vouchers or work permits had to be obtained prior to entry for applicants with a recognised skill or qualification (that was in short supply); applicants who had been offered employment in the country of origin and, finally, workers without specific skills or job offer. Quotas were set up for each category but with room for adjustment according to British labour market needs. However, the Act also allowed for family reunification in terms of wives ('dependents') and children under 16. Despite having the appearance, as Hampshire (2005) remarks, that other criteria for entry had been considered but rejected as impractical (e.g. state of immigrant's health or housing situation) it points to a slight exaggeration of admissions being purely based on labour demand. In addition, a distinction was made between citizens who 'belonged' (born in the United Kingdom or holding UK issued passports) and those who did not (everyone else).

In addition, one of the features of the 1962 Act included a provision that British citizens living in the newly independent commonwealth countries were exempt from the introduced immigration control given that they held a British passport. This referred to a number of white settlers in East Africa but more importantly it also included a large number of Asians living in Kenya and Uganda. There had already been a flow of migrants to the United

Kingdom from these countries during the mid- to late 1960s and in 1967 Asian – in addition to Black – immigration began to be perceived as 'problematic'. The Labour government had already been pressured to introduce firmer immigration control and it was therefore not surprising that a second Commonwealth Immigrants Act was passed in 1968. This act suggested further restrictions and targeted the East African Asians specifically in that any Citizen of Britain or its colonies would be subject to immigration control unless they (a) were born in Britain or (b) had at least one parent or grandparent that had been born, adopted, naturalised or registered in Britain as a citizen of Britain or its colonies (Solomos, 2003). Given the historical pattern of migration of the Asian communities in East Africa, this new legislation effectively excluded these groups from 'belonging' to Britain. As Karatani (2003) mentions, the criterion for exemption of immigration control was changed in order to establish a qualifying connection with the United Kingdom in terms of ancestry, mirroring the German understanding of belonging to the *volk*. Furthermore, the 1968 Act was established in line with its 1962 counterpart but the Nationality Act from 1948 was kept intact. Consequently, although the nominal citizenship from 1948 continued to be maintained, the criterion for free entry and rights and privileges connected to being a national was narrowed and were now reserved for those with ancestral links to the United Kingdom.

Following Powell's infamous 'river of blood' speech in April 1968, immigration, especially of non-whites, was popularised as leading to a total transformation of British national identity and white Britons eventually becoming a minority in their own country as well as leading to similar racial 'wars' as seen in the United States. Despite facing stark criticism for these views and being forced out of the shadow cabinet, Powell's opinion had a profound impact on the immigration debate even leading to calls of halting immigration completely.

Having played the 'immigration card' during the election campaign, the Conservatives returned to power in 1970 and set out to further limit the channels of entry by introducing yet another immigration bill which became the 1971 Immigration Act. The need felt here was to bring order to the confused legislation and create a logical basis for immigration control. This new Act introduced the term of 'partial' citizens, meaning that they were considered to have a link with Britain if one of their natural or adoptive parents was at the time of their birth or adoption a citizen of the United Kingdom and Colonies by reason of birth in the United Kingdom or in any of its Islands (i.e. the Channel Islands and Isle of Man). In contrast to the previous two Acts, the 1971 Act included those Commonwealth citizens that the Acts of the 1960s had prevented from entering Britain. However, the ancestral link was limited to only one generation and the parent in question had to be born in the United Kingdom rather than naturalised, registered or adopted in the United Kingdom as previously stated. Despite the Conservatives arguing for tighter immigration control on Commonwealth immigration, the new Act in fact removed a number of, especially Old Commonwealth, migrants from immigration control and as such the Act could not be judged to be a measure to reduce immigration. The results of the new act were however somewhat confusing or even contradictory in that the new act freed up several million Commonwealth citizens from immigration control rather than reducing the number as seemed to be the general intention. Interestingly enough, the impact of the Act, as we shall see in the following section, could be found primarily in the area of British citizenship. Invoking Karatani's (2003) extensive study on the development of British citizenship, the opposition to the bill demanded further work and legislation on the nationality act instead of redefining immigration law and the supporters of the creation of a 'new' definition thus consisted of an unlikely alliance between more liberally orientated MPs and Powellites. Although agreeing on the principle of a necessity to create a British citizenship, the two partners differed with regard to its ingredients. The former arguing for an extensive understanding which was to include East African Asians whereas the latter favoured a more exclusive citizenship type based on ancestry. Despite being an optimal time for the government to re-negotiate British citizenship given the timing (the United Kingdom joining the EC and the dismantling of colonies was well underway) there was little debate in parliament in terms of defining a British national and in the end the following two understandings were put forward:

1. persons who are citizens of the United Kingdom and Colonies or British subjects not possessing that citizenship or the citizenship of any other Commonwealth country or territory, who, in either case, have the right to abode in the United Kingdom, and are therefore exempt from UK immigration control;

2. persons who are citizens of the UK and Colonies by birth or by registration or naturalisation in Gibraltar, or whose father was so born, registered or naturalised (Karatani, 2003; see further Treaty 22 January 1972)

Of interest here is that given the context, the British government was still not in a position to create a British citizenship due to the overall negative sentiments regarding immigration. The government was reluctant to closer define 'Britishness' since it was unclear what this should be based on and besides, the current legislation was already filtering out those who the government wanted to keep out. Therefore the rational by the British government was to narrow down criteria for entry, that is, by means of immigration control, rather than to put forward further definitions of British citizenship in order to establish who belongs to British society. This meant that issues of belonging became a technical issue and the government pursued different ways in order to include Old Commonwealth citizens as much as possible within the definition of who was considered a legitimate citizen while at the same time trying to avoid to appear racist. This was a way out of the dilemma which could potentially be created by focusing on issues of Britishness and nationhood. Moreover, these debates were in a sense already settled with the British Nationality Act from 1948 and as a result, the imperial definition of citizenship – formal membership established on the basis of the Empire – survived into the 1960s. Belonging was consolidated within the realms of immigration control. However, after almost two decades of immigration to the United Kingdom, the gap between those holding nominal and substantive citizenship continued to widen. This in turn contributed to the resurrection of a proper citizenship debate which culminated in the introduction of a British citizenship in 1981.

Pursued primarily by the Conservative government, subsequent changes were intended to come to terms with the perceived dangers posed to British society by already settled ethnic minority communities and immigration control became a tool to prevent further flows of dependents and marriage partners of those settled legally (Gordon, 1985). A main goal for the Thatcher administration was to construct the question of nationality along racial lines (Solomos, 2003), which the 1981 Nationality Act signalled. Here, the existing nationality and immigration legislation would rationalise British citizenship with an automatic right to take up residence in Britain. This was created by dividing the category of Citizen of the United Kingdom and Commonwealth into three categories: British citizen; British Dependent Territories Citizen and British Overseas Citizen. This distinction further strengthened the racial connotations of previous divisions by disguising it within the overall framework of British citizenship (MacDonald and Blake, 1995).

However, the 1981 Act was still more of a legal term (who had the right to entry) than a definition of substantive citizenship and any references to 'Britishness' were kept silent.

### Citizenship policy

Given the blurred border between immigration and citizenship policies, the concept of citizenship has had a notoriously weak presence in the British history especially when it comes to serving as a tool to define national identity and 'Britishness'. Despite aims to make immigration more exclusive, the United Kingdom has not pursued an exclusive citizenship policy as such but has rather been one of the prime users of the *jus soli* principle which has a long and well established tradition (Cesarani, 1996).

Until the 1981 Nationality Act was laid down, anyone born within British territory – regardless of the parents' legal status or whether they were British nationals – could claim British nationality. As pointed out in the previous section, this meant that persons born in any of the Commonwealth countries with only a slight connection to the United Kingdom had the right to British citizenship. However, the introduction of immigration control on

British subjects – which went against one of the fundamental rights of citizenship, the right to free entry and settlement – meant that citizenship definition had to be narrowed. The changes introduced in the early 1980s thus suggest a mix between *jus soli, jus sangunis* and *jus domicili*. Persons born in the United Kingdom by parents who are British citizens have the right to citizenship. If born in the United Kingdom but not entitled to citizenship at birth one is entitled to be registered as a citizen by the age of ten given certain conditions relating to residence. For resident migrants who are not British citizens, naturalisation can occur through two ways. First, registration for those with the right to claim citizenship (i.e. British overseas citizens who have not acquired the citizenship of their country of origin at independence or citizens of British dependent territories provided they have resided in the United Kingdom for at least five years). Second, through naturalisation for all adults who do not qualify under the first rule. However, this is subject to a number of conditions, for example, length of stay (three to five years, or stemming from Gibraltar or the Falkland Islands); knowledge of the English (or Welsh or Scottish) language at an Entry 3 level;[17] that the person is of good character and has the intention of residing in the United Kingdom permanently.

There was also a transitional period for Commonwealth citizens to register given that they were residents in the United Kingdom on 1 January 1973 or who had the right to abode and were living in Britain on 1 January 1983 (also included were women married to British nationals prior to this date). These transitional agreements ended on 31 December 1987. Furthermore, applicants must show that they have not been in violation of immigration laws (De Rahm, 1990) although it is unclear whether an applicant needs to show a clear criminal record. New citizens are now also required to attend a citizenship ceremony.

In contrast to other European countries, Britain has a remarkably relaxed attitude towards dual nationality. As Hansen (2002) notes, the British Home Office views dual nationality with indifference and does not encourage or even pressure individuals to give up their previous citizenship. Given the heated, and almost hysterical, level of debate regarding colonial and non-white immigration it is surprising that dual nationality has never been considered a problem. Hansen continues by suggesting two explanations for the lack of suspicion or hostility to this situation. The first relates to how policy is generated more generally. UK policies are not guided by abstract legal principles or philosophical aims but do rather have a more pragmatic approach according to a 'if it ain't broke, why fix it?' – mentality. The second aspect relates to the beneficial effects that dual citizenship has on integration and also how it can serve as a tool for integration. By becoming British nationals, the identification process with British society was considered to be facilitated which, in turn, creates healthy 'race relations'. This term is particularly important in the UK context since it has formed the basis to many important legislations and policymakers use and refer to it constantly. The aim is to create harmonious relations between ethnic groups and the absence of a threat to public order by any one group or groups.

The three Race Relations Acts of 1965, 1968 and 1975 (plus the Amendment Act of 2000) are key elements of British integration policy and the issue, or relevance, of dual nationality plays a secondary role to these acts which have outlawed discrimination in employment and housing and allowed the active recruitment of ethnic minorities (see further Solomos, 2003). The labour market is especially important since the British policy of integration places a great emphasis on the role of this sector. As such, multicultural thinking has led to creating equal opportunities to stimulate economic integration, with social and political integration following on naturally from this (Soysal, 1994).

Citizenship in Britain has therefore until recently been viewed with some indifference. This relates to the complex historical relationship that Britain has had both with herself and with its colonies. When a formal definition was made of British citizenship in 1948 this was perceived by politicians as being alien to British traditions (Hansen, 2002) and the link between citizenship, national identity and political rights appears to be more of a post-war, post-immigration invention. Here, there appears to be an urgency to create a sense of 'Britishness' which has been lacking in previous centuries. This is not to say that the concept has been missing in history but that it has been constantly changing and has included ideas of shared language, customs, religion, colour, and so on. As Cesarani (1996) discusses, the British identity has been dependent on place of birth; as being non-Catholic or non-Jewish; as being white. The last category is closely related to the creation of the Empire in which race played a central role for domination. However, given the paradox of British citizenship legislation which meant that even colonial migrants identified as being 'non-British' could settle freely in the United Kingdom, the definition of Britishness had to be narrowed down and take on an increasingly more racialised appearance. Especially for New Right representatives, this redirection of national identity meant that migrants, and especially Black migrants, were considered to be an enemy within and source of disruption to the social and moral fabric of British society. Again, one finds emphasis given to differences amongst the ethnic communities in terms of culture, attitudes and values with a sense of migrants 'failing' to integrate and adapt to a 'British way of life'.

The emphasis on creating healthy race relations is thus symptomatic of the problems that British identity has faced over the years as well as how migrants are perceived by the state and how integration is supposed to be achieved. In terms of migrant policies in the United Kingdom these are far more individually orientated and decentralised compared to the corporatist incorporation patterns found in Sweden and the Netherlands.

In the United Kingdom, migrants' status is not defined by their corporate standing but as individuals whose position in the host society is determined by their participation in the labour market. The key here is the individual and less faith is put into centralised policy instruments as the AMS in Sweden or the NCB in the Netherlands. As such there is also less state support or sponsoring of migrant identities or migrant organisations which is considered to be a more private matter. Migrants are thus expected to integrate as individuals into the communities where they reside.

Similarly, British policy has emphasised racial equality (in the sense of opportunities rather than outcome) and apart from some important legal implementations, few other direct measures exist. The key player in this respect is the Commission for Racial Equality which was set up under the Race Relations Act 1976 to facilitate integration by providing equal opportunities and good race relations (CRE, 2004). The main focus is to eliminate discrimination within various spheres of British society, for example, in education, housing and employment. In stark contrast to the closely co-ordinated systems of integration in Sweden and the Netherlands, the British case's main aim is to remove obstacles to individual migrants and providing the settings for equal participation in order for these to enjoy the benefits offered by the system in a similar fashion to French integration policy. This means that policy instruments are there to formulate a legal strategy and action in order to protect individual migrant interests and abolish restrictions that affect foreigners as individuals. This means that, for instance, funding for ethnic cultural associations is very limited and mainly directed at general organisations offering legal support (see further CRE, 2004 for list of funded organisations).

Apart from the general activities in the field of combating discrimination, Britain does not have any centrally defined policies and migrants are by and large taken care of by their locality. In the education area, funds are available for extra English lessons for migrant children but few schools offer mother-tongue education which is regarded as a private concern. Keeping with this line, the general policy instruments aimed at serving the rest of the population are also intended to work for the migrant communities although one direct source of income stems from the 1966 Local Government Act, Section 11 which provides local financing services for what has loosely been labelled the special needs of immigrants. This, however, has almost exclusively been within the educational sector (Soysal, 1994; see also Fitzgerald, 1986). The emphasis lies, again, on projects and programmes that will facilitate integration and make use of mainstream services rather than developing a separate collective identity and organisation.

In terms of how incorporation is organised, the goal of healthy race relations serves as the guiding principle. The CRE is the main institution for this purpose which reports directly to the Home Office which also includes a minister of state who is responsible for race and immigration matters but with few co-ordination or supervising activities. As such, the agency's main tasks are to eliminate discrimination and to promote equal opportunities. In addition, a major task is also to provide legal services and representing individuals in cases of discrimination. The CRE plays a very important role in British race relations by being the main channel through which the government is informed about the current state of affairs regarding issues that affect immigrants and ethnic minorities.

# 3
# The Role of Institutions in Shaping the Opportunities and Constraints on Actors' Behaviour

## Introduction

This chapter will deal with the role and importance of institutions in structuring the political environment. The institutional make-up and its impact on the political actors' scope of options and actions, in combination with the creation of modes of conduct and dominating discourses, are key issues in understanding how political parties and migrant organisations respond to and utilise ethnicity as a territory for mobilisation. Furthermore, national models of citizenship are an important additional institution that sheds light on important cross-national differences in the modes of inclusions and exclusion of migrants and ethnic minorities (Brubaker, 1992; Koopmans and Statham, 1999). The institutional framework will also enable us to explain variance in identification levels and what role identification plays with regard to political participation. This will be explored in Chapter 4.

Institutions, it will be argued, do matter in that an institutional approach helps us to explain differences with regards to macro outputs and outcomes as civil and political rights (Lane and Ersson, 2000). This chapter argues that formal institutions, by means of context-specific entities as well as serving as constraints and facilitators for specific types of policies and priorities, also manage to filter out certain questions and issues in favour of others. Furthermore, the presence and historical emergence of certain institutions within a polity will also influence the behaviour and actions available to actors. Political institutions do thus contribute to shape the process through which decisions are made and implemented (Weaver and Rockman, 1993). This filtering mechanism is transmitted out to other parts of society influencing levels of host society identification by creating norms and ways of conduct.

The chapter is divided into three parts. First, it offers an overview of neo-institutional theory, its importance, relevance and variety, as well as arguing for the historical development of political institutions as the main source of influence with regard to actors' choices and positions. Second, this chapter seeks to examine how different types of democratic options create certain institutional conditions that can either facilitate and/or constrain certain type of issues and actors within the Dutch, French, German, Swedish and British context. Here, attention will be drawn to the specific POS that these institutions have given rise to in the five cases. The historical development and emergence of the prevailing institutions will also point to whether competition will take place in an environment which is either more plural or more corporatist in character. Third, the chapter will focus on why certain types of questions dominate the political agenda over others and the consequences this has for actors' choices. This will be exemplified with reference to why party formation, as a strategy, was adopted in the Swedish case (The Rainbow Party), but not in the Dutch, when attempting to bring ethnic issues onto the agenda.

## The emergence of neo-institutionalism

Over the years, re-emphasising the importance of societal institutions has led to a scholarly fatigue within political science. Immergut (1997) discusses a number of potential explanations as to why the institutional approach might be much 'ado about nothing'. First, institutions have been one of the fundamental pillars within the political science discipline since its beginning and one might wonder why any researcher needs to underline the need for further affirmation on the topic. In fact, the study of political institutions has been so central to political science that, as Eckstein (1963) points out, it can be deemed to be its raison d'être. Second, can the study of institutions offer any new insight into an area that has been dominated by a primarily European approach, that has given prime weight to interest-group pluralism? Third, what relevance does institutional theory have for societies characterised by strong states rather than a weak (American) state? Immergut proposes further that perhaps the relevant question to ask is why institutions do not matter since this proposition would be more interesting from a counter-intuitive point of view.

Indeed, this was at the core of the criticism raised by the political behaviour movement of the 1950s. 'Old' institutionalism was mainly concerned with a descriptive account of different administrative, legal and political structures. It was argued from the behavioural side that merely lining up a number of institutions and explaining how they worked did not provide fully explanatory tools to understand why political behaviour shifted between institutions – and often also within institutions – as well as not providing any satisfactory arguments for difference in policy outcomes. On the contrary, institutions were secondary compared to the importance played by informal aspects such as power distribution, attitudes and, of course, political behaviour (Steinmo and Thelen, 1992). Political behaviour was here defined as an orientation or a point of view that aimed at stating all of the phenomena of government in terms of the observed and observable behaviour of actors (Dahl, 1961a). This approach was concerned with observed behaviour and empirically testing how people vote, what type of policies are passed through and the like. Behaviouralists were thus concerned with dismissing the formalism of politics, institutions, organisational charts, constitutional myths and legal fictions as pure sham (Goodin and Klingemann, 1996).

As a reaction to this approach, a body of literature emerged during the 1980s that aimed at combining the study of institutions with that of political behaviour. Coined 'new institutionalism', this theoretical stance rejected observed behaviour as its starting point for political analysis. Observation of behaviour as such was not considered the main problem, instead the objection was rather that behaviour was not a sufficient basis in order to explain all the complicated phenomena of the political world. Since behaviour occurs in the specific context of institutions, it would therefore only be understandable with specific reference to what institutions, and the extent to which these institutions, influence this behaviour. In Tsebelis's (1990) opinion, the pre-eminent role of institutions can be understood as a simple contribution to studying the way in which human interaction takes place. First, there are a number of players (individual or collective) that are involved in interaction, these players have strategies (which jointly determine the outcome) and the players anticipate some form of payoff at the end of this interaction. Institutions are thus important when we want to understand what type of strategies are involved in terms of sequence of move, set of choices and information available to the players. These parameters, it is argued, are ultimately determined by the institutional structure of the situation.

This theoretical re-routing was a response to the under-socialised accounts of social, economic and political behaviour, proposed famously by March and Olsen (1984, 1994), in which they strongly emphasised the importance of the organisation of political life and asserted a more autonomous role for institutions in shaping political behaviour. One can find three types of neo-institutionalist critiques directed at the behavioural approach. The first one relates to preferences and to what extent a certain type of behaviour reveals the actor's preferences. For the behaviouralist, a person's preference is equalled to his or her behaviour since someone's 'true' preferences are unobtainable. The neo-institutionalist, on the other hand, finds the distinction between 'expressed' and 'real' preferences to be at the core of the analysis, since this serves as support for the assumption that institutions affect the choices that the individual makes. Definitions of interest are viewed as political results rather than starting points for political action that should be taken at face value. Second, institutional theory views the conception that preferences can be aggregated as problematic. Institutions do not serve as mechanisms that sum up interests and preferences but rather distort them. Here, institutions serve as chaos-organisers rather than as aggregating a total of preferences of the individuals. Third, the institutionalist challenge is normative in that this approach recognises an in-built bias in the institutions. This suggests, according to Immergut (1997), that much political behaviour and collective decision-making is an artefact of the procedures used to make decisions. If political processes are to be perceived as decisive, then the analyst's evaluation of politics will change, and interests are no longer regarded as subjective assessments of individuals and collective decisions are no longer viewed as the sum of those individual choices. In the following section, I will explore further how neo-institutional theory can offer insight into the opportunities and constraints facing actors in the political process.

## Defining institutions

Neo-institutional theory has been criticised for its vagueness in terms of defining its programme but also with regards to the term 'institution' itself. Since neo-institutionalist interest lies in the formal as well as the informal side of institutions, this prompted opponents to argue that such an expanded definition would run the risk of 'conceptual stretching' (Collier and Mahon Jr, 1993; see also Sartori, 1970). That is, its meaning and impact would become diluted as it would come to include everything that guides individual behaviour (Peters, 1999; Rothstein, 1996). The word 'institution' has been used loosely in, especially, political science to refer to everything from a formal structure (e.g. a parliament) to more abstract entities (e.g. social class), but also to describe such components dwelling in the socio-economic world such as laws and markets. Although providing some insight into what serves as a structure or constraint to behaviour, the term needs further specification. According to Lowndes (2001), new institutionalists are not only concerned with formal rules and structures but also with informal conventions, paying closer attention to the way in which these institutions embody values and shape power relations as well as to study the interaction between individuals and institutions. Similarly, March and Olsen (1984) remark that an institution does not necessarily have to be understood as a merely formal structure but also as a collection of norms, rules, understandings and routines deriving from the structures in place.[18]

More concretely, Diermeier and Krehbiel (2001) define institutions as a set of contextual features in the setting of collective choice that defines constraints on, and opportunities for, individual behaviour in the setting. Comparatively, Hall (1986) suggests that institutions are also procedures and standard operating practices that structure the relationship between individuals in various units of the polity and economy. Lane and Ersson (2000) find the term to be more or less impossible to define but do propose that the wide variety of definitions tend to boil down to the following five terms – rules, behaviour, practice, organisation and order. This suggests that institutions can be interpreted as behaviour, norm and organ. The problem that arises here is that each concept tends to incorporate elements of the others. Using the behaviour interpretation, an institution could be an organisation since it assumes a particular type of behaviour in a given environment. As a norm, an institution can indicate a term such as democracy or a certain rule of law. Finally, as an organ, an institution can mean behaviour, for example, meeting procedures tend to shape the behaviour of its participants. Conversely, organisations act but rules are never said to be actors or to have preferences. Political organs or bodies such as the parliament or government are often referred to as political institutions since behaviour in such bodies is heavily institutionalised; that is, certain rules, codes and practices prevail in these environments which structure individual politicians' actions. However, as Lane and Ersson point out, the institutions of these bodies and their rules have to be understood as an aspect that is separate from other characteristics such as their resources or capacities to undertake actions.

This gives a series of interpretation issues, which in turn has given rise to several sub-disciplines within the overall neo-institutionalist framework. Reich (2000) develops this conception further when, in the tradition of Lowi (1964) he proposes that there is no need to assert the development of a general theory of political behaviour. Instead, Reich suggests that the different strands within neo-institutionalist theory should be used when addressing specific types of problems. In his article, Reich discusses four types of neo-institutionalism, where each type has unique features which makes them systematically more suited to the study of particular forms of public policy by virtue of the distinct character of politics in that domain. The four major approaches have been identified as historical institutionalism, new economic institutionalism, institutions as cognitive frameworks and institutions as actors, although other authors suggest the inclusion of rational choice institutionalism as well (Eggertson, 1990; Weingast, 1996).

Historical institutionalism emphasises the role of institutional choices made early on for the development of political systems or policy areas (Peters, 1999; Skowronek, 1982). Crucial for this perspective is that the initial structural as well as normative choices will have persistent effects on future public choices. Institutions, understood in this way, determine the identity and number of legitimate actors, the ordering of action, the information available to actors about each other's intentions and relevant agenda. In this understanding, the institutional organisation of the polity or political economy becomes the principal factor for structuring collective behaviour and generating distinctive outcomes in which the institutional arrangements determine the opportunities available as well as the level of acting risk (Hall and Taylor, 1996). New economic institutionalism assumes as its point of departure the actor driven by rational cost/benefit assumptions.

Institutions are conceptualised as tools that are available for the individual actor in order to solve collective problems. Actors' preferences are seen here as being independent from institutions to which actors come and engage in an institutionalised game, with a fixed set of preferences that they are able to rank. Change in institutions leads to change in strategy but not necessarily to a change in preferences (Reich, 2000). Rockman (1994) states that institutions play such an important role for co-operative behaviour since institutionalised practice makes it much more difficult for deals to come unstuck by providing an enforcement mechanism. In addition, a rational choice perspective on institutional theory has emerged from this line of thought. The rational choice option, it is argued, has clearly understood that most political life takes place within institutions (Tsebelis, 1990). This perspective can be defined as the analysis of the choice made by rational actors under conditions of interdependence (Immergut, 1997). It suggests that choices are structured by the rules of the game – for example, which player is allowed to move first; although institutions do not determine actors' preferences, they seem to affect individual and collective choices. Scholars of this tradition interpret institutions as important features of a strategic context, imposing constraints on self-interested behaviour (Steinmo and Thelen, 1992). When the rules change, the choices available to the actor change. In this way, political and economic institutions are important for rational choice theorists because institutions define the options that the actors can adopt in order to pursue their goals. In contrast to historical institutionalism, this version theoretically frames preference formation by assuming that political actors are rational and will act to maximise their self-interest, although the context will make them operationalise self-interest and also tend to assume the preferences of actors from the institutional structure itself. For the rational choice approach, institutions are seen as being primarily rules that work in order to prescribe, proscribe and permit certain types of behaviour. Institutions are conceptualised as being aggregations of rules that members of the bodies have agreed to follow in exchange for benefits that these actors receive from being members of these structures. Peters (1999) highlights how the rationality aspect becomes apparent by referring to how individuals can gain benefits from membership of an institution and would therefore, presumably, be willing to sacrifice options to keep those benefits. There is also an incentive for leaders to have their rules followed. This would suggest that there is a crucial moment of rule-setting that would hinder exploitative behaviour from actors trying to maximise their utility at the expense of other, perhaps less fortunate, actors. Rational choice approaches deal to a lesser extent with the relative justness of a particular institution and more with what interests can come from having a privileged position due to a certain set of constitutional rules.

By contrast, normative institutionalism stems primarily from a sociological tradition, and finds institutions to be normative contexts in themselves

(Olsen, 1988; Powell and DiMaggio, 1991). This view emerged as a reaction to the previous distinction made between means-end rationality and culture. This distinction suggests on the one hand that the variety of institutional forms available were adopted simply because they were the most efficient. In contrast, these forms and procedures should be seen as culturally specific practices which are incorporated into societies and organisations, not necessarily in order to enhance formal means-ends efficiency but rather as a result of processes associated with the transmission of cultural practices more generally. Cognitive explanations thus emphasise cultural explanations in order to understand even the most obvious of bureaucratic practices (Hall and Taylor, 1996). This form of institutionalism addresses matters of the relative degree, type and character of institutional homogeneity and/or heterogeneity, while attempting to investigate how values and practices are diffused. The key here is that the actors are socialised into a certain type of behaviour where action is said to be normatively based rather than based on a calculation of the return that the actors expect from alternative choices. Hence, political behaviour is influenced by duties, obligations, roles and rules that are determined by the particular institutional setting (March and Olsen, 1984). Jepperson (1991) takes this approach a step further. In his view, institutions are social patterns that, when reproduced, owe their survival to relatively self-activating social processes. Institutions are not reproduced by action but rather by routine and its reproductive procedures support and sustain this pattern of behaviour. This definition should not be confused with 'institutionalisation' – a term that indicates the ongoing or social reproduction of such patterns. Democracy can be a norm but it is not institutionalised unless there are formal aspects such as elections available that reproduce that norm. Jepperson thus proposes that institutions are frameworks of programmes or rules that establish identities, and activity scripts for such identities.

Finally, institutions can be perceived as actors themselves. This approach has been labelled international institutionalism (Peters, 1999) since it adopts an international relations perspective and views, primarily, states as institutions with the ability to act. However, international institutionalists are not particularly keen on using the 'institution' term. Instead one finds the term 'regime', which refers to institutions with specific rules, agreed upon by governments, that pertain to particular sets of issues in international politics (Keohane, 1989). States are viewed as being composed of organisationally coherent collectives of state officials and career officials who are relatively insulated from ties to currently dominant socio-economic interests (Skocpol, 1992). This perception implies that institutions have a certain degree of autonomy and internal coherence that enables them to act. This claim is necessary in order to treat institutions as decision-makers. States are thus seen, to some extent, as independent actors, depending on contingent factors including foreign and domestic challenges and resources that they can utilise. However, as Peters (1999) points out, it is not clear within this strand of neo-institutionalism how international regimes have sufficient capacity to produce changes in behaviour of members to say that they are really comparable to other types of institutions such as governments or political parties. Similarly, Powell and DiMaggio (1991) argue that a number of other institutions display similar types of characteristics to those found among states, whether defined as hierarchical, collectivist or not. Market-driven actors, for instance, may also have organisational features that are similar to those found among states.

Generally speaking, these different approaches can be divided into two categories, related to the familiar structure–agency debate. That is, do institutions govern behaviour, which in turn gives rise to determinate results, or do actors take institutions into account when they act, suggesting that behaviour is orientated in terms of institutions?

On the one hand, structure-dependent interpretations such as historical institutionalism and the normative sociological understanding of institutions tend to emphasise the structural element, in that the options available to actors are more or less already in place with little or no opportunity to influence institutional change. On the other, agency-dependent interpretations such as new economic institutionalism and the rational choice perspective tend to emphasise the agency side, portraying actors as fully informed individuals who are able to calculate and manipulate institutions in order to maximise utility. Similarly, Lane and Ersson (2000) discuss this problem in relation to an atomistic versus holistic perception on institutions.

Structure-dependent interpretations would argue that political institutions such as governments and ministries and the judiciary are not acting randomly in favour of individual agendas but are rather the aggregated outcome of several different bodies working in a predictable fashion. This behaviour also tends to be institutionalised, that is the process through which rules and norms are implemented in the sense that they are met with acceptance by the parties involved and that violations of these conditions are met with sanctions in one form or another. The key here is that whatever norm is said to be institutionalised has a backing from the groups concerned. On the other hand, agency-dependent interpretations would emphasise that although institutions play a key role in shaping collective behaviour they do in fact only constitute one part of collective behaviour, that is, rules direct interaction. In this understanding, behaviour is framed by institutions as rules and not, as structuralists would state, that collective behaviour establishes institutions as organisations which have interests of their own. In the case of parliamentary voting, agency advocates believe the outcome of such a procedure to reflect historical legacies, national interests and community needs. For agency-dependent interpretations, whatever the outcome, the result is nothing more than the aggregation of individual choices stemming from the participants' preferences into a group of collective decisions in accordance with rules. As a compromise, Lane and Ersson propose the following definition: political institutions are rules that shape the interaction between individuals when they focus on power and the public sector (structures). Within these settings, it is always persons who act (agency), but the setting varies depending on the nature of the political institutions or the rules of the game. Political institutions frame the setting in which individual actors participate and act in accordance with their interests and preferences (agency), which could also be viewed as organisational choice-setting institutions (structures). The important issue remains, though: if institutions provide the rules of the game and seem to regulate and/or facilitate behaviour to such a large extent – for whom are they important and why?

## How and why institutions are important

The key issue that new institutionalism addressed – that institutions do matter – does still need to be clarified. Since this lies at the core of the neo-institutionalists paradigm, it is important to clarify how one can be sure that institutions are so important and why they seem to play such a large role in society. Do institutions that govern human behaviour give rise to determinate results such as policy outputs or social outcomes? Or do actors take institutions into account when they act (which suggests that behaviour is orientated in terms of institutions)?

Lane and Ersson (2000) recognise the importance of institutions as proposed by the new institutionalists, but suggest that there needs to be a more sophisticated statement. The authors distinguish between what they perceive as an institution's 'intrinsic' and 'extrinsic' importance. The intrinsic side is associated with the problem generated by 'old' institutionalisms' emphasis on the study of institutions for their own sake. Here, public institutions in a country are interesting objects to analyse purely by the fact that, an institution like the national assembly, for example, is an institution that has been there for a considerable amount of time. Extrinsic importance, on the other hand, addresses institutions by asking more specific questions about the consequences of institutions and the relationship between the institution and the individual or collective. The word 'importance' is crucial here since it suggests a number of different interpretations. First, the orientation of behaviour in terms of the institution in question. This implies that since institutions have been in place for a long period of time they have most likely been able to exercise some form of influence on both actors' behaviour but also on other institutions. Second, the moral value attached to the institution. Here, institutions are the carriers of moral and social values and might therefore have a number of groups contesting in what way and how valuable existing institutions are. Finally, institutions have a causal impact upon social results. This statement relates to the conception that institutions might impact on or bring about other results rather than simply being objects of existence.

The same authors argue that the usefulness of neo-institutional theory lies in its use as a counter-factual tool; that is, when one's claim goes beyond saying that an institution exists, one needs to show what the consequences would be of that particular institution not being present. This presupposes the presence of empirical research, since counter-factual testing must involve generalisations (Goodman, 1965). The institutional counter-factual models the likelihood of certain outputs and outcomes in relation to certain institutions. This proposition links in with Diermeir and Krehbiel's (2001) argument concerning the usefulness of neo-institutionalism. Here, they suggest that neo-institutionalism is perhaps better understood as a method rather than as a body of substantive work that is motivated by the so-called chaos problem. They argue that institutionalism should guide us through the more-or-less stable features of collective choice settings that are essential to understand collective choice behaviour and outcomes.

Shepsle and Bonchek (1997) suggest that institutions are relevant since they are at the core of the political communities' way of functioning and make participation, organisation and exercise of authority possible. Collective action, for instance, comes to pass in the political community since institutions provide standardised procedures for actors who, with appropriate incentives, undertake action necessary to secure, provide or control a public good. Adopting a rational choice perspective, the authors state that institutions matter since the tasks or choices that face actors often lend themselves to preliminary structuring. Here, institutions do not so much determine a group's preference but set out the action plan or strategy that the individual or group opts for. These procedures define a context in which individuals may consider whether to engage at all, in what parts of the sequence and in what manner they participate. Similarly, Easton (1990) comments on the issue of the importance of institutions when stating that politics takes place within structural conditions that usually take the appearance of social conditions such as class, culture, economic and even psychological conditions. Easton's position is that political conditions represent the immediate environment of any political act or structure itself, taken in the broadest meaning of the term, on any action in or on any part of the political system. Although there has been a rediscovery that political action takes place within an institutional framework, Easton argues that the more relevant question should not be that the structure of the state is the central phenomenon to investigate, but rather why different states assume such different structural forms. He does, however, recognise the importance of bringing the state back into social analysis since there has been a previous conviction that placed an emphasis on the extent to which the state as a major political actor consists merely of aggregations of individual actions, or simply a direct response to external societal forces (Lowndes, 2001).

Other scholars point to the importance of institutions when refocusing on the state. Here, the central character is the state's authority as the determining factor for the political life of the nation. Important characteristics are the nature and the composition of the state, its actors, functions and abilities to withstand challenges from within as well as from outside. In order to do this, one must consider the prevailing institutional structures of the political system and in particular those from which power and influence flow (Kamrava, 1996). However, what most authors seem to agree on is the way in which constraints and consequences are influenced and shaped by institutions (see e.g. Calvert, 1995; Riker, 1980). Furthermore, Putnam *et al.* (1993) suggests that neo-institutionalists seem to be in agreement on two fundamental points. First, that institutions shape politics. The key issues here are that the rules and standard operating procedures that make up the institutional foundations leave an imprint on the political outcomes by the way in which they structure political behaviour. Second, institutions are shaped by history. Even though institutions are subject to change, most major institutions have inertia and a certain robustness which roadblocks rapid change (unless by extreme measures such as wars or revolutions). Institutions do therefore embody historical trajectories and turning points. The historical development influences the appearance of the institutions since it makes them path-dependent – the former event conditions the latter. Although Putnam states that most neo-institutionalists seem to agree on these two points, it is difficult to see how a rational choice institutionalist could agree with this historical institutionalist view.

The former emphasises that institutions are important primarily since they are features of a strategic context. This suggests that when the rules are changed, the actor's choices change as a consequence since these new rules affect the choices that will maximise the actor's self-interest. Furthermore, when rational choice institutionalism deals with preference formation, this is done at the level of assumption invoking the idea of the all-knowing, rational maximiser. Rational choice theories assume that the actors can use institutions in order to pursue a certain goal by adopting an institution-specific strategy. The main focus here is on the individual or group of actors as agents in relation to a fairly static structure (see e.g. Lees, 2002).

However, the rational choice perspective raises a number of questions. First, it pays little attention to the possibility that the institutional environment might also influence the goals of actors. For example, the choice of pursuing ethnic-specific interests could be related to the socio-economic or ethnic hierarchy position rather than as a result of individual choice. Furthermore, the presence of certain institutions could also hinder or constrain actors or issues from gaining access to the political arena. This becomes especially hazardous if the polity is characterised or dominated by certain cleavage lines which these new claims do not correspond with.

The following sections will deal more thoroughly with the issue of how institutions are able to shape the opportunities and constraints for actors to pursue certain interests.

## Governing institutions

The Lijphart model (1984) contrasts two ideal-types of governing institutions – the (1) Westminster and the (2) Consensus democracy model (see Table 3.1). This discussion came about as a critique of Almond's (1956) typology, which put forward three main categories: Anglo-American political systems, Continental political systems and a third, unlabelled category. Almond's categories are embedded in the old institutionalist school, that is, an emphasis was placed on describing different political systems while emphasising political culture, social structure and political stability. Lijphart's typology is mainly concerned with showing how state stability and performance differed depending on what type of institutions prevailed, but it can also be used as a tool to analyse what type of policies stand the best chance of being passed through and why they tend to do so. Lijphart's model follows the following three-fold set-up: state and executive structure; state legislature and election system; party system and executive structure. This distinction is portrayed in the following table.

Lijphart was originally interested in showing – by means of a single-country case-study – how Dutch democracy managed to survive for so long given that it was characterised by potential threats to stability. The Netherlands is marked by social fragmentation in the sense of religious and political cleavages, and Lijphart pointed out that the key issue here was that a certain type of elite behaviour – consociational attitudes – compensated for the instability one might have expected to be more apparent. Government by an elite cartel could thus turn a democracy with a fragmented political culture into a stable democracy.

Lijphart labelled this the 'politics of accommodation' since the political process was characterised by bargaining and agreement rather than the

*Table 3.1*   The Lijphart typology of governing institutions

| Westminster democracy | Consensus democracy |
|---|---|
| 1. One-party or bare-majority cabinets | Executive power-sharing |
| 2. Fusion of power and cabinet dominance | Separation of power, formal and informal |
| 3. Asymmetric bi-cameralism | Balanced bi-cameralism and minority representation |
| 4. Two-party system | Multi-party system |
| 5. One-dimensional party system | Multi-dimensional party system |
| 6. Plurality system of elections | Proportional representation |
| 7. Unitary and centralised territorial parliamentary | Territorial/non-territorial federalism and decentralisation |
| 8. Unwritten constitution and sovereignty | Written constitution and minority veto |

rivalry politics found in, for instance, an American- or UK-type (and to some extent even a French-type) democracy (Lijphart, 1975). A successful consociational democracy would be characterised by the governing elites' capability to accommodate divergent interests and demands of subcultures by means of transcending cleavages and joining up with the elites of competing subcultures. This would depend upon the elites' commitment to maintain the prevailing system and in what way cohesion and stability could be improved, given that the elites were aware of the perils that a fragmented society could potentially mean. Initially, Lijphart was primarily concerned with what politicians did, and not so much why they did it, but then redefined this view in later writings (1977). Here, he took a much more explicit institutional stance when arguing that deep-rooted cleavages, such as ethnic or religious ones, were much easier to handle in Consensus-type democracies since these involved power-sharing to a much higher degree than a Westminster-type democracy. What this tells us more explicitly is that a certain institutional setting does make an impact on what type of political behaviour we can expect to find. Contrasted with the latter, this is said to promote power-fusing rather than power-sharing. Although ideal-types like this tend to exaggerate certain characteristics, it could still be said to be one of the key distinctive elements. For instance, a two-party system with majority election rules sets serious limitations for new actors to enter. Similarly, majoritarian executive institutions strongly favour well-established actors and issues. That is, systems that score high on the Westminster check-list would most likely see a limited amount of actors and certain types of issues on the political agenda, considering that a Westminster-type democracy is more orientated towards governmental efficiency and parliamentary sovereignty as compared to the Consensus-type emphasis on maximum representation and the recognition of veto-players.

Furthermore, the different characteristics portrayed by these two models do also help to shape the political environment in which particularly non-political party actors, such as organised interests, are able to operate. Westminster-type democracies are predominantly characterised by a pluralistic model of competition whereas Consensus-type democracies generally have strong corporatist traits. The former suggests a predominance of pressure-group politics and the use of lobbying of government agencies and parliament by fragmented and competing interest groups, and a low degree of effective participation by unions in policy-making (Lehmbruch, 1982). The latter indicates a situation of effective participation of labour unions in policy formulation and implementation across all sectors with regard to those policy areas that are of central importance for the management of the economy. Sweden and the Netherlands score high in terms of degrees of corporatism since they display a system of interest representation in which units are organised into a limited number of singular, compulsory, non-competitive, hierarchically ordered and functionally differentiated categories, whereas Germany is usually considered to be in the mid-range with France and Britain displaying few or none of corporatist traits (Siaroff, 1999). These interests are recognised or licensed – sometimes even created – by the state and granted a deliberate representational monopoly within their respective categories in exchange for observing certain controls on their selection of leaders and articulation of demands and supports (Schmitter, 1979). The institutional set-up is thus the key for the understanding of why certain societies tend to lean more towards a pluralistic or a corporatist arrangement of interest access. Dahl's (1961b) work on individual and group influence in the United States points out that the diversity of preferences and values is reflected in political decision-making. Due to the open and competitive American political system, this prevents any single group from regularly seeing its preferences realised in political decisions. That is, influence is widely – but not equally – dispersed, and among many groups rather than a few. Given this situation, the countervailing power of interest-groups vis-à-vis the state increases. Few groups embedded in this type of institutional arrangement lack the capacity and opportunity to influence at least some officials somewhere in the political system in order to achieve their goals.

This pluralist notion acknowledges that individual participation is limited since direct involvement in decision-making is usually confined to a smaller number of leaders of concerned organisations while interest-group activity plays an important role as a supplement to electoral politics. The competitive element in the pluralist approach also suggests that members who are not satisfied with the current direction of a given interest-group can have a substantial amount of influence in that they are able to attend meetings and exercise voting power or, alternatively, exit the organisation and form a rival association.

According to the pluralist view, associations enjoy success in influencing decisions taken by governments because the elected officials are interested in the preferences of the citizens due to electoral reasons and are most likely to respond to those associations with the largest number of members. Implicit in these propositions lies the notion of the 'neutral' state. The state is here an arena where group pressure is brought to bear and focuses primarily on democratically elected and accountable governments as the key actors. Here, the state acts as a referee and guarantees the legitimacy of the system by harmonising interests and building consensus. The state thus serves as a counterweight to the role of interest organisations by preventing these interests from becoming too powerful. The main argument suggests that since the state is of a fundamentally neutral character, it does not act collectively against the balance of societal preferences but simply reflects them or attempts to keep them in balance. However, the concept of power and its treatment differs in a Consensus-type democracy. Williamson (1989) suggests that the pluralist concept of power is too narrow since it does not include a more fundamental form of power which enables an actor to exclude issues from the political agenda in the initial stages. The prevailing institutions are of key importance since they manage – along with social and political values – to filter out issues or define a particular *modus operandi* well before the issue is able to enter the decision-making arena in the first place. The greater the extent to which the state is actively involved in political life and is able to influence the agenda and which actors are to be involved, the more difficult it is for the unrecognised actors to compete. This suggests that interests might be less determined autonomously by individuals and more influenced by social, political and organisational factors that in effect limit the choices and options available. Furthermore, if the state recognises certain interests as being 'more' legitimate than others, then their share of power might become cumulative. Licensed interests may not only use this influence to shape current decisions but also to increase their amount of influence in the future.

Institutionally, corporatism implies that competition amongst organised interests is not as open as in the pluralist understanding, but is to varying degrees dependent on the state and consequently has to be aware of what constitutes justifiable behaviour. Membership is significantly embedded in the organisations through pressure to join and the absence of significant alternative channels. This points to some form of control exercised by the leadership. Associations are furthermore not private but rather semi-public, and group politics is mediated through hierarchies of authority rather than through structures based on the sovereignty of the constituents.

As noted previously, the Westminster/pluralist and Consensus/corporatist dichotomy is of an ideal type; and elements from both types are present in real-world democratic systems. However, whether one adopts a pluralist or a more corporatist stand is furthermore influenced by the prevailing institutional settings of the given society. This issue remains implicit in, for instance, Dahl's (1961b) study of democracy in New Haven. Here, he focused on controversial decisions where different interests would come into conflict and posed the question of who was able to initiate or veto policy changes. Dahl's conclusion was that different actors were able to be successful in different policy areas, suggesting that political power was spread across a variety of individuals and institutions, which in a sense provided evidence for the pluralistic view of the American political environment. Furthermore, the country-specific examples provided in Dunleavy and O'Leary's (1987) chapter on pluralism in *Theories of the State* do all mostly refer to Westminster–Presidential systems such as those in the United Kingdom and the United States, which support the link between institutional set-up and the characteristics of the scope available for action.

The corporatist mode of interest representation is closely associated with the politics of production while pluralism is related to variants of consumption politics. This facilitates the incidence of corporatism and pluralism but does not exclusively state what type of interest-group politics are at play (Saunders and Klau, 1985), giving it a 'more pluralist, less corporatist' dimension. Therefore, in the more pluralistically designed system of the United States, interest groups can gain access and exercise influence at numerous points in the policy-making process. This setting generates relatively open channels of access in that interest-group influence may be broadly dispersed and variable over time. The pluralist approach offers some important insight into the interest-group process. A pluralist conception of a politically active interest group suggests that individuals take part in lobbying or protests to influence political leaders only on issues that are very close to their own preferences. This means that it will be difficult to get people involved unless it genuinely addresses issues of significance to their members and the leadership can show that voluntary participation pays off. Pluralists have more faith in the internal democratic nature of interest groups compared to, for instance, political parties due to the greater experience that the members will have on the relevant issues; and subsequently, if members are dissatisfied, they can easily exit the group and form an alternative interest organisation. Pluralists also consider interest groups to be able to exercise influence over policy-making since the competitive nature of the political environment in terms of democratic considerations is related to sufficient public support.

In contrast, parliamentary systems will have a more corporatist flavour if the centralisation of legislative power decreases the alternatives open to interests groups and party discipline makes appeals to individual legislators, an unobtainable strategy in terms of changing policy outcomes. In the Swedish case, the presence of a dominant party – the Socialdemocrats – with its close ties to the labour federation gives the latter a privileged position in that they have a relatively easier access to the bureaucracy and to cabinet ministers compared to other actors. However, it is usually difficult to reverse the government's position once a decision has been taken with a majority. Also, open campaigns against the governing party or the bureaucracy may be associated with some risk since the recognised actors deal with the government repeatedly. The structural relationship between interest groups, political parties and cabinet members are even more direct in countries such as Sweden and the Netherlands since one of the main characteristics in these countries is the presence of multiple parties and coalition governments. Furthermore, labour unions, business organisations, agrarian and environmental groups are to some extent already represented by individual parties. This gives these groups privileged access to government through the particular type of corporatist arrangements.

The following section will thus exemplify how governing institutions shape the political environment and how these institutions can serve as constraints and facilitators to certain types of interests.

## Political institutions in France

France has experienced a number of different political frameworks over the past two centuries. Whereas Sweden, the Netherlands and the United Kingdom have had fairly long lasting constitutions, the average life of the French constitutions has been around fifteen years. Despite this apparent lack of continuity, Theen and Wilson (2001) identify two enduring patterns of French political life. First, a democratic pattern which features an elected and powerful parliament that dominates politics with a subsequently weak executive. Second, an authoritarian pattern, which emphasise the power of the executive which could be found in the monarchies, the empires and during the Vichy regime.

The current regime, the Fifth Republic, has since its establishment in 1958 aimed to fuse the two patterns by increasing executive power but at the same time retaining democratic values through an independent legislature and free elections. As an attempt to correct the long history of governmental instability, the current constitution mixes parliamentary and presidential types of political frameworks. The result is a hybrid of both these organisational patterns. First, the parliamentary elements include a prime minister and a cabinet of ministers who are accountable to parliament and who can be voted out by the National Assembly. Second, the presidential elements include a popularly elected president who in turn appoints the prime minister who enjoys a variety of constitutional prerogatives and powers. This famously mixed system results in a dual executive sharing responsibility in the direction of the government with a generally strong presidential leadership along with parliamentary government.

Although being characterised as a mixed system, Theen and Wilson continue by pointing out that, in practice, the French system is much more 'presidential' than 'parliamentary'. The reasons, they suggest, can be found in two areas. First, efforts had been made to rectify the weak position of previous presidents by granting substantial power to the president through changes in the constitution. The president is elected for a seven-year period using the absolute majority system with the possibility for re-election. These 'new' powers allow the president to appoint and dismiss the prime minister and members of the cabinet; preside over the meetings of the Council of Ministers; control the agenda of these meetings; require the parliament to reconsider previously passed legislation and declare a state of emergency. In addition, presidential elections use France as one big electoral district enabling the president to claim that he represents the nation as a whole (compared to all other elected officials who come out of relatively smaller electoral districts). Furthermore, the election process contributes to the growing role of the president. Here, the president makes a number of promises on what will be done if he gets elected which will then have to be followed through post-election. Consequently, one therefore often finds the French president to be actively involved in directing politics as well as being a leading figure in policy-making. The prominent role of the president is, however, dependent on having a majority in the National Assembly. The parliamentary side of French politics consists of two chambers, the National Assembly (NA) and the Senate. The former is the more powerful of the two with its membership elected directly by the people for five-year terms whereas the latter is elected indirectly for nine-year terms by an electoral college made up of locally elected public officials. Although both chambers act on all legislations, the government is only accountable to the NA.

On a local level, France displays a number of differences compared to other Western European countries in the sense that local government is heavily dependent on central government and serves mainly to implement decisions taken centrally. The underlying reasons for this high degree of centralisation lies in the French striving for national unity and equality stemming from the historical fear of regional and group-specific interest separation. This means that policies and services are uniform and apply equally to all regions in France. Traditionally, local self-governance has been weak and has been seen as part of the state's bureaucracy according to the ideas of the one and indivisible republic. However, the reforms that were introduced after Mitterand's victory in 1981 meant that more responsibilities were given to the local level. This meant that, formally, the 22 regions are now responsible for economic development, physical planning and labour market strategies; the 96 departments cater for infrastructure, health and social service and the 36,000 local councils are responsible for building plans, local infrastructure and social service. The local authorities are however very much in the hands of the central government since they have little influence over, taxation, for example, and are generally dependent on grants from Paris.

Similar to the Dutch pillar division in society, France has for a long time been divided into various ideological 'families' both amongst the electorate as well as amongst the political elite but has lacked the politics of accommodation of the Netherlands and, as such, has more in common with the conflict ridden Britain. Four cleavage lines have been dominating in the post-war era: class, religion (traditionally between secular-clerical but today also an important part of integration politics), foreign policy (protectionism – EU integration) and form of governance (president – parliament) (Wahlbäck, 1991).

The issue of distribution of societal resources has been dominating in French politics and has divided the parties in a traditional Left–Right dimension but the way in which this conflict has been fought differs from, for example, Sweden and the Netherlands. In contrast to Sweden, the issue of distribution has not been fought according to an overarching goal of achieving equality but has been rather concerned with achieving an effective market economy.

This angle has had a significant effect on the competing parties. In France, especially since 1981, the communist party saw its power diminish substantially while the power of the (Socialist) president has increased. The Socialist Party also differs from its Dutch and Swedish counterparts by having moved rapidly towards the centre and also embracing market-economy principles in the same vein as Britain's New Labour and the German Social Democrats. This is reflected in the blurring of the traditional Left–Right division of the electorate where socio-economic differences have dropped dramatically since the 1970s. Consequently, another dominating cleavage line now appears to be the centre–periphery division with a strong agricultural sector (compared to other Western European countries) as well as a still populated countryside. In combination with large proportion of the workforce employed in small-to medium-sized enterprises, this has meant that the traditional settings for a strong labour-based mobilisation by and large has been absent in France. Consequently, the Left has had a weak presence in politics. However, despite a rapid increase in GDP and general living standards, great disparity in terms of income still exists between different social groups relating to the fact that taxation has been mainly placed on consumption rather than on wealth and inheritance. However, France displays a number of 'leftist' traits in the sense that a significant proportion of industry, banking and insurance have been under the state's control which has also included generous wealth re-distribution schemes.

The four dominating cleavage lines in French society is also reflected in the ideological division of parties as well as displaying a large number of political contenders almost on a Dutch level with parties representing the full spectrum from Maoists and Trotskyites on the Left to the Front National on the Right. In practice, the major French parties have tended to group into two loose coalitions: the Left (dominated by the Socialist Party with the French Communist Party) and the Gaullist and Giscardian coalition on the Right. The French political system has, as noted above, been characterised by friction and instability due to the high degree of ideological, as well as emotional, polarisation between parties and coalitions which has been notably higher than in the United Kingdom. However, even though the discrepancies due to ideology have diminished, there is still a sharp division between parties in terms of style, discourse and personal relationships which makes a divided government increasingly volatile (Frears, 1991). As a consequence, France has seen a quite unique electoral success of the Front National in recent decades. Profiling itself through a mix of populism (erosion of traditional values; decline of public order; large, ineffective government), nationalism (anti-EU; protectionist) and an explicit anti-foreigner stance, the FN has exploited the fears of voters from both the Left and the Right (Kitschelt and McGann, 1995). The comparative success of the FN reached a peak in the May 2002 election when Le Pen got through to the second round of the French presidential elections after scoring 17.9 per cent in the first round, but failed to match these results in the June 2002 general election getting only 18.5 per cent in the second round. Despite not gaining any seats and being ousted by Chirac in the second round, the results are alarming and above all show the presence of a quite significant space for an ethnic cleavage in French politics.

## Political institutions in Germany

Germany provides an interesting and contrasting example to the other four countries covered in this book since Germany has experienced a sharp departure from a totalitarian, fascist regime towards a democratic system within the space of just a few years. Up until reunification in 1990, Katzenstein (1987) describes Germany as a semi-sovereign state over which the Western Allies exercised a substantial influence over policy. But these limits to sovereignty were also key features in the temporary constitution from 1949, the Basic Law, which proscribed that Germany may by legislation transfer sovereign powers to inter-governmental institutions and, for the sake of peace, enter into a system of mutual collective security by consenting to limitations in state sovereignty. This situation of being a 'penetrated system', that is, being controlled by external actors gave way to an 'integrated system' in the 1950s when Germany joined the European Coal and Steel Community in 1952 and the European Economic Community and Euratom in 1957. The integrated system consolidated the handing over of national rights to sovereignty to supranational institutions but with the main difference being that this decision was now made by Germany rather than by external forces.

There was no question in the early post-war period that Germany should have a federalist structure given the pressure by the Allies as well as the fact that the Länder had existed prior to the Federal Republic. The constitutional order of the Federal Republic is based on a principle of representation and that authority should emanate from the people by means of elections, voting and specific legislative, executive and judicial organs. In terms of Germany's institutional make-up, the Federal Republic has three characteristics: legislative competences are allocated to both the federal government and the Länder; administrative tasks are divided and financial resources are shared between the two units. This means that the Länder have got a substantial degree of self-governance possibility compared to even highly decentralised countries like the United Kingdom. Exclusive federal administration exists in only a few areas, for example, foreign policy, immigration; financial administration and national security but apart from these issues, the Länder have sole responsibility when it comes to implementing federal law (Glaeßner, 1996).

Given the federal structure, the central level government thus governs in a way but does not directly control the administration of its policies. The consequence of this particular institutional set-up is that implementing legislation involves a number of players such as state-level administration and government and parapublic labour and social-policy institutions. Furthermore, the central government aims at making legislation as detailed as possible in order for its intentions to be carried out in the implementation process. Policy-making in Germany thus includes a variety of actors who are not only involved in the latter stages but who also play an active role early on in the legislative process. This means that the parliamentary majority and state government are under pressure to harmonise legislation and to achieve consensus relatively early on, echoing the Swedish approach of reaching agreements before hand. Further similarities with Sweden (and the Netherlands) is the presence of corporatist type consultation by the administration with the relevant interest groups in pre- as well as post-legislative procedures in all policy areas. Organised interests are expected to speak for their concerned group and this participation is seen as necessary and legitimate. Interest groups are in a favourable political position in Germany given the decentralised state structure which allows them a number of access points at national, Länder and local level as well as in the numerous parapublic institutions (Schmidt, 1996). However, in contrast to, primarily, Sweden, the German liberal version of corporatism is of a sectoral nature and confined to a limited number of policy areas such as income policy and health care. The major recognised interest groups are business and industry; labour; agriculture and churches. Business and labour have traditionally played a dominant role but compared to Britain and Sweden, farming and religious groups have also enjoyed a prominent role in German society. Conradt (2001) points to the close relationship between German political institutions and business and industrial interests by referring to the high degree of organisation and specialisation of business as well as their active involvement in policy-making. Local, national and state employer organisations are further represented by three umbrella organisations, the Federation of German Industry (BDI); the Federation of German Employer Associations (BDA) and the German Industrial and Trade Conference (DIHT). The BDI is by far the most politically active unit encompassing 39 industrial associations which together have a membership of more than ninety thousand firms. This federation enjoyed very close ties with the CDU government for almost two decades and tended to dominate over the trade unions given the commitment of all major parties for a free market. The BDA, on the other hand, has been mainly concerned with issues of wage policies whereas the DIHT concentrated on maintaining the economic viability of small independent business owners.

The major labour organisation, the German Federation of Labour (DGB), is a post-war construction whose aim has been to, independently from any political party, emphasise the basic economic objectives of wages and working conditions rather than radical and social changes. The DBG has backed a further strengthening of workers' representation and input in the decision-making within firms through co-determination. It has also moved away from its previous Marxist framework towards emphasising collective bargaining to improve the economic status of the workers within the existing social, economic and political framework. Although being represented in parliamentary delegations of both the SPD and the CDU, the labour unions' sympathies have in general laid with the Socialdemocrats similar to the situation of its Swedish counterpart.

The agricultural lobby in Germany has been comparatively well organised in relation to similar interests elsewhere in Western Europe. The so-called Green Front organises Germany's around two million farmers within three organisations: the German Farmer's League (BD); the Association of Agricultural Chambers (VL) and a co-operative association called the Raiffeisenverband involved in banking, mortgage loans and retailing. In addition, there are around 50 parliamentary deputies who constitute a relatively unified farmer's group within the legislature and who also dominate the parliament's agricultural committee. The significance of the highly organised agricultural interests can be found in the maintenance of EU's Common Agricultural Policy in Germany. Despite high food prices, poor international competition and diminishing farming sector, opposition to this policy has, according to Conradt (2001), never been high. The reasons for this, he argues, are that the farming interests constitute a critical voting bloc in many districts and the overall net gain from Germany's EU membership.

Finally, religious interests have enjoyed a privileged position in Germany society for both legal and traditional reasons. Churches, Protestant as well as Catholic, benefit from church tax and a state subsidy which finance a number of charitable activities. These two major churches also operate social welfare organisations, including hospitals, nursing homes, nursery schools, and so on for children, women, the elderly and the unemployed all over Germany. These charities are also significant employers with over 700,000 employees making the churches the biggest private employer and provider of health and welfare services. Similarly to the Dutch religious pillars, churches in Germany are also present on the boards of control of radio and television networks and represented on a number of advisory commissions at both the federal and state levels. Despite sharing a common legal and political status, the two churches differ in terms of their policy goals. The Catholic church has traditionally been well organised with extensive lay organisations and has sought output from the political system in accordance with the church's claim that it has the right to intervene in certain political, social and spiritual matters. The church has been especially active in the field of education striving for the right of parents to send their children to state-funded Catholic schools. The political arm of the Protestants – the Evangelical Church – has on the other hand placed greater emphasis on the support of the basic political values of the Federal Republic than on matters affecting the immediate interests of the church. In contrast, Germany's substantial Muslim population, primarily within the Turkish communities, receive no financial support from the state but since the change in citizenship policy, Conradt (2001) expects greater pressure from these new voters claiming equal religious recognition.

The Federal Republic is furthermore characterised by its high degree of fragmentation with the freedom of action by the federal government being highly restricted. These historical restrictions on the government also impact on the way in which policy-making is conducted in Germany, with changes being gradual and incremental rather than dramatic. The outcome of Germany's institutional make-up is a mix between a majoritarian and consensus democracy with a trade off between state power and legitimation for political parties.

In terms of the German electoral system, this consists of a proportional variant with two-track representation on the basis of universal suffrage for German nationals aged 18 or over. The two votes are for, on the one hand, constituency candidates and, on the other, party lists. Half of the 656 basic seats in the Bundestag are allocated through relative majority in constituencies and the other half through party lists in each of the 16 Länder. The decisive vote is the second one, through which distribution of party seats in parliament is dependent on how many constituency seats have been won. These are then deducted from the total on the basis of the second vote. This vote is then distributed and transformed into seats according to Hare-Niemeyer formula that is calculated by dividing the number of valid votes by the district magnitude. Parties are given as many seats as they win quotas and any remaining seats are awarded to parties with the largest remainder of votes (unless a party wins more constituency seats than its proportional share of the second votes, which in that case means that the parliament is enlarged accordingly). Parties gain seats if they pass the electoral threshold of five per cent. In other words, the German election system is a modified system of proportional representation. On the Länder level, the voting system is similar to that of the central level but with the main difference being the greater variance in public support relating to the party the electorate vote for indicating that the party or parties in power in the Bundestag may not necessarily be in a majority in all Länder.

In terms of cleavage lines, Germany shows similarities with the Netherlands having class and religion as the traditional way of structuring electoral politics (Dalton, 1996). These cleavages have shown a remarkable stability throughout German political history, surviving the constitutional monarchy, the Weimar Republic and the Nazi dictatorship and eventually becoming consolidated in the post-war era. In relation to these dividing lines, the issues of German reunification and increased communist presence in German politics have also been important features. This was especially apparent in the early post-war period when the Socialdemocrats were labelled as unreliable by the Christian Democrats and the more conservative forces (Lindahl, 1991). Class has however been dominating in Germany which is also reflected in the country's party system built upon the traditional struggle between capital and labour. Despite the dominance of class, Dalton (1996) suggests that this division has declined, especially in terms of class voting. Religion has historically been an important cleavage line especially in the western parts relating to, primarily, the separation of church and state whereas in the east it has taken on a more secular – religious division. This has created two sets of electorates, the religious in the west and the secular in the east. Given these societal divisions and the five per cent threshold, German politics were up until 1983 dominated by Christian Democrats (CDU/CSU); the Socialdemocrats (SPD) and the liberal Free Democrats (FDP). In the 1983 election, the Greens changed the political landscape by getting 5.6 per cent of the votes becoming the first left-wing opposition party to enter the parliament since the 1950s. Their electoral success was by and large due to the support they received from younger voters with university background. Similarly, another party, The Party of Democratic Socialism (PDS) managed to get enough votes in the 1994 and 1998 elections, indicating that the German electoral system was not impenetrable for new contenders.

## Political institutions in the Netherlands

The two main case countries, Sweden and the Netherlands, show a number of primarily economic similarities. They are both on the upper scale on the OECD country ranking with regard to governmental outlays as a proportion of GDP. Both have large public sectors that offer benefits from 'the cradle to the grave' to most of the population. They are also relatively small countries with open economies relying heavily on international trade. However, they do also display a number of important differences. Although the two countries are parliamentary democracies and elect legislators according to a principle of proportional representation, the Netherlands has a single national list while Sweden divides the country into multimember districts, each with its own list. Sweden has had one dominant party, the Socialdemocrats, since the 1930s; whereas the Netherlands has been characterised by generations of small, multiparty coalitions. The Swedish cabinet displays a high degree of integration whereas the Dutch is highly heterogeneous (Andeweg, 1988). In Sweden, the government is compartmentalised into ministries – which serve as the policy-making organs – and agencies – which implement the policies – and usually consist of members from the same party who meet regularly and are in close proximity to each other. Dutch ministries are more diversely composed with key ministers from different parties who tend to meet less often and in a more formal setting. Sweden has an encompassing labour movement with strong ties to the dominant Socialdemocrats, whereas the Netherlands has long been a segmented society in which social cleavages are managed through the politics of accommodation (Schick, 1993). Also, Sweden is dominated by horizontal type cleavages (class) compared with the more vertical types found in the Netherlands (religion).

Early writings on the nature of the Dutch political system described it as being a segmented pluralistic society (Lorwin, 1971). Here, social movements, voluntary associations and political parties were organised along religious and ideological lines. By pluralist, the author referred to the recognition of religious, socio-economic and political affiliations; while segmentation indicated an institutionalisation of the different forms of mobilisation according to these cleavage lines. Implied here is that these cleavages produced neutral and competing networks of schools, media, interest-groups and voluntary organisations, falling into one or the other of the prevailing pillars. This process of pillarisation or verzuiling became a concept shortly after the Second World War, when these pillars would serve as integrating mechanisms to the diverse Dutch society. The pillars were thought to sustain an overarching unity above the diversity of the nation's social and political struggles. Social groupings made up on the basis of religion or ideology formed pillars which were more or less closed communities in which social life for the members was played out from the cradle to the grave. This organisational mode meant further that each group had its own specific societal institutions ranging from schools, hospitals, newspapers, to broadcasting networks, trade unions and political parties. Little cross-pillar interaction existed, apart from on the elite level where accommodation between pillars was arranged. In a sense, the existence of the pillars reflected Dutch society's division into a number of minorities. This situation meant that inflexibility would reduce actors' influence in the political sphere, whereas power-sharing would mean that at least some form of saying in the matter would be gained. The pillar system started to unravel somewhat in the 1960s. During this period, the role played by religion and ideology began to decline, alongside the size and density of the pillarised organisations, in favour of an increase in non-pillarised organisations. By the mid-1970s, the politics of accommodation had by and large been replaced by what Daalder (1986) considers to resemble more the system found in the United Kingdom and the United States. The previous way of conducting politics, in which the prime objective was to achieve consensus by means of proportionality, depoliticisation and summit diplomacy, was now being replaced by conflict based on a polarised and politicised environment. This particular description was however challenged by Andeweg and Irwin (1993), who suggest that accommodation politics did in fact still exist. Pillarisation in itself was one of the potential threats to a stable democracy, leading to a situation in which the minority position of the subcultures may have been a crucial incentive for the elites to co-operate rather than compete. Indeed, if one looks at the number of parties within the parliament one sees that they are still far away from holding a majority position which according, to these authors, explains how accommodation could continue without the presence of the pillar system.

However, even though this system was losing its important role, organisational pillars were closely involved in the set-up of the welfare state, exercising influence on the creation and implementation of government policy, especially in the distribution of social goods and services to their members. The presence of these pillars has had a strong impact on the Dutch political system. First, the main political players are still divided along two cleavage lines – class and religion (Gladdish, 1991). In the former, the two most important are the Labour Party (PvdA) and the Liberal Conservative Party (VVD). The religious cleavage accounts for one religiously oriented party, the Christian Democratic Appeal (CDA), which came about from a merger of one Catholic and two Protestant parties. There were strong links between parties and their equivalent pillar in terms of recruitment but these ties lost importance during the process of de-pillarisation. A number of smaller parties can be found to the left and right of these three main contenders. The four large parties are surprisingly close to each other in terms of positionality on the Left–Right (1: Far Left and 10: Far Right) dimension scale (Klingemann, 1979), with the PvdA being furthest to the left (3) and the VVD furthest to the right (6). This close proximity facilitates the understanding of government formation. For a period of almost forty years, coalitions were formed by the PvdA and the VVD together with the Christian Democrats, with the latter being the dominant party since, by virtue of being in between the two other parties, the CDA has been able to exercise coalition formation veto. The Dutch system has been criticised for having an electoral system of extreme proportional representation giving rise to fragile multi-party coalitions. These delicate coalitions could induce internal instability leading up to the break-up and reformation of governments between elections, which in turn might cause changes in the ideological balance of government without popular ratification (Daalder, 1986).

The Dutch understanding of 'Left' and 'Right' differs slightly from the understanding found elsewhere. Here, the concept of 'Left' refers to non-religious and anti-confessional elements and includes the Liberal Democratic, Socialist and Communist parties, whereas parties considered as 'Right' are based on religious principles. However, if one includes issues of economic and social affairs, then this positions alters. This means that the position of the VVD and CDA shifts more to the right for the former and more to the centre for the latter. Seeing that the religious aspect of Dutch politics does not seem to play the same important role as before, the Left–Right division has come to resemble the appearance found in other Western multi-party systems.

In terms of the Dutch electoral system, its use of extreme proportionality echoes the societal composition and allows for a high number of effective parties, making single-party dominance the exception and multi-party coalitions the rule. The Dutch system can be classified as being a multi-polar bargaining system (Laver and Schofield, 1990), indicating the presence of a fairly balanced distribution of votes among the major parties. Despite displaying a large amount of parties, six parties can be considered to play a central role – CDA, PvdA, VVD, D66 (Liberal Democrats), Groen Links (Green Party) and SP (Socialist Party). This structural setting directly influences the way in which governments are formed, giving the process dynamic character where government composition and programmes have been decided after lengthy bargaining in the post-election period (Narud, 1996).

Elections are held on the basis of proportional representation, with the Netherlands as a whole serving as the constituency. The total number of voters is divided by 150 and this determines the electoral quotient – the number of votes a candidate needs to be elected. The country is divided into 18 election districts and parties may put up a different list in all districts. Only 25 signatures are required for the submission of a list (but with a financial guarantee). The existence of these 18 electoral districts are beneficial for candidates who are known in a given area and to small parties that can gain parliamentary seats by winning the required votes. Votes are cast for persons on the list and for the party as such, but the vote is counted for the party. Naturally a strong candidate can attract a great number of votes helping the party to gain additional seats beyond their own vote. Thus, charisma and personality play an important role, but votes tend to be cast for the party first and foremost.

The extreme proportionality trait of the Dutch political system is evident in the subdivision of local municipalities, of which there are around 700. These are structured more or less in the same way as the provincial government but differ in that the elected aldermen (who form the executive branch of the local government) are elected from among the council members (as opposed to ministers).

## Political institutions in Sweden

Similar to the Dutch pillar system, political institutions in Sweden display many of the traits associated with a corporatist structure. This has been manifest in what Micheletti calls 'a cross-class collaboration and labour peace situation that to a large extent has become part of the Swedish collective identity' (1995: 72), with the key words being dialogue and consensus. It became a general practice for the government and the collective-action organisations to solve political problems in a pragmatic way. These groups were legitimised and institutionalised into the public realm since they were considered to be able to provide rational and expert opinion and the necessary information to evaluate policy proposals. Trade unions became so fully integrated into the process of policy-making and implementation that Sweden was often regarded as the paradigmatic case of corporatism. Swedish trade unions – primarily the blue-collar union LO (Landsorganisation) but also the white-collar union TCO (Tjänstemännens Central Organisation) and to a lesser extent the smaller academic SACO (Svenska Akademikers Central Organisation) – were all allowed to participate in policy-making, especially on issues regarding economic and labour policies. This relationship included systematic consultation on proposed legislation and representation on commissions of inquiry into new policy proposals before they were passed on to the parliament (known as the remiss procedure). Furthermore, it gave unions the opportunity for submissions to parliamentary committees and representation on the governing bodies of major executive agencies such as the labour market board (Arbetmarknadsstyrelsen). This system was developed by the Socialdemocrats during their extensive 44-year rule (1932–1976) but was also in effect during the two conservative governments (1976–1982, 1991–1994). In accordance with the pattern of governing consensus, there were few disagreements with regard to the direction of the economic policy. The close relationship between the Socialdemocrats and the LO – in terms of interlocking office-holding and frequent high-level meetings – enabled the government not only to follow union-preferred economic policies for securing full employment, but also facilitated agreement on less traditional Socialdemocratic policies such as the deregulation and monetary policy for the 1982 recovery programme. In general, agreements were reached in advance, even on the crisis package following the recession of the early 1990s which included a ban on strikes, approved beforehand by the LO leadership.

In the same vein as the Dutch consociational tradition, this meant that the political institutions in Sweden enjoyed a substantial amount of settled agreement. This tradition traces back to Sweden's late but rapid industrialisation at the end of the nineteenth century which also spawned a number of new social organisations and served as an important catalyst for the political changes. Much of this organisation had a voluntary and collective foundation which served as an educational influence in democratic procedures, and particularly the trade unions and the industrial associations that expanded rapidly both in terms of influence and size.

Seeing that economic, social and political changes happened in a relatively short period of time, this prompted the Swedish state to become more actively involved with the large number of grass-root organisations. One of the earliest examples of this formalised variant of negotiation was the 1933 Socialdemocratic/Agrarian Party compromise that resulted in the Basic Agreement (the so-called Saltsjöbaden Agreement) in 1938. Here, the state managed to settle an agreement between the two main economic competitors, the Swedish Confederation of Trade Unions and the Swedish Employer's Federation, which prompted long-term stability on the labour market with high levels of employment. The essence of this compromise was that unions were to co-operate with management as partners in an effort to rationalise and maximise production; production decisions were to be left to management in an industrial structure which was overwhelmingly under private ownership and control; and the state, while staying out of labour negotiations, was to see an equitable distribution of the product and use Keynesian means to counter unemployment. The state would also promote structural changes directed to increase economic efficiency (Elder, 1988; Ugelvik Larsen and Ugelvik, 1997).

Although the combination of parliamentary democracy, market economy and welfare state did not differ substantially from many other Western European countries, a number of special traits help to explain the rise of those particular characteristics that have been commonly associated with the so-called Swedish model. Petersson (1994) suggests that the lack of a feudal past, of foreign intervention, of revolutionary incidents and of a federal system have had a decisive impact on the formation of contemporary Swedish political institutions. Also, the presence of centralised bargaining and a consensus culture, in combination with a long period of full employment and a strong welfare society, has created a situation in which the state has managed to successfully function in a close relationship with organised interest groups.

As with the Dutch pillars' legacy within the political party system, political parties in Sweden mirror the class cleavage that was established in the late nineteenth century. Since industrialisation, the introduction of parliamentary government, democratisation and the formation of political parties occurred more or less simultaneously; this facilitated the set-up of the five-party system, divided into two blocks. On the one hand was a Socialist bloc (Socialdemocrats and the Left Party), and on the other a non-Socialist bloc consisting of a Conservative, a Liberal and an Agrarian–Centre party. The introduction of proportional representation during the early twentieth century provided the ground for establishing new parties but this did not occur on the same scale as in the Dutch case. This overview proves a valid description of the system until the early 1990s when the five-party system expanded to encompass eight (the Greens, New Democracy and the Christian Democrats).

Initially, the political parties displayed slightly different internal structures. The left-orientated parties by and large emanated from the labour movement and were thus structured as large collective organisations, while the conservative bloc more resembled regular parliamentary groupings. However, in terms of the local branch–central party relationship, all parties share the same characteristics. The basic unit of the political party is in most cases concentrated around a specific geographical area, for example, the city or the municipality. This local branch is in turn part of the district party which is county-based and usually identical with the electoral constituency. These two units elect representatives for the supreme decision-making body at the national party congress. Here, a smaller committee is elected by the congress to serve as its executive and is usually fronted by the party chairman. Those elected as representatives of a particular party form an organised group who in turn elect a leadership and have a secretariat at their disposal. The events surrounding the national assembly are of key importance since they by and large provide the only opportunities to determine the party agenda as well as what candidates will appear on the party list.

In contrast to the United Kingdom for instance, political parties in Sweden do not rely on monetary contributions from the private sector but are instead eligible for state subsidies, depending on the number of seats won in parliament or whether they gained more than 2.5 per cent of the votes in the national election. The presence of state subsidies favour the well-established parties over newcomers and could potentially serve as an additional barrier-threshold for new competitors.

## Political institutions in Britain

British political institutions have commonly been considered to have endured an extraordinary stability, surviving two world wars and two social and political revolutions. The British parliamentary government, with power centralised in a Cabinet supported by a partisan majority lower house, emerged in 1868 and has, in essence, not been altered since. Despite standing as a model for a number of other countries' political institutions, Britain does ironically not have a written constitution. Regulations of a constitutional character are laid down in a number of basic laws and the current constitution is said to be a combination of these laws, interpretations of said laws and tradition (Dearlove and Saunders, 2000). The fundamental constitutional principle is the sovereignty of the parliament and its possibility to pass laws on any subject without interference from the judiciary. In this sense, Britain is a unitary state but with devolved government in Scotland and Wales due to the historical incorporation of these two areas into the United Kingdom. Despite these extensive powers, there are some practical limitations to the majority exercise in power, for example, central government has no direct field administration in most domains and as such is largely dependent on other bodies to implement its policies. The strength of the government in relation to the parliament is dominated by the idea of the party mandate. As Budge (1996) notes, this is the constitutional doctrine that the electoral programme of the party – given that the party has a majority of the parliamentary seats – is implemented while the party is in power. This, Budge continues, brings other potential roles for the parliament such as to scrutinise and revise proceedings. All parliamentary activity is overshadowed by the results of the most recent election or by the prospect of the next and is a forum for debate in order to influence public opinion for or against the government. Control over the parliamentary proceedings is thus in the hands of the leadership of the two main parties and primarily in that of the government. The parliament is in turn divided into two Houses, the House of Commons and the House of Lords. The former consists of 651 directly elected MPs with debates being very much partisan in nature compared to the Lords. The latter consists of hereditary nobles, bishops, judges and life peers who are nominated by the major political parties, who are also actively involved in parliamentary discussions. Although their speeches tend to be influential, their actual power is diffuse and indirect and has merely delaying, and not veto powers, over legislation. The role of the parliament, and especially the House of Commons, is to be interpreted more as a context in which the government operates rather than as constraint on its governing powers in which partisan contenders meet and discuss. These limitations to parliamentary power puts a premium on tight party discipline and loyalty which makes independent action of the party leadership difficult. Further limitations to independent action is prevented through the system of every minister being responsible for the administration, that is, all decisions taken are taken in the name of the minister and he/she can be held responsible for these by the parliament (Christoffersson, 1991).

The British political system is further characterised by its Westminster model of governance which makes it distinct from the other countries covered in this book. First, its electoral system is characterised by its single-member, simple plurality system or 'first past the post'. Consequently, this means that parties win seats if they have a strong local support and are in a position to win a majority of seats and form government if this support corresponds to other constituencies. This also means that local minority interests face a lot of difficulty gaining representation even though they may have a large national percentage of the votes, as has been the case with Liberal Democrats. This system thus consolidates and stabilises the existing party system and resists and deflects major movements for change. Second, the system tends to over-represent the public support for the major parties and enhances the effects of electoral success. The chances are in other words big that either of the major parties will achieve single majority in parliament and as such enjoy a considerably stronger position than in countries with proportional representation.

Third, the electoral system enables national parties to ignore many political movements and their demands. However, once they gather enough national support this will generate a succession of changes in a short period of time given the long period of non-attention and non-response from policy-makers. Fourth, the Westminster system serves as a filter to reduce the number of parties competing for votes by restricting effective parliamentary representation to mainly two parties (Budge, 1996).

As an effect of this system, the major cleavage line has been around class-based issues which has been much more apparent compared to other Western European countries. This class identity, being based on education, accent, life-style, place and type of residence and income, was intensified during the inter-war era when religion and the territorial Irish cleavage began to lose its importance. However, the class dimension became less important from the 1960s onwards resulting from improved industrial and economic conditions which was mirrored in the increased electoral volatility of the 1960s and 1970s with many Labour votes going to the Liberal Democrats (Lib Dems), thus strengthening the Conservative government in power from 1979 to 1997. More recently, scholars have identified a differentiated pattern of regional voting relating to the rise and decline of heavy industry and manufacturing in the northern peripheral regions of Leeds, Manchester, Cardiff and Glasgow. The classic industrial proletariat thus started to develop here, reinforcing the pre-existing North–South division (see e.g. Taggart, 2004). In the aftermath of the Conservative government's emphasis on monetarist policies, the 1980s and onwards saw a new class–territorial cleavage where Labour draw its electoral support from the north of England, Scotland and Wales while the Conservatives draw a majority of their supporters from London and the South-East thus penalising the Lib Dems through a system that privileges regionally strong parties.

On a local level, Britain displays an interesting scenario of centralised control and local self-governance. The central government relies on the local government and so-called Quangos to implement its programme in detail and also exercises a degree of control through the provision of government revenue to local authorities and through parliament (passing legislation which is binding on lower bodies). However, the central government relies heavily on local initiatives to go forward with decided decisions but does rarely intervene (apart from requesting compliance and progress reports). The central government also faces further complications of control given that local elections take place over a three-year period and serve as a form of mid-term test of government popularity, and as such can create a situation in which the party in power locally is not the party in power centrally.

Finally, Britain also presents a different relationship between parties and interest groups. As in other Western European countries, the United Kingdom has a large variety of organised interests but with the difference that individual MPs often have close connections with a particular interest which means that this MP can act as a spokesperson for the interest group. Ministers have their 'own' policy networks on which they rely for information and gaining compliance for their policies and in turn tend to adopt a majority of the views stemming from these networks. This creates an exclusive 'insider' situation which can be very beneficial for the concerned group but is also subject to heavy control by the civil service and ministers that restrict their scope of action. It is in other words a quasi-corporatist arrangement with a significant imbalance of power. Given the strong class presence in Britain, the various trade unions have tended to be the organisations with largest membership and power brought together under the umbrella organisation of the Trades Union Congress. The employer equivalent is the Confederation of British Industries which serves more as an interest organisation than a representative for the employers during negotiations. Both organisations tend to tie individual MPs to their organisation as spokespersons and economic support is usually given to these MPs through becoming a member of the board or through consultancy. The strong presence of organised interests was severely damaged during the Thatcher years when this relationship was broken due to a belief that these organisations would subvert government policies instead of supporting them which today still leaves the trade unions in a weak position compared to previous decades.

## Political institutions as constraints and facilitators

When behaviour becomes institutionalised, it suggests that behaviour is framed by standard operating procedures. Proceedings within political institutions reflect the ways in which behaviour has become routine and how the actors within these institutions are supposed to handle certain types of procedures. Institutions have a number of procedures to choose from, and use rules to select among these. The rules may be applied and enforced by direct coercion and political or organisational authority, or may be part of a code of appropriate behaviour that is learned and internalised through socialisation or education. The particular institutional set-up can thus be said to create fairly stable patterns of norms that have systems of sanctions and rewards attached to them (Jepperson, 1991). These sanctions and rewards influence the actions of actors within institutions by providing abstract scripts that regulate behaviour and learning theories that emphasise how individuals organise information (Powell and DiMaggio, 1991)

As the outline of the French, German, Dutch, Swedish and British political systems suggests, certain codes or rules of behaviour dominate. First, the presence of a certain type or types of ideological cleavage lines make issues that do not correspond to these divisions difficult to place on the political agenda. As Mény and Knapp (1998) emphasise, every political society is split by a number of cleavages. However, these cleavages do to a great extent vary in terms of origin, nature and magnitude. Depending on the importance of a particular cleavage in a society, its impact upon the formation of political attitudes and behaviour is different. This means that the range of cleavages that separate groups within societies and set them against each other vary in intensity, distribution and manner of combination depending on time, socio-economic circumstances, and so on.

France has had less clear-cut cleavages and the ones that have been present, seem to have been less relevant than in the other four countries. Instead, Mény (1996) suggests that the French electorate has become more volatile and appear to vote more in accordance to the political moment and what 'message' they want to send to an increasingly weak partisan allegiance. The effect of this change can be found in the success that previously minor parties, such as the Greens and the National Front, have had in the past 20 years. This indicates that despite displaying some traditional cleavages (class, centre–periphery) there is also room for other, less traditional, issues to mobilise around (foreign policy, secular Catholic-national identity, Islam) depending on the political climate. In addition, France displays a different way of channelling political discontent through what Mény calls 'the periodic eruption of violence and protest that contradict or counterbalance choices expressed through the ballot box' (1996: 107). The reasons for this, Mény suggests, can be found in the institutional set-up of French society which has not managed to channel violent social protests into peaceful and formal expressions. Parties, unions and interest groups have had difficulties to effectively organise group activity as a consequence of extremely varied electoral rules which has helped to fragment the formation of wings and factions within parties and to set up alliances. The successive changes of the main ideological organisations have not put forward an alternative framework of conflict resolution for actors who are not part of the political apparatus. Instead, social movements and new contenders face resistance from the state since they, as non-elected entities, are not considered legitimate. Therefore in order to be heard, they must resort to extreme measures such as violent demonstrations or large-scale strikes which has been proved to pay off. This is due to the paradoxical nature of the French state which is on one hand haughty, all-powerful and disdainful but faced with violent protests tends to become ready to concede and forgiving since there is no other way out (see also Andrews and Hoffman, 1981). This is exemplified with what Guigni and Passy (2004) refer to as a selective, inclusive system in which a closed system is generally accompanied by exclusive prevailing strategies. This is also reflected in the case of migrants' political activity which creates high levels of obstructive strategies for claims-making related to recognition of cultural difference.

German political life has been dominated by the dividing lines of class and religion which has, until the entry of the Greens, created a two-tier system with parties representing the broad categories of capital – labour and religious – secular groups. However, explicit political competition and conflict has by and large been absent in Germany due to what Conradt (2001) describes as a striving for absolute solutions in order to eliminate the causes of conflict. This aversion of conflict has thus led to both the elite as well as the general public being unable to accept the need for strong opposition parties or extensive bargaining within and between parties in parliament, opting for a more expert-orientated and legalistic conception of politics. Consequently, this has generated a strong state presence in the political order that has generated a public sphere which is both highly centralised and bureaucratic despite its federal political system. Furthermore, the corporatist elements present in the German system provides opportunities for class and religious interests such as trade unions, welfare organisations, churches, business organisations, and so on, to participate in public policy-making (Soysal, 1994). At the same time, migrants and minorities are excluded from decision-making and influence by the exclusive nature of German citizenship as well as the limitations for the dominating cleavages to incorporate an ethnic as well as the, primarily, Islamic dimension (Koopmans and Statham, 1999).

In contrast, British political life has been dominated by, first a class cleavage and later on a class–geographical cleavage, juxtaposing the Labour stronghold in the north with the Conservative south. However, in contrast to Germany, France and the Netherlands, these cleavages have become less dependent on collective identities and have since the 1980s moved in a more individualistic direction. This has forced the parties to adjust and re-invent themselves (most famously in the case of New Labour) in order to adapt to an increasingly more complex and diverse social structure with a substantial challenge from social movements such as the peace- and anti-capitalist mobilisation. At the same time, the relationship between organised interests such as the trade unions and political parties was weakened during the Thatcher era and Britain moved away from this (light) corporatist situation towards a more plural environment. In this sense, opposing movements tend to direct their efforts more towards the state than to the party in power. The class perspective has also been weakened by the presence of New Labour which has taken a centre-right position thus profiling themselves towards both traditional Labour voters as well as Conservative supporters. Following on from the shift in a neo-liberal direction, the main source of action and authority has now become the individual whose interests supersede other institutions in society (Soysal, 1994). This means that most political action stems from individuals and/or private organisations lobbying the state. In Britain, then, the consequence of these institutional arrangements is that migrants are in a, theoretically, better position to participate politically since these actions are facilitated by the state through the emergence of anti-discrimination legislation and the various bodies in place which report and advice on practices for ensuring equal treatment.

In the Swedish case, successful mediation of class conflict proved to be the basis for not only the Socialdemocratic political hegemony but also became the main source of mobilisation potential. The class angle managed to supersede other types of cleavage such as religious–confessional (religion as a private rather than public matter), centre–periphery (de-centralisation of power to local governments) and minority–majority (strong sense of national identity coupled with local governance for certain linguistic minorities). As noted previously, this fitted in with the societal norm of equality. Seeing that the government did not assume a passive role but rather engaged actively in the negotiation with organised interests in decision-making, conflicting interests regarding the allocation of material welfare resources became neutralised.

Especially important was the fact that both the socialist and the non-socialist bloc had welfare distribution as a common goal (Uddhammar, 1993). An explanation for the long-lasting Socialdemocratic rule could be made with reference to exploiting the conservative bloc's emphasis on lower taxes rather than full employment. Pontusson (1988) argues that the two key issues surrounding this political hegemony was the Socialdemocrats' firm position on economic growth and strong grounding within the trade union movement. This reassured the confederation of trade unions and other collective-action organisations that parliamentary democracy through consensus agreements could be successfully used to solve socio-economic problems. Similarly, the Dutch case displays two main cleavage lines, class and religion. Religious groups were ensured equal rights in the late eighteenth century although the secular claims of the Dutch state provoked Calvinists and Catholics to demand church autonomy and a certain amount of control over education. This development proved to be paradoxical since religion simultaneously became a dividing and a uniting force. As pointed out previously, this process fragmented Dutch society but simultaneously united it by the fact that religious conflict was kept away from the central government and steered towards the regions. This consociational situation was the outcome of deliberate attempts to neutralise potential immobilising and destabilising threats that cultural fragmentation could bring about. Thus, Dutch policy was a deliberate attempt to accommodate difference in a pluralistic society by a ruling elite (Lijphart, 1975).

In contrast to the Swedish situation of de-politicised and limited cleavages, the Dutch experiences shows how elites who are in a position to successfully balance different competing actors also have the opportunity to determine the type of cleavages around which mobilisation can occur. In addition, they can exercise influence on how these are to be handled in society, to what extent they will become politically loaded and to what degree subcultural divisions are to be solved without stimulating violence and repression.

Furthermore, the formal structure of the political system itself directs the actors towards a particular type of action. Depending on whether a proportional or a majority system is in use, the strategy adopted by the political parties changes. In a proportional system, one can see a larger number of parties competing for votes compared to a majoritarian system as in the United Kingdom. One could also potentially expect a higher presence of single-issue, geographically, gender and/or ethnically orientated parties since there is at least a theoretical possibility of achieving seats. That is, votes are competed for on the basis of multiple dimensions – as opposed to a Left–Right dimension in two-party systems – but with relative importance given to each dimension being weighted differently by each actor. However, issues that parties struggle to make their 'own' must be able to fit within the prevailing cleavage.

Therefore, issues such as public spending, crime, welfare, morality or education are relatively easier to incorporate into existing dividing-lines of class and religion since they could potentially cross-cut these cleavages. It has been argued that parties tend to occupy a particular area within the policy space – marked by their ideology – sometimes even specified by the party name, for example, Christian Democrats, Socialdemocrats or Greens (Budge and Farlie, 1983; Robertson, 1976). In the Swedish case, notions of class and improvement of class position were also more compatible with the Socialdemocratic guiding line of equality and thus applicable to all citizens. Representation according to more narrow characteristics was seen as a threat to the status quo. Similarly, the Dutch case shows few signs of deviating from the class/religion cleavage, even though it might be argued that the massive, but unanticipated, success of Pim Fortuyn in the Rotterdam election of 2002 was due to the exploitation of an, until that point, non-existent ethnic cleavage. Britain also displays a similar situation where race and ethnicity appears to be off the national political agenda. However, as Solomos (2003) points out, this does not mean that ethnicity was not an important force for mobilisation amongst grass root activists and local community groups addressing the failure of local governments to develop adequate policies in response to the increasing diversity of the population. This situation points to varying institutional opportunities for actors depending whether they are situated on a local or a national level. In contrast to Sweden and the Netherlands, Britain shows more space for politicians profiling their policies towards specific ethnic groups. Following the urban unrest of the early 1980s, local black politicians strived to bring issues of racial equality onto the local political agenda as a response to the failure of central government to deal with these issues suggesting the possibility of an ethnic cleavage on a local level but with class and north–south cleavages dominating on a national level. Germany also displays variance on the regional level and especially so within particular cities with Berlin and Frankfurt deviating from other places in having more political space available for issues relating to migrants (Koopmans, 2004). France on the other hand, displays very limited opportunities, both nationally as well as locally, due to its centralised state system, concentration of power in the hands of government, a strong and coherent administration, in addition to a particular understanding of citizenship (Guigni and Passy, 2004). However, in terms of how public policy is formulated, the Dutch, as well as the Swedish corporatist system, is predominantly characterised by a class cleavage. In the social and economic sphere the corporatist features are apparent in the form of a number of agencies that are brought together at the negotiating table together with the main representatives of employers and organised labour. Germany displays a similar scenario but with the addition of powerful financial actors involved in the negotiations between the state, business and labour (Hicks, 1988) whereas France and Britain have had a traditionally weak interest representation with the French state exercising comparatively more power over which groups are 'good' and which are narrow and self-serving (Cole, 1998).

In the Netherlands (and Germany), these interests are commonly referred to as 'social partners', a term that corresponds to the importance placed by Dutch society on an ideology of social harmony and co-operation. The two main interest groups consisted of a collection of actors that reflected the pillarised network and were co-ordinated by the Social and Economic Council. The principle of corporatist decision-making had become a central ingredient in the style of national policy-making and as such had profound consequences for the strategies adopted by the government as well as on political activities. Even though the Netherlands shares a number of important similarities with Sweden in this sense, the political sphere has lacked a long-term dominance of a Socialdemocratic movement which would theoretically provide more space for unorthodox types of mobilisation. Germany displays a similar scenario but with the addition of also having remarkably stable coalitions with a right-of-centre coalition involving the Free Democrats (FDP) being in power from 1949 to 1966 and then being replaced by a coalition of the FDP and the Socialdemocrats from 1969 to 1982 (Glaeßner, 1996). Britain, on the other hand, has enjoyed long periods of Conservative rule with occasional Labour rule until 1997 with France displaying a comparatively unstable case with shifts from right to left-wing governments and presidents following the long period of Gaullist-centrist rule (Mény, 1996).

Despite the long tradition of coalition governance in the Netherlands, the political arena has been similar to that found in Britain due to the two-party dominance of the PvdA and the CDA, and to a lesser degree the VVD. The CDA has tended to be the dominant force during most of the post-war years and did in fact outperform the Swedish Socialdemocrats when in government from 1945 to 1994. As Bruff (2003) notes, the CDA's ability in the early post-war years to capture most of the confessional votes, and the way in which the party marketed itself as the key responsible centre party moderating between PvdA and VVD, proved to be highly successful and showed the path for rival parties to profile themselves. This situation echoes that found in the German 'two-and-a-half party system' up until the mid-1980s with the small and liberal FDB having the same function between the two big 'catch-all' parties, the SPD and CDU (Lees, 2002).

The exception to this uninterrupted rule occurred between 1994 and 2002, when the so-called purple coalition of the PvdA, VVD and D66 managed to become the first entirely secular government under universal suffrage and proportional representation. Indeed the position of the PvdA has always been relatively weak by West European standards. It played an important role in the process of post-war reconstruction but it never came within sight of exercising exclusive authority and its role was reconciliationist – not redistributionist. Equally, when a cabinet with a strong Labour component held office in the mid-1970s, its performance was largely characterised by a desperate struggle to sustain commitments, already undertaken by governments without a Socialdemocratic presence against a downturn in economic fortunes.

In terms of political party input one has to outline the matter of how policy consensus developed during the 1960s to early 1970s. Here, one finds two distinct elements. One is the nature of policy reconciliation within a centre-based coalition polity. The other is the extent to which central planning and the various forms of corporatist consultation and recommendation created a policy climate which propelled social and economic strategies outside the frame of direct management by the cabinet and parliament. The dynamic of such a centre-based system has meant that the centre has been able to absorb and accommodate the contentions of the time, apparently without ideological brakes or the need for ideological accelerators.

A second important feature of the governmental dimension of the Dutch policy process was the growth of sub-corporate advisory bodies to departments (the so-called adviesorgaan). Attempts to control their proliferation were made at that time but as the less formal inputs of the verzuiling network gave way to more structured consultation, their number increased inordinately. By 1975 there were almost 400 permanent advisory bodies, 60 per cent of which had never been sanctioned by parliament and 40 per cent of which had been assembled since 1965. In addition to the web of corporatist and advisory organs, interest groups also had some purchase within the cabinet itself. Van Putten (1982) described this phenomenon as 'sectorisation' and points out that, for example, the Minister of Agriculture is normally recruited from the agricultural sector, the Minister of Social Affairs is often a former trade union leader and so on. This situation is highlighted by the intimate relationship between political parties and the Dutch interest-articulators, and the lack of cross-party polemics. As van Putten points out, differences between parties 'disappear like snow under hot sun' (1982: 179) when the interests of involved groups are at stake. This particular situation arises from the fact that interest groups not only have access to their own political platform but in addition that every parliamentary party tends to have one or more representatives from the concerned group.

This situation has also been a characteristic feature in the Swedish case. As Ruin (1982) points out, there has been a long tradition of close contact between interest groups and government. As in the Netherlands, these groups have been indirectly represented in Parliament in the sense that many parties who have had interest group links have also been systematically nominated. This means that these groups also tend to be well represented on government commissions which formulate new policy proposals – acting within the 'remiss'-system – thereby enabling comment and potential amendments to the proposition. In addition, a number of informal contacts occur between the government and the more important interest organisations, primarily within the labour area. This suggests that conflict avoidance has been a cornerstone in policy-making which runs through not only policy-making but also the comparatively large public apparatus and the central agencies. As a consequence, even though the central agencies have their independence, they often tend to maintain very close relations with their sponsoring ministries. This link has been particularly close during the long Socialdemocratic period of governance. The individual ministers thus held office for a very long time and often appointed people as heads of central offices whom they had worked with or knew well; the senior officials of these agencies also tended to regard politicians as partners for co-operation rather than as disturbing elements (Melbourn, 1979).

This is in contrast to Germany's variant of corporatism involving a few 'peak organisations' who enjoyed close contacts with government on a regular basis but similar in the sense that these corporatist arrangements where supported by both Labour in terms of their relationship with the German Federation of Labour as well as the Christian Democrats/Free Democrats through their ties with the business community. France, on the other hand, falls in between both pluralistic and corporatist explanations and shares similarities with Germany and Britain but few with Sweden and the Netherlands. On the one hand, as mentioned above, France lacks a tradition of strong interest groups mobilisation with a lack of cohesion among groups as well as little involvement by labour and capital in economic policy while the institutional set-up enables the president and national assembly to monopolise the power. On the other, the main social partners (employers and trade unions) are institutionally incorporated into the state through the tripartite system which points to a strong public sector corporatism. This means that certain sectors, the so-called grand corps (especially the Mining, Highways and Bridges, and Rural Engineering Corps), are present in numerous public policy decisions (Cole, 1998). Britain conforms to a limited version of pluralism in the sense that competition between interests is greater than in the other four countries but limited in that central ministries have developed distinct relationships with particular interest groups, for example, between the Department of Employment and trade unions; the Department of Trade and Industry and the Confederation of British industry. These relationships are furthermore not initiated by the British state but by individual ministries which sets the British situation apart from the other examples (Budge, 1996).

## Outcomes of institutions: political opportunity structures

Having outlined the institutional settings and discussed how these institutions shape the political sphere, the following section will analyse in more detail the effects or outcomes of these settings. The analysis will be framed by Tarrow's four categories of POS (Tarrow, 1994; see also Kitschelt, 1986; McAdam, 1996; Tarrow, 1998; Tilly, 1978) and the way in which these dimensions shape the choice of action for political parties and migrant organisations.

The state provides most of the institutional settings that make up the political environment and determines the rules and boundaries that political actors are obliged to adhere to. In this environment there are certain conditions which can either facilitate or constrain the political opportunities that these actors face in order to pursue their strategic goals. These opportunities can be expressed in terms of the relative openness of the institutionalised political system, the stability of elite alignments, presence of elite allies and the state's capacity to repress actors (McAdam, 1982, 1996). But POS are not only determined by the presence of the state. Other factors include specific configurations of resources, institutional arrangements and historical precedents which determine how and what type of groups mobilise.

The ideas behind POS are not of a monolithic kind but can be analytically divided into four categories: (1) formal institutional structures; (2) national cleavage structures; (3) informal procedures; and (4) alliance structures.

The first concerns legal and institutional arrangements, which set the relationship between the state and the political actors. Dimensions involved here are the degrees of centralisation of political institutions, type of electoral system and separation of powers (Lees, 2002; Stepan, 2001). These dimensions establish the channels of access and opportunities for mobilisation based around manifest social cleavages available for the potential challenger. The second defines the political space available for challengers to introduce new conflicts into a polity. Opportunities for mobilisation are related to the prevailing politicised cleavages in society. The third dimension maps out the rules and procedures that have emerged within the polity for conflict management and resolution. As opposed to the cleavage approach, the informal channels refer to the modes through which political conflicts have been dealt with by political elites. Finally, alliance structures determine the specific balance of power between different actors at a certain time and place. This includes party composition, party systems and the relative strength of political parties and the government (Tarrow, 1994).

The extent of political opportunities available also depends on the relative openness of the political system. On the input-side, the number of political parties, factions and groups that are able to articulate demands, influences the degree of openness. If established actors are concentrated in cartels of entrenched interests, the system will tend to be more closed for new actors. Second, if the capacity of the legislature to develop and control policies is independent from the executive body, openness will increase. Third, if links between interest groups and the executive branch are fluid, access to decision-making is facilitated. Fourth, new demands must find their way into the process of policy formation in order to aggregate these demands. Openness is constrained if there are no viable procedures on which to build effective policy coalitions. On the output-side, the political structure can be either

*Table 3.2* Political opportunity structures in France, Germany, the Netherlands, Sweden and Britain

| | | Political input structures | |
| --- | --- | --- | --- |
| | | Open | Closed |
| Political output structures | Strong | Sweden, the Netherlands | France |
| | Weak | UK | Germany |

weak or strong, in the sense of transforming demands into action. National policies are implemented more effectively if the state is of a centralised character. The degree of state control, co-ordination or exclusion of certain actors influences political efficiency and limits the resources available for challengers. Finally, policy implementation becomes more difficult if the courts are able to influence executive branch control (Kitschelt, 1986). The five countries covered in this book can thus briefly be summarised by this modified Kitschelt typology in Table 3.2.

## Formal institutional structures

The five countries in question can be categorised on a scale indicating the extent to which they display corporatist or pluralist characteristics. The main distinction is whether a liberal polity is dominated by a monopolised and centralised system of interest organisation in which the state formally designates and recognises only a limited number of encompassing interests (corporatist) or multiple, overlapping, spontaneously formed, voluntaristi-cally supported, easily abandoned, and politically autonomous associations (pluralist) (Schmitter, 1981). Countries that have traditionally been described to show high levels of corporatist elements are Sweden and the Netherlands, whereas Germany displays some elements with France and the United Kingdom having weak to no corporatist tendencies (Lehmbruch, cited in Nollert, 1995).

Sweden and the Netherlands have a number of corporatist features, both with regard to general policy-making as well as in the area of integration in which incorporation of immigrants has been dealt with in a corporatist style. This involves the assertion of individual influence through party channels as well as that of group influence via organisations. These settings constitute an institutional framework – driven by a top-down perspective where the government recognises and identifies the needs and rights of immigrants – and provide the context in which immigrants and their inter-ests are organised. The institutional arrangement in Germany, with limited corporatist influence, is reflected in its way of organising resident migrants.

Migrant organisations are not given a special role or status in the integration policy formulation and formal links with organisations, as in Sweden and the Netherlands, are less well established. Instead, labour unions and churches play a more prominent role than migrant organisations. In addition, few provisions exist on a federal level for the collective participation of migrants although due to the institutional nature of the German polity, one finds significant variance on a municipal level depending on whether the local government is positively orientated towards these organisations or not. Furthermore, there is also a high degree of variance in terms of funding for migrant organisations, which is often left to the discretion of the local government (Berger *et al.*, 2002; Koopmans, 2004). Despite these unfavourable settings, Germany displays a relatively large amount of migrant organisations but of a very fragmented nature which lacks the centralised and representative character of Sweden and the Netherlands (Soysal, 1994). Again, we can see that more liberal and multiculturally orientated cities, such as Berlin and Hamburg, have created favourable settings for funding of and contacts with migrant organisations. France and Britain, on the other hand, display relatively few migrant organisations and less available funds. There are however two major differences between the two countries if one considers the characteristics of these organisations. In France, migrants are predominantly organised and unified with respect to specific political issues, especially related to citizenship and religious concerns, and as such emerge as a response to the particular political climate and environment. In this respect, they very much correspond to how interests are generally manifested in the French polity. To contrast, British race relations attempted to create national level umbrella organisations catering for the interests of primarily the Asian and Afro-Caribbean communities but with limited success. Instead, most organisational activity takes place on a local level where political, religious and professional ethnic associations have been active in electoral and racial politics. However, these organisations do more resemble traditional pressure groups than cultural organisations which can be explained by the lack of funding for groups or activities that promote collective identities or ethnic organising.

In Sweden, membership is organised around belonging to a particular group, defined primarily by occupational or socio-economic membership, and to a lesser extent ethnic, religious or gender identity, with a strong emphasis on equality. Immigrants are seen as a natural social grouping and are thus on an equal level with other incorporated groups. In the Netherlands, a main goal has been to provide the immigrant groups with opportunities to become emancipated. This key term originates from the process of religious liberation which, unlike Sweden, resulted in a division along religious lines. The effect of this has been the organisation of social, cultural and political functions according to pillar groups. Each pillar was allocated its own school, welfare system and union. Immigrant communities were subsequently perceived as yet another pillar in the Dutch system (Soininen, 1999; Soysal, 1994).

A central feature in both countries is the high level of centralisation and organisation of migrant management. In Sweden, the national board of immigration (Migrationsverket, MV) is the prime authority on the state level. The MV makes decisions about entry visas, employment visas, residency permits and naturalisation. Once legally resident, migrants are co-ordinated and supervised by the Swedish board of integration (Integrationsverket, IV). There is a close working relationship with the national labour market board (Arbetsmarknadsstyrelsen, AMS) which deals with training and employment projects aimed at immigrants. Although highly centralised in one sense, integration policy is administered primarily on the local level. The main responsibility lies with the ordinary administration: the social welfare offices, local housing authorities, schools, and so on (Hammar, 1985). This way of incorporating migrants is in stark contrast to the methods prevailing in the United Kingdom and France, where 'racial equality on the labour market' is emphasised in the former and 'equal state access' in the latter through legislation (United Kingdom) or general state bodies (France). Germany on the other hand displays a mixed case with little institutional recognition for migrants as collectives but with a number of measures (e.g. vocational training) aimed at specific migrant groups within local state ministries of labour and social affairs.

The Netherlands does not have an MV equivalent dealing with migrant matters *per se*. Instead ministerial bodies and intermediary institutions take charge of different aspects of incorporation. Although autonomous in relation to the state, they are fully funded by state spending and are centrally organised. Co-ordination is an important aspect of the administration, and is executed by a group of ministerial committees, including the Directorate for the Co-ordination of Minorities Policy (DCM) under the Ministry of Justice and the Interministereal Co-ordinating Committee on Minorities Policy. The DCM is the central body liaising between the national government and the migrant groups. In both countries, state funds support institutional frameworks for collective organisation. The state allocates certain functions – such as interest representation and consultative participation – thereby creating a unified and bureaucratic network. Even spontaneous and oppositional movements are incorporated into this scheme by being dependent on state funding (Soysal, 1994). In Sweden and the Netherlands, the level of finance allocated to a movement or an association is dependent on compliance with a number of specific objectives[19] and the number of members enrolled, making recruitment a prime task for the associations, and is also a rather complicated procedure.[20] If a migrant group or a coalition of groups intend to place issues on the political agenda, this has to be done through an organisation which is closely connected to the state. That is, political action in Swedish politics is not taken based on an individual but as a member of a recognised organisation. The Swedish system arranges matters in such a manner that results can only be achieved if participants play a clearly distinguished role in group settings requiring the assent of other designated group representatives (Heclo and Madsen, 1987). In Sweden, the traditional source of political mobilisation, outside of the mainstream parties, has been through the so-called folkrörelser (people's movements). These movements are highly institutionalised popular movements with a symbiotic relationship with an enlightened and reforming state-bearing elite (Ålund and Schierup, 1991; Micheletti, 1995).

The most famous example is the Swedish national labour organisation, who not only enjoyed a close working relationship with the Socialdemocratic party but also managed to influence the shape of the welfare system (Kjellberg, 1988; Lundquist, 1992). Immigrant associations are part of this organisational system and Sweden displays a comparatively high proportion of organised immigrants in Europe (Soysal, 1994). These associations are organised in a parallel fashion corresponding to nationality and/or ethnicity under supervision by the MV and the local authorities.

This mode of incorporation aggregates interest groups into federations, which are formally or informally involved to some extent in the policy process. The result is either direct consultation of interest groups or self-administration by federations at the local, regional or national level (Janoski, 1998). In the Netherlands, the relationship is very similar. The government supports associations financially and is supervised by an intermediary body, the National Advisory Council for Ethnic Minorities (LAO). Claims and requests are made through the LAO, which then channels these claims via sub-councils.

These formal institutional structures to a large extent determine the levels of access to the state as well as the capacity for different actors to participate. States can in this case be characterised as being either strong or weak in terms of three institutional arenas – the parliamentary, administrative and direct-democratic arena. In the parliamentary arena the critical indicators are the number of parties, factions and groups as well as the possibility of forming viable policy coalitions (Laver and Schofield, 1990). The number of parties is a function of the national conflict structure and the electoral system. The hypothesised relationship is that a more heterogeneous national conflict structure and a higher degree of proportionality will generate a larger number of parties. As a challenger, the proportional system facilitates access compared to plural or majority systems. Seen from the established parties' point of view, this means a greater risk of being subjected to competition from challengers than in the plural or majority case. A higher number of parties will also make it easier for non-party actors to find established support within the party system, as opposed to political systems with a limited number of parties such as Britain where the option may create separate ethnic fractions within the major parties (Adolino, 1998).

The second aspect, the administrative arena, concerns formal access as well as the capacity to act and is determined by the amount of resources at the disposal of the administration, the structure of interest groups and the structural arrangements established between the two. In general, the greater amount of resources available for the administration and the greater degree of coherence and internal co-ordination within the group, the better the connection between the two. Both Sweden and the Netherlands have multiple levels of state co-ordination and are able to steer migrant associations as well as the intermediate bodies that handle working relations between organisations and the state apparatus, which are absent in the other three countries. Challengers not part of this highly institutionalised and encompassing arrangement of policy negotiation will find the system inaccessible and difficult to influence. The corporatist trait prevailing hinders certain types of new challengers, especially those not based on social class (Sweden) or on social class/religious grouping (Netherlands), from entering. But these limitations are also present in Britain depending on whether a pressure group has achieved an 'insider'-status or not and in Germany where migrant claims are generally excluded from the policy process but less so in France where spontaneous movements can exercise influence.

This exclusive situation is most apparent within the Swedish Socialdemocrats where decisions have to be anchored in one of the party's many sub-branches such as the labour union or labour communes in order to be perceived as 'legitimate'. Immigrants are not perceived to be representing any social class or organisation and are therefore prevented from making certain claims (Westin, 1998). This is highlighted by the following quote.[21]

> It wouldn't be possible to give special privileges to particular migrant groups, it has to be from a general perspective ... I would tell them to get involved in the party and raise those questions from inside, I am rather sceptical about lobbying attempts. (Socialdemocrat C, 2001)

The Dutch discourse follows the same path. However, these interviewees seem to be more concerned with problems of heterogeneity amongst the ethnic groups rather than being opposed to the idea as such, which a member of the Socialist Party points out.

> If you look at the Turks, there are as many views as there are Turks so it's problematic to accommodate these people together because they all have such different backgrounds. (Socialist Party B, 2001)

> You can't call for instance the Surinamese an ethnic group because within them you have Muslims, Christians and Hindus, it's too diverse even within groups. (Christian Democrat A, 2001)

The final point is in regard to the direct democratic arena. Here, formal access is a function of the degree to which direct democratic procedures are institutionalised, most commonly in the form of referenda. This allows challengers to place an issue on the agenda and then ask the electorate to vote on the subject (as practised in Switzerland). The downside to this option is that it only allows oppositional intervention after an elite decision has been taken. In the Netherlands, citizens have rights to appeal against the course of implementation of public policies (Duyvendak and Koopmans, 1992).

In the Swedish case, this option has been largely absent due to a political culture characterised by a consensual democratic appearance and its emphasis on stability and predictability. The former involves low levels of opposition to the framework of rules and regulations for the resolution of political conflict within the state (Elder *et al.*, 1988). The latter indicates the status of the political structure. First, the 349 seats in the parliament are distributed proportionally to the parties who manage to pass Sweden's four per cent barrier to electoral representation. Although a certain amount of the governing power is decentralised to the regional and municipal levels, there is still a close relationship between the different authorities since the municipal assemblies are responsible for implementing national decisions on a local level. However, local authorities have a large degree of independence in relation to the central authorities when it comes to managing their own affairs, such as health and educational issues. Local politics are furthermore strongly focused on local needs, giving the participating parties an opportunity to sharpen their profiles as well as facilitating smaller parties to pursue specific questions (Wallin, 1991). Setting up a local party is relatively easy, since there are no significant formal requirements involved apart from a simple registration procedure.

As pointed out previously, both countries practice a system of proportional distribution of parliamentary seats. This system converts the Netherlands into one constituency and has weakened the basis for strong regional identification (Goudsblom, 1967). The party system is characterised by a multitude of parties, more so than in Sweden. Parties are organised according to the basic social and religious cleavages developed through the process of pillarisation. This division has rendered the creation of a number of parties that are not only of a purely local kind, but which also extend nationally and beyond 'one-issue politics'. Since the proportional system was introduced in 1933, the relative access to entry became easier in terms of establishing new parties attempting to access the political arena. However, as in Sweden, five parties have dominated the electoral system in the post-war period. Despite being decentralised to a certain extent, the Dutch regions and municipalities have a limited impact on policy-making as such and operate similarly to their Swedish counterparts (Andeweg and Irwin, 1993). Constitutionally, two concepts are prominent for the local government: autonomy and co-government.

The former refers to the policy domain in which the municipal government has independent authority, whereas the latter states its position in terms of national legislation implementation. Both systems can hence be characterised as being relatively open. Closer defined, this means that determining factors for this 'openness' are present in both the Swedish and the Dutch political structures, that is the capacity of the political system to convert demands into public policy. Both countries have several political parties and modes of interest groups to channel their demands. The intermediary structures between interest groups and the executive branch are plural and fluid, which facilitates access for new interests to access decision-making. This contrasts with France which has a much more closed system where the executive branch dominates over the weak legislature and policy-making access is limited to a few selected groups. In similar vein, the German political input shares common features with the French – centripetal party system, weak legislature and inaccessible executive (Kitschelt, 1986).

## National cleavage structures

However, there also needs to be a certain amount of political space available to new challengers (Tarrow, 1994, 1996). The chances to mobilise are here shaped by prevailing politicised cleavages in society, such as class or national identity conflicts. If an issue divides the elite and creates internal conflict, new movements can exploit this or make allegiances with opposing parties. This was, for example, utilised by the labour organisation in Sweden during the 1930s and 1940s. Despite its strong ties to the Socialdemocratic Party, they opted to co-operate with the Agrarian Party when the latter pressured for extended citizenship and workers' rights, which the Socialdemocrats were reluctant to pursue at the time (Lewin, 1988). As pointed out earlier, conflict in Sweden has tended to evolve around class-based issues, juxtaposing the two dominant parties, Socialdemocrats and Conservatives, over time. Therefore, the Socialdemocrats have tried to establish links with different immigrant organisations in order to gain their electoral support since a majority of the Swedish immigrants have been considered to belong to the 'working class' (Widgren, 1982). This class division appears to be a relatively common feature. In Britain, for example, a majority of the Asian and Afro-Caribbean labour migrants have tended to vote for the Labour party but with a significant Asian minority voting for ethnic reasons, especially if there is an Asian local MP, which indicates the possibility of parties to 'fish for the ethnic vote' by making specific appeals to these groups (Adolino, 1998).

In Sweden, an explicit attempt was made to challenge the left's dominance over this 'the immigrant vote'. A report put forward at the annual Conservative congress in June 1999 suggested that the party needed to profile itself more explicitly towards the different migrant communities (Friborg, 1999; Rojas, 1999[22]). The opportunity available here suggests an affiliation with the party that provides the best outcome. The Rainbow Party tried to take advantage of this competitive element by approaching a number of parties and proposing a coalition. However, the interest received was moderate and in some cases even hostile. The Socialdemocrats in particular became very concerned with this new challenger. The following quote highlights this situation.

> As we joined the campaign in 1998, the Socialdemocrats became very interested and preoccupied with the Rosengård area (an immigrant-dominated area in Malmö – author's note) ... on election day they asked, 'Are you going to vote?' and a lot of people understood that as 'Are you going to vote for us?' (Ex-Rainbow Party B, 2000)

However, in retrospect, after the election 'failure' of the Rainbow party, its impact was described as minimal by a Socialdemocrat.

> It's very difficult to do something that specific, look at the attempts to form a women's party, they were a serious threat when they weren't mobilised, but then when they did, they didn't get any support. It takes so much more than just being a woman or an immigrant. (Socialdemocrat A, 2001)

The Rainbow Party was also a response to the lack of initiative showed by other migrant associations. These organisations had not used this channel to introduce their demands as much as one might have had expected. Migrant organisations have been preoccupied with sporting and traditional cultural preservation activities, and had not functioned as platforms for channelling immigrants' social or political interests. Since voting rights for denizens[23] were introduced in 1976 (Hammar, 1985) and certain linguistic rights had already been implemented, specific immigrant interests tended to be given less attention in the political process (Soininen, 1999).

The opportunity available for individual migrants is thus to affiliate with a certain party or an interest group. The difficulty with this approach is that the corporatist model of representation is primarily based around class interest which prevents or hinders, for instance, labour unions from recognising interests stemming from other causes. Immigrant questions tend to be given a low priority and politicians with an immigrant background face difficulties obtaining party support for nominations in elections (Ålund and Schierup, 1991), an experience which was also true for the Rainbow Party candidates.

> We had the experience that it was not easy to get involved in the established parties and we did often discuss the alternative to go to other parties ... we did see some immigrants who had succeeded, but they were forced to transform themselves, so suddenly they were no longer part of 'us' but of 'them'. (Ex-Rainbow Party B, 2000)

The Dutch case differs in this sense in that it gives rise to a rather paradoxical situation in terms of the political system. As Lijphart (1975) observes, the Netherlands should be overshadowed by conflict and antagonism rather than consensus and co-operation. Pillarisation created a form of civic organisation, which was interconnected through personal links at the elite level. This condition determines the mobilisation potential (Klandermans and Oegema, 1987) or the extent to which people could be mobilised. This potential varies according to the degree to which cleavages constitute social groups that are clearly segmented from each other and internally highly integrated. Bartolini and Mair (1990) refer to this as the relative degree of closure, where the cleavage is a structure of processes that restrict mobility in a variety of ways including marriage, educational system, social customs, religious practices, and so on. The notion of closure is important since a highly integrated group in a fragmented surrounding constitutes a suitable foundation for political mobilisation (Oberschall, 1973). In this respect, France provides an interesting example in that one finds two ethnic minority pressure groups operating within the Socialist Party. The first one, the Cercle des Socialistes de Culture Musulmane, was set up as a reaction to the institutional environment which denied difference on religious grounds as well as in reaction to French society perceptions of Muslims during the so-called headscarf affair. The Cercle's aims were to gather Muslims with socialist beliefs and to combat prejudice and spread greater knowledge of Islam in French society. The second group, the Conférence natuionale des Élus Socialistes Originaires du Maghreb (CEESOM), was set up to outline how the Socialist Party's integration policy would better achieve integration amongst North African migrants (Cole, 1998).

A second aspect is the degree to which a certain cleavage line dominates conflicts in the political arena in relation to other cleavages. The more institutionalised a political cleavage is, the more regulated it becomes by established procedures. Furthermore, groups involved become more integrated into the political networks of the administrative and parliamentary arena. Thus, the Dutch system of class and religious cleavages constitute highly integrated groups. These enjoy peaceful relationships with each other marking an instrumental stabilisation of the relationship on an elite level, where elites are able to exercise control over the grassroots movement. Since immigrant communities are seen as yet another form of 'pillar' in the Dutch society, they are also subdued to work within a system that promotes the maintenance of the existing system (Bagley, 1973). However, this representation often proves to be difficult in practice, as described by both a Turkish and an ethnic Dutch councillor, which echoes the Swedish equality mentality.

> I represent not only the Turks but all people in Rotterdam, you can't make ethnic claims in my party, definitely not, we have our programme and our ideals. (Socialdemocrat D, 2001)

I think it's dangerous, it's not a position our party wants to promote and it shouldn't happen because you should represent the whole population. If certain groups support you because you promise certain things to certain groups then you automatically get a clash between the party interest and the group interest. The party interest should always be the main priority. (D66 A, 2001)

As in Sweden, organisational activities are primarily concerned with non-political performances such as community development, cultural or emancipation activities. Seeing that the Netherlands display a similar amount of migrant organisations, a unified organisation of, for instance, specific Turkish interests requires the collaboration of internally diverse groups[24] and this has proven to be difficult in practice (Soysal, 1994). Because of the Netherlands' pillarised society, political competition takes place along vertical cleavages such as religion, rather than through the horizontal class cleavage, as in Sweden. As a result, alignments with different parties would have to be based along these lines as well. The two major religious groups are Protestants and Catholics but among the four dominating migrant groups, two of them (Turks and Moroccans) are mainly of Islamic belief, which could make religious collaboration somewhat problematic. Therefore, alignment with any established party is more difficult in the Dutch case, which the following quote points out.

It's very difficult because you get this fear, not so much here in Rotterdam but on the national level, there is a fear of Muslims, especially in the smaller villages and some people seem to think that Muslims and Christians can't work together. (Christian Democrat A, 2001)

## Informal procedures

Tarrow's third dimension deals with the indirect channels that have developed within a polity when it comes to conflict resolution. For instance, one could view the extensive nature of rights and benefits available to immigrants in Sweden and the Netherlands as working in the opposite way and pacifying these groups since there is not much more to struggle for. As the president of the Association of Women from Turkey in Sweden expressed it, 'we cannot mobilise the Turkish population around any real demands .... Most rights and freedoms are already given by the state, and there is already an organisation for every problem that migrants face in this country' (Soysal, 1994: 99). This quote highlights the effective ways of neutralising any challenge to the status quo by immediately making them part of the system and appointing a representative that deals with these issues (e.g., an ombudsman).

In the Netherlands, attempts were made to establish separate immigrant parties, but their life-span was relatively short and their impact minor, especially after local voting rights were introduced in 1985 (van der Wusten and Roessingh, 1997). However, immigrant parties could theoretically stand a chance of obtaining parliamentary seats. Due to the highly proportional Dutch system of electoral representation (Gladdish, 1991; Steiner, 1998), small fringe parties have a relatively better chance of winning parliamentary seats. For instance, there is no four per cent electoral threshold like there is in Sweden.

Yet one-issue or highly specific parties would most likely face two types of problems. First, once they become institutionalised they would have to put forward an ideological line of action relating to other areas (Taggart, 2000). This could prove to be highly problematic and disruptive for the party, as for instance the case of Leefbaar Rotterdam has shown. Second, one-issue parties will most likely face intra-council resistance from other parties, as the following quotes suggest.

> If you are a Jew, a Turk or if your grandfather was Hindustani, that should not be made into a political issue because that only feeds stupid nationalists and we don't want that development. (Socialist Party A, 2001)

> An immigrant party would have the possibility but would first have to solve the problem of being a one-issue party, if they do that then they have another problem, that is what do all these people have in common apart from being migrants? (Socialist Party B, 2001)

However, in Sweden emerging parties are not eligible for governmental party funding aid unless they manage to obtain seats. This threshold singles out a majority of prospering parties, in that they might not otherwise have the economic resources to continue. As discussed previously, conflict management in corporatist states revolves around negotiations between the state and the sanctioned corporate groupings. In Sweden this has traditionally been done between the labour movement and the state. The former needs to display high membership rates in order to be taken seriously by the negotiating partner. This also applies for migrant organisations. However, membership rates have tended not to be sufficiently high (compared with other actors) and lack intra-organisational cohesiveness. Similarly in France, given the lack of contacts between organised migrant interests and the political elite (a situation which also applies to the population at large), political activism has been seriously undermined for, in particular, the vocal Maghrebi groups (Cole, 1998). Migrants wishing to put their interests on the political agenda in Sweden have been redirected towards the major actors rather than through their own organisations. Moreover, migrant associations are dependent on a healthy relationship with the authorities in order to receive funding for their activities, constraining their independent position. This precarious relationship is described by an ex-Rainbow Party member as a major obstacle for migrant political participation.

[T]hrough these structures and mechanisms those organisations are tamed and practically all they think about is getting funds for their activities, so they are really tamed and don't dare to think about those questions that we have, They know they will be punished, just like the IPF got punished, because all aid and funds will disappear. (Ex-Rainbow Party A, 2000)

The Rainbow Party emerged from the The Political Association of Immigrants (IPF), an association with a focus which is rather unique compared to the activities performed by other immigrant associations (Ålund and Schierup, 1991). The interviewees argued that being a migrant organisation trying to make demands and political claims was not perceived as appropriate associational behaviour by Swedish society, and continuing as the old association proved to be very difficult. By forming a party, they would be perceived as more serious and would also become more independent in relation to the Swedish state. It was also suggested that other alternatives such as joining one of the established parties or a trade union were not an option since immigrant interests seemed to get lost given the emphasis put on class. Although migrant membership rates in unions are similar to that of native Swedes, immigrants are less likely to be union representatives and are also notoriously under-represented in both interest groups and political parties (Bäck and Soininen, 1993).

Dutch migrant organisations appear to be in a similar position, although migrant representation is more developed by the presence and use of, for instance, the LAO. Since this central administrative body serves as a mediator it provides migrant associations with a channel for participation on the national level through sub-councils representing nationality and minority groups. This has enabled, primarily, the Turkish community to become very active and influential in establishing an Islamic identity in the Dutch society. The Turks in Germany have had a similar, although more fragmented, experience especially after some local states started developing more participatory policies in order to cater for the representation of non-nationals (Soysal, 1994).

However, migrant associations in Sweden and the Netherlands are subjected to tight directives in order to get funding from the state. Funding is available if these organisations promote migrants' interests and provide informational, cultural and emancipation activities for their national constituencies (the Netherlands) or if they have activities for youth and children that promote integration (Sweden) (Soysal, 1994). Although categorised as relatively open (Kitschelt, 1986), corporatist states often limit the number of relevant interest groups, in essence one group for each interest sector. Gaining entry to the political arena is constrained by the state through a number of requirements, and the goal of the organisation is to be 'representative' of its members, which in turn forces the association to accumulate large membership rates. Corporatism can thus be viewed as a way to domesticate uncontrolled (and unrecognised) political claims by channelling action into acceptable forms.

## Alliance structures

Finally, in terms of opportunities for challengers to mobilise when political elites are internally divided and/or form strategic power relationships, both countries display a rather stable scenario. In Sweden, the Socialdemocratic party has enjoyed a long-term stay in government, more or less uninterrupted since the 1930s. Traditionally, they have relied on support from the Left Party in order to secure their minority government position. This ideological cleavage has created a block system in which a Left–Right division prevails. The Dutch have a similar but much weaker division due to the high degree of minority fragmentation. No party, either religious or confessional, has enjoyed a majority situation, so the Dutch have instead relied on multi-party coalitions (Andeweg and Irwin, 1993; see also Lucardie, 1991). This situation creates decision difficulties for new parties in terms of rationally choosing which side to align with what Smith (1991) calls the 'third party problem'. Here, a small party positions itself between the two dominating blocks and becomes a potential coalition partner. In contrast, this option seems to be more accessible in Sweden which has also been the case in Germany but less so in Britain and France. In the 1988 election the Green Party managed to influence the agenda by forming an alliance with the Socialdemocratic bloc. In Malmö local politics, this traditional Left–Right division and alliance was disrupted when the xenophobic Scania Party (Skånepartiet) appeared in the 1985 election and managed to gain five seats in the local municipality.[25] The presence of anti-immigrant sentiments produced a counter movement in the form of an explicit immigrant party. In France, similar anti-immigrant sentiments did not produce a party, but rather the emergence of externally located pressure groups which were apolitical and represented ethnic groups in general (SOS-Racisme) and the Maghrebian migrants in particular (France-Plus). As with the Anti-Nazi League in Britain, the French organisations were initially closely affiliated with the Labour party but have since tried to distance themselves from being associated with one particular party (Cole, 1998; Solomos, 2003).

However, alignment formation for the Rainbow Party turned out to be difficult despite considerable media coverage and access to political platforms through debates and press conferences. The party formation strategy proved to be far more problematic than initially perceived, not only in terms of resistance faced by a majority of the established political actors, but also in terms of financing the movement. Seeing that governmental party support is only available after a party gains representation, the Rainbow Party had to rely on voluntary work and donations from sponsors. This obstacle relates to what McCarthy and Zald (1977) label resource-mobilisation. This term not only refers to the need to bring in monetary resources from outside, but also to the ability of obtaining political, legal and media support.

As mentioned above, when attempting to establish working relationships with the dominating parties, the response received was moderate,[26] and in some cases even hostile,[27] except from the Green Party.

> [T]hey tried to establish a dialogue with us from the start. They said that their manifesto was compatible with ours. The Green Party took it more seriously, they wanted to co-operate with us and they wanted us to join their organisation. We got invited to debates, which we re-named a dialogue, because there wasn't much to debate against, more of a discussion about questions that were similar for the both of us ... that was very positive for us, it made us look more legitimate, that they took us seriously. (Ex-Rainbow Party B, 2000)

The positive response from the Green Party is not very surprising given that the Rainbow Party's manifesto is, if not identical, at least very similar to that of the Greens,[28] something that the interviewees openly admit to. By affiliating the Rainbow Party with the Greens, the party gained access to a wider scope of opportunities to influence the local agenda. The candidates could use the means offered by an established party, but this also meant that their previous profile had to be re-negotiated.

In the 1998 election the Rainbow Party only managed to receive 0.7 per cent of the votes in Malmö and thus were not entitled to either municipal seats or monetary support. This outcome and the previous engagement with the Greens generated an outflow of Rainbow Party candidates to the Green Party. In retrospect, the Rainbow Party not only shares similarities with a social movement utilising available opportunity structures and organising a suitable strategy accordingly, it also shares similarities with what Johnson (1981) identifies as a 'tribune party'. Drawing on the experiences from the French PCF party, Johnson suggests that tribune parties work according to a principle in which gaining political representation is not the prime directive. Although, this line of thought seems rather contradictory, the idea of a tribune party can highlight the particularity of the Rainbow Party. Its function was to organise and defend a social group who were excluded and/or felt themselves to be excluded from the political participation process and from the benefits of the economic and cultural system. The existence of a tribune party relies on three preconditions. First, there must prevail a large and relatively homogenous group to represent. A group which, despite its size, is poorly integrated into the political and cultural system and thus placed in a position of inferiority. Second, the political structure in which such a party operates must tolerate a tribune party's actions by legitimating the right of political defence. That is, the recognition of the party's right to oppose the perceived imperfections of the system. Third, the group or groups must be willing to settle primarily for political defence rather than passiveness or open revolt.

## Conclusion

This chapter has discussed three things. First, it has explored the role and importance of institutions in terms of shaping the political environment as well as setting a framework for actors' choices and space for action. Second, this has been concretised with reference to the French, German, Dutch, Swedish and British context and the historical development of certain institutions have been examined more closely. This development has produced a number of norms and regulations for political behaviour, which in turn determines the scope available for certain types of issues and what mobilisation ground exists. Third, the particular institutional set-up has then been examined in relation to the concept of POS. The importance of institutions and the role of different types of POS have been used to examine the opportunities for non-established actors to influence and challenge the political system.

More specifically, the chapter focused on migrant organisations, the opportunities available for them in a corporatist as well as less corporatist environments and – in the Swedish case – the specific option of party formation as a strategy. Migrants are encouraged by official policy to become integrated in the receiving society. Citizenship regulations are liberal (Sweden, the Netherlands, the United Kingdom, to some extent France) public funding is available for organisational activities (Sweden, the Netherlands, Germany) and the state supports and recognises difference in ethnic or cultural backgrounds (Sweden, the Netherlands, the United Kingdom). Sweden and the Netherlands are also relatively more open in terms of their capacity to convert demands into public policy. However, this seems to be limited to larger, more established parties or interest groups. Small-scale social movements lack the necessary means to pursue their goals and are thus re-directed towards the major actors. Taking advantage of political cleavages is a second form of opportunity structure through which a movement or group can establish an alliance with a party. In Sweden this has been done according to class-membership through large corporatist groups. The channels available for immigrants here are to use their organisation as a platform, although this has predominately been limited to non-politicised activities. Given that class issues dominate public discourse, an explicit ethnic agenda appears difficult to pursue. The Dutch case is slightly different, mainly relying on religious affiliation rather than class, but this strategy has been under-utilised since the dominating religious beliefs differ from the main religious practice of immigrants. Britain and France lack an explicit group focus and migrants are thus directed, as individuals, towards other institutions (legal or general welfare bodies) to address their particular concerns. Germany, on the other hand, displays certain elements of corporatism but only in the sense of class representation and migrant interests are catered for by other actors, such as trade unions and religious institutions.

Formal and informal ways of conflict resolution constitute a third possibility. Once again, non-party affiliators have to rely on a strong organisational back-up, which means a large organisation that will not be ignored by the negotiating partner. Immigrant interests are not actively promoted by their representing associations, steering them towards other organisations in which their particular interest might get a lower priority. However, this channel seems to be used more often in the Netherlands than in the other countries. Finally, challenging groups can find opportunities to mobilise when the political elites are internally divided over a specific issue. This does however presuppose that the political system is unstable. The internal division has to be such that challenging actors have a realistic chance of gaining influence by affiliation with a certain party. Germany, Sweden, the Netherlands and Britain have enjoyed rather stable scenarios over time, and even though France is the exception, this last dimension has also largely remained under-utilised.

In conclusion, regardless of whether a country has an explicit multicultural agenda or not, pursuing immigrant-specific issues seems to be rather difficult. The challenger can experience numerous thresholds in order to become an influential actor on the political arena. However, these types of claims still exist and migrant actors try to find different strategies as a response to the institutional environment. As highlighted by the example of the Rainbow Party, choosing the party strategy was an alternative to group-orientated pressure in the short run. However, as a long-term strategy it was only partially successful and Rainbow Party candidates were eventually compelled to adopt a new strategy and join the party that responded most positively to their demands.

# 4
# Identity, Citizenship and Identification

## Introduction

Immigration policy in Sweden and the Netherlands has experienced a radical shift regarding the emphasis and preferred outcomes since it was officially recognised that the 'new population' was becoming permanent settlers. The shift took the direction of acknowledging cultural pluralism and the acceptance of Swedish and Dutch society as becoming more and more diverse in its ethnic demographic composition. The inflow of migrants from countries both geographically and culturally distant from the host societies put pressure on the integration regimes. This new situation led the authorities to reconsider the provision of societal support for the maintenance of cultural practice and/or a cultural identity that was considered to be different, while at the same time encouraging the integration of the new population in the social, economic and political areas of society.

The purpose of this chapter is threefold. First, it sets out to examine different notions of identity, its perceived relevance and subsequent construction. Second, closer attention will be paid to the impact of citizenship policy and 'politics of belonging' on the expression of specific types of identity. Here it will be argued that the state's conception of identity and citizen management and the choice of integration regime provide structural limitations and opportunities for identity expression. Furthermore, these settings influence potential movement between different types of identities and thereby determine the level of host-society identification. Third, the importance of relating these two concepts – citizenship and identity – to each other lies in the potential impact that identification has on political participation. The final part of this chapter will compare levels of identification with the levels of political participation and political interest, using results from a questionnaire survey distributed amongst the target groups in Malmö and Rotterdam.

## Identity – relevance and construction

The public recognition of difference is an integral part of multicultural policies and theory. This recognition is crucial since it is supposed to be linked to the concept of identity. This term offers the means to understand the interplay between subjective experiences of the world and the cultural and historical settings in which those meaningful subjectives are formed. As a concept, identity has been applied to several issues in political discourse. It has been branded in speeches of belonging, ethnicity and nationality, constantly repeating the message that racial or ethnic conflict are the product of, or should at least be understood as, incompatible identities that mark deep cleavages between cultures and civilisations (Gilroy, 2000).

This concept is, however, not uncontested. As with catch-words such as 'Globalisation', 'Integration' or 'Multiculturalism' the term 'Identity' has been used and applied in such a multitude of ways that no one seems to be really sure what it means any more. Therefore, a brief overview of the different understandings, or definitions, of the concept will be made. The main point will not be to try and establish the 'true' nature of identity, but rather to discuss its relevance as a political concept and how an identity is constructed in a given environment.

The idea of identity has come to play an increasing role in modern politics in that it influences the way in which people perform their duty of civic participation as well as how this duty is to be executed. That is, the identity possessed by individuals determines their views on interpersonal relations, conflict resolution and/or what the appropriate legal frameworks should be. This suggests that identity be linked with the concept of 'culture'. Waldron (2000) observes a common tendency to equate culture primarily with something that is detachable from personal identity, such as a club or a hobby, picked up at one's convenience. Indeed, culture and identity seem to be more difficult to distinguish from one another if the latter is understood as a social practice, subsisting as a way of life for a whole collective of people. What Waldron addresses here is a set of guiding tools used as a compromise for dealing with issues from the organisation of the economy, transmission of knowledge, the punishment of offences to the rearing of children. Therefore, identity seems to be bound in a given setting, dependent on previously existing structures but also open to restructuring and adopting new definitions of the identity when overall society changes. In that way, when a claim is made to belong to identity group A or B, it not only refers to seemingly superficial practices of traditions such as dances or cuisine, but goes further into a situation of historically developed and distinct practices addressed to settle and solve issues of life in that particular society. However, the question that Waldron avoids is how identities emerge and in what way they can be constructed. Identities seem here to be given, or at least left unproblematised; they simply exist and run into conflict. What can then be said about identity and its origins?

In its most basic understanding, identity is the term that flags who we are, where we come from; working in a symbiotic relationship of choosing the person you want to be while negotiating your individuality with others by the attachments being imposed upon you (Taylor, 1994). Identity is the background against which our opinions and aspirations make sense; that is, identity serves as the navigator through a turbulent and chaotic world.

Taylor strongly favours that identity expression, or practice, has to be recognised in its public forms of manifestation. But, as Rath *et al.* (2001) point out, the politics of recognition is intrinsically ambivalent since it simultaneously refers not only to the equal distribution of rights and provisions to all those regarded as citizens but also to the distribution of special rights and entitlements. The latter then suggests that individuals and/or groups possess a unique identity which distinguishes them from others and it is therefore a recognition revolving around specificity and not universality. Others suggest that identity implies a perception of an overall coherence within the experiences and expressions of an individual (Nelson and Kavolis, 1973), or adoption of a more sociological standpoint, claiming that identity should be considered as images, knowledge or assessment of positions, performances and attributes of social actors (Burkhart and Robertson, 1980). Identity has often been used interchangeably with the term 'self' but this should rather be viewed as two distinct notions which have to be distinguished from each other. First, identity is the appearance of self – that is, the way in which the self is perceived and understood by persons. Second, self is a component of the psychological process by which behaviour is explained, and identity is the appearance of self in that process (Du Preez, 1980).

In the literature, two strands of identity discussion have come to the fore. The first one deals with national identity and its late-eighteenth-century construction and reconstruction of the nation as an 'imagined community' (Anderson, 1983). Here, an emphasis is put on the collective narrative referring to a shared, deeply rooted history of the ethnically common people, with a unified common territory, language and tradition signifying the uniqueness of the community, which distinguishes it from other nation-states. Even though the concept of ethnicity or the ethnic basis of the nation was fictive or imagined, it proved to be a powerful tool in order to play down conflicts relating to gender and class by asserting that the 'we' of the state were all part of the same community, regardless of social status, sharing the same identity origins and, more importantly, a shared understanding of culture and its practical manifestations. Hjerm (1998) argues that national identity not only supplies individuals with a sense of who they are in the world but also provides a sense of belonging in order to claim that they are part of a certain community. This particular relationship is manifested through the introduction of citizenship, which creates an emotional bond between the citizen and the state. In addition, national identity can be framed in an ethnic or a civic manner. The former indicates an emphasis on a community of birth and a presumed descent in which the people are constituted as one *volk*. Similarly to Smith's (1986) ethnie characteristics, this understanding emphasises the ethnic national identity as a product of commonly shared characteristics and the institutionalisation of one particular national identity by attachment to the state. More importantly, as Oommen (1997) suggests, national ethnic identity only became relevant when it was experienced in psychological and emotional terms. That is, it is necessary, but not sufficient, to only provide the tangible characteristics when trying to pinpoint the ties between state and the individual.

The civic understanding encompasses a well-defined territory with a common set of laws, single political will, equal rights for members of the nation and a minimum of common values, traditions or sentiments that bind people together. The factors used to determine who is to be perceived as a legitimate member or not, are dependent on, amongst other characteristics, birth in the country, duration of stay, knowledge of language, respect for laws and regulations, being a citizen and having a sense of being a national. Compared to the ethnic understanding, the civic model provides easier access for individuals lacking the traits described above to transfer from being outsiders to insiders.

The second strand concerning the concept of identity involves societies that are characterised by a majority–minority relation. Here, cultural identity is the focus of interest. Cultural identity has been used to refer to one shared culture with a collective of people sharing a common history and/or ancestry. This cultural identity reflects the common historical experiences and those shared cultural codes establishing a stable frame of reference in order to bring in a notion of 'one people' (Hall, 1994) – that is, the dominating culture is the norm which other cultural expressions are compared to. To receive acknowledgement for one's cultural identity can be a way for the state to signal that cultural practices differing from a stipulated norm are a condition that is not only supported by the society but also one that could be encouraged (Kymlicka, 1995). However, identity – being either in the form of national identity or a cultural identity – in a new environment, is to a large extent dependent on the recognition received by the state or by institutions operating within the framework of the state. In other words, a specific form of identity does not emerge by itself but does rather depend on the interaction between different groups and between different competing notions of identity expression. This recognition is essential for the maintenance of a certain identity and is practised in relation to other identities as negotiated through social interaction (Du Preez, 1980). Discussions of identity, either with reference to the individual or to the collective dimension, often include the construction of boundaries between those with whom one shares likeness juxtaposed with those who are marked by difference. A distinction is made in order to first, establish those with whom one is identical with, and second, those whose difference, or 'otherness', signifies the 'sameness' of one's own group. Dimensions of identity are built up of a set of instinctive, yet dynamic, meanings which are self-evident, reconfirmed and reinforced via the interaction of a particular space of practice and discourse (Pred, 2000).

Mouffe (1995) follows a similar line of thought when stressing the importance of placing identity within a diversity of discourses, where identity creation is not so much a movement from one to the other but rather a constant movement which is constituted by something she calls 'subject positions'. Identity is here shaped by multiple and contradictory subject positions in which self-understanding of 'who I am' is temporarily located at the intersection of those subject positions and dependent on specific forms of identification, by the self as well as by others. As I will argue later on, this flux in identity can be facilitated or constrained by means of public policy, in this case very much dependent on the opportunities determined by the prevailing societal and institutional structures. More explicitly, this suggests that identity expression – primarily in the public sphere – will rely on the space available within the dominating structures in society. However, this interaction does also give rise to competition between social agents, either individual or collective, in order not to change or vanish. According to Turner (1975), groups or collectives aim to achieve a more positive value compared to other groups in order to ensure a place in society which can only be assured if the group can be positively evaluated in relation to other groups. Hence, the existence of an individual or a collective identity is dependent on the existence of at least one other point of reference in order for the identity to be established. Weber (1968) describes this as 'social closure', in which he compares the way in which the market operates and the way social groups interact. These groups generally attempt to form monopolies or restrict this competition of other identities similar to the behaviour found in the economic sphere. Here, identity exists within a framework of systems in which its definition becomes meaningful first when placed in relation to something considered as the opposite or in relation to a competitor. This line of thought corresponds to what Zolberg (1994) describes as the negative criteria of identity, that is 'we are who we are by virtue of who we are not' (1994: 142). The negative 'others' have in Zolberg's terms been those commonly close neighbours with whom perennial wars have been fought, outsiders within one's own society or non-nationals in general.

As a recurring phenomenon in history, tracing back to the Middle Ages, being a Christian meant not being a heretic, a Jew or a Muslim. Similarly, during the crucial phase of nation-state building, 'the German' was created by distancing him/herself from the Latin or the Slav, while 'the French', along with other nationalities, became 'the non-German' along with other competing nationalities. Furthermore, an individual or group establishes their peculiarity by being different, in one way or another, in terms of cultural forms, practices or way of life. Group affiliation stems from similar experiences or way of life which ties its members to one group, more than those perceived as not belonging to the group (Young, 1990). Consider the following example: the Socialdemocratic political identity becomes meaningful first when contrasted to that of a Conservative identity, since context has a marked effect in differentiation as a process (Doise *et al.*, 1978). In its most simplistic way, to be considered as a member of the former could for instance be that one subscribes to the belief that a general policy of child support is a better option than one based on income. Or consider Marx's theory of class-consciousness. Here, a class is transformed from a category of persons sharing a similar position by the means of common grievances and interests into a class for itself, rather than in itself. The establishment of communication and organisational patterns distinguishes them from the bourgeoisie by establishing social boundaries (Burkhart and Robertson, 1980). In practice, markers of identity may focus on any one of a broad variety of characteristics, or a combination of traits, including religion, national origin, language and race. But identity can also invoke more abstract or diffuse concepts attributed to groups, such as political culture or alleged moral personality.

However, to speak of a group or an individual having an identity also implies a situation of continuity or that the identity can be placed in a context of different relations. Identity thus requires both difference and coherence in order to be comprehensible. That is, identity hinges upon what makes a difference. Or as Zizek (1994) points out, 'what I am "for the other" is condensed in the signifier which then represents me for the signifiers' (1994: 45). Outside of these relations, the identity ceases to be of any significant matter since identity is constituted through an externalisation of the other by drawing frontiers (Norval, 1994).

Therefore we must speak of locating the identity within a social space and time in which the social actor exercises a degree of reflexivity (Guiot, 1977). Here, the individual needs to be conscious of the self, or in the group-case be conscious of social boundaries and other collective actors. The limits or constraints of boundaries lead to the determination of the 'sameness' of the identity over a period of time in relation to other competing identities. By reflexivity, the identity is established but will vary since the degree to which the boundaries are perceived, the variety of boundaries to be considered and available symbols might be limited. Furthermore, as identity is part of a more or less imagined community or a non-material world that is socially constructed, it therefore needs to be constantly re-created and maintained. This can be described as being a process of constant confrontation of views, ideas and projects. Through this 'dialogue' individuals negotiate their identity in relation to others.

Similarly, in more psychological terms, identity formation can be described as an evolving configuration which responds to inner drives and social pressures which experience change in different stages of life (Bloom, 1990). Max Weber's work on ethnic groups describes the creation of an identity in a similar vein. In Weber's understanding, a specific group evolves when human groups (other than kinship groups) cherish a belief in their common origins of such a kind that it provides a basis for creation of a community (quoted in Stone, 1995). The important issue that Weber centres on is the set of beliefs of group membership, and that identification with a shared origin is largely fictitious. Therefore, group membership as such does not necessarily entail or result in in-group formation but rather provides the resources that may produce group mobilisation.

Another strand in the discussion of identity formation is put forward by the notion of symbolic interaction. This term concerns itself with the actor's point of view as well as the nature of the situation in which collective action is constructed. This point of view emphasises social processes rather than social structures as the imagery appropriate to the study of ongoing human group life. This concern with the ceaseless and indeterminate change of experience and events lends itself to what is called a 'process model of culture' rather than a 'pattern model of culture'. More explicitly, it takes a historical and social setting approach in which context, once again, provides the explanatory frame in which collective organisation is formed (Ballis Lal, 1995). Furthermore, a theory of symbolic interaction stresses the importance of self as an object of self-definition. This is grounded in the way in which the actor is perceived or treated by the so-called significant other, such as parents, teachers, acquaintances, as well as the way in which the actor interacts with others in a variety of situations – as friend, neighbour, party affiliate and the like. This suggests that the self or the personal identity is constantly defined and redefined by waves of significant others (Goffman, 1961).

## Interpretations of citizenship

One of the key points of reference that establishes at least a formal identity is the possession of a particular citizenship. This historical development has come to mark the relationship between the state and the individual in that the citizen status sets out the rights and obligations which are appointed to those individuals who are conceived as members of that particular society. This modern notion of citizenship stems from the development of the Western liberal state, going back to the early sixteenth century (Skinner, 1978). Rights and obligations were no longer to be limited to individuals from a certain class or in a privileged position due to heritage. Hobbes (1973), who recognised this new pattern early on, argued that in contrast to previous ages, the individual would now enjoy a direct relationship with the state which required a more developed sense of citizenship, through which this relationship would be mediated. Introducing the idea that the ruler and the state were indivisible meant that the individual's allegiance now shifted from the monarch or the feudal lord to the state itself. Hobbes's state sovereignty theory also highlights the paradoxical nature of citizenship in which citizenry as consent is opposed to the state as the enforcer of order, a situation which has greatly influenced the context and extent of the term.

Furthermore, citizenship, understood as an attachment to a certain community, originates from the development of the modern nation-state, especially following the aftermath of the French revolution. Compared to previous attempts at uniting and homogenising 'the people', the idea and practice of the nation-state proved to be far more stable and lasting than other efforts of state formation. As commonly practised during this formative period, the nation-state supplied centralised units of administration that structured, predominately, the Western European states into single states rather than as a looser federation of connected regions. What worked in favour for the nation-state was not only the provision of a rational administrative infrastructure, but also the introduction of an effective judicial framework allowing for individual and collective action. When the nation-state established a citizen from the non-citizen, it also enabled a way to determine membership status of a community (Habermas, 1995). This is most commonly associated with an ideology of citizenship (Rath *et al.*, 2001). The members, or citizens, of the nation were assumed to have certain common features – origin, culture or religion. This perceived bond and key distinguishing factor from 'others' was expressed in the formalised notion of citizenship where 'full members' of the nation-state were juxtaposed with 'foreigners'. This relationship was manifested more directly in terms of the state's sovereign role of making the decision of admittance and deportation of foreign nationals. On the other hand, identity as stipulating a communal sensation can be interpreted in an ideology of residence. According to this line of thought, deciding on membership for newcomers was not dependent on possessing certain characteristics but on spatial placement. Here, social goods and services were not exclusive to those identified as citizens but available for all long-term residents regardless of nationality (Held, 1995; Riesenberg, 1992). Citizenship indicated a level of mutuality, including rights against and duties towards not only a political but also a social and economical community.

Following this distinction, the notion of citizenship has been analytically divided into three categories or elements – a civil, a political and a social dimension (Marshall, 1950). These three different aspects of citizenship emerged during the past three centuries in such a way that each new type built on the pre-existing one. The first type, civil citizenship, emerged in the eighteenth century and established those rights which were necessary in order to protect the freedom of the individual – including free speech and religious, property and judicial rights. Relating this to the notion of identity, the civic aspect provides the framework for the maintenance of an identity differing from a stipulated norm. Here, this practice is safeguarded by the state in the form of regulations or constitutional rights. Second, the French Revolution can be said to have sparked the inclusion of political citizenship into the term. This aspect implies equal opportunities to participate in the practice of political power. The establishment of political rights and political democracy provided the means whereby the mass of the people were given the opportunity to shape their social worlds through collective action and public choice. More specifically, this means that no one identified as a citizen should be excluded from the possibility to hold a governmental position or to participate politically. Finally, social citizenship was introduced in the twentieth century, closely linked to the emergence of a welfare state. This notion indicated a guarantee for each individual citizen to be granted a basic form of social security in which specific institutions were responsible for providing public service goods such as education or social services (Twine, 1994; van Steenburgen, 1994).

These different expressions of citizenship were to be, if not directly following on after one another, at least overlapping. The unifying characteristic of the three elements, despite displaying differences from society to society, was that of equality. To be a citizen indicates a position in which the individual shares the rights and duties attached to the concept of citizenship with other members of society (Petersson *et al.*, 1989). Marshall understood citizenship as a set of rights enjoyed by all societal members on an equal basis. If these were fully developed, they would embody an idea of social justice. Citizens would here enjoy certain entitlements that were separate from, and in some cases in conflict with, the outcomes of the efficiency-driven market economy. According to this understanding of citizenship, the concept carried strong redistributive overtones, for instance the guarantee of free schooling and health care, which would not have been accessible if left solely to market forces.

Invoking the idea of citizenship into a polity has the basic purpose of interlocking the individual with the state in a symbiotic relationship (Heater, 1999; Prior *et al.*, 1995). Another important distinction is that of interpreting citizenship as a judicial and/or rights-based sign of belonging. In the former case, being a citizen simply indicates a legal status. In this sense, citizenship tends to be used interchangeably, or confused with, the idea of nationality in that it expresses a distinction between someone considered as a national of a particular country contrasted to one being a temporary resident (Faulks, 1998).

From this point of view, the right to a particular citizenship is determined by the principle of *jus sanguinis*. Here, parental heritage determines the citizenship of the child, rendering it almost impossible to become a legitimate member of such a society unless one is able to prove a historical bloodline attaching the individual to a certain enclosed community. This line of thought could also stipulate an important legal position when coming to terms with who is entitled to participate in the political arena. The principle of heritage prevents individuals from becoming political citizens or full members of a new society by proscribing or neglecting naturalisation based solely on residence. The implication of this particular understanding of citizenship is that it is resistant to converts by enforcing social closure on the basis of a prescribed collective identity of national ethnicity. Rights are thus strongly connected to an ethnocultural belonging to nationhood.

In contrast, a *jus soli* or *domicili* principle bases citizenship on territorial residency rather than blood. In this case, loyalty to the community is determined by duration of stay and a voluntary wish to become part of a new community. This interpretation allows citizenship acquisition by the means of a contractual assimilation by the individual to nationhood, which is done either through ritual conversion or automatically by birth (Brubaker, 1992).

The latter interpretation regards citizenship as a right stemming from membership. This understanding defers from the judicial meaning of the term by adopting a more sociological view of the term. Here, citizenship is associated with rights and obligations manifested via the individual possession of membership of a certain community where rights signalled by the citizenry status apply to all those defined as members of the community. Relating back to the nation-state development, this conception of citizenship aimed to replace previous local or regional loyalties in favour of the new state. The two understandings are linked together in the sense that judicial citizenship determines the degree to which the individual is able to enjoy the rights constituted by the sociological interpretation of the term.

This distinction is slightly blurred when non-nationals are brought into the equation. Despite not having full legal citizenship, they might still be entitled to most privileges associated with the civil, social and, to a certain extent, political sphere. This state of limbo has given rise to what Hammar (1985) has defined as the denizen category. However, it is important to note that the state distinction between 'the citizen' and 'the foreigner' is still highly present. There are several reasons for the state to be concerned with who is to be characterised as a citizen or not. First, from the receiving state's point of view, it must be in control of who enters the boundaries of the polity in order to determine who is subjected to the particular legal system which dominates the designated area. Since the state exercises sovereignty and monopolises the use of force, it must also be able to control which part of the population this sovereignty and monopoly refers to. Second, one of the key characteristics of the state is its taxation power. In order to be able to collect taxes, the state must also be able to define who is going to be taxed and what their status on the labour market is, which suggests that the notion of legitimate citizen versus illegitimate citizen seems to be highly relevant. Consequently, nation-states have opted for different types of responses to the challenge that incorporating migrants presents. For instance, one distinguishes between the degree and form of inclusion and exclusion in the national polity in relation to ethnic difference – that is, the criteria for formal access to citizenship and the cultural obligations that such access entails. The access criteria are linked to the distinction between the ethnocultural and the civic territorial basis for full citizenship acquisition, in which the former is more closed than the latter. The cultural criteria relate to the extent to which the state favours assimilation or cultural pluralism as a condition for attributing citizenship, the former more demanding than the latter.

To complicate this matter further, states can choose to emphasise one of two sides of the concept of citizenship[29] – on the one hand, the state can stress rights and on the other, duties. This is linked to ideas of what the role of the state should be, thus giving rise to a liberal and a civic republican style of citizenship in practice. As Heater (1999) discusses, the former stipulates that the function of the state is to ensure the protecting of citizenry rights – to liberty, property, security and from oppression. Heading along the traditional libertarian school of thought, citizenship indicates a status of the individual being left alone to be an individual, where the pursuit of one's self-interest should not interfere with that of others. The role of the state is hence to safeguard these rights rather than to intervene or dictate interindividual relationships. Citizenship is not so much valued for its own sake, but as a means in order to secure goods entitled to the individual by the status of being a 'citizen'. If the liberal conception of citizenship is taken to its extreme, as in the case of Nozick's (1974) arguments, the state is an enterprise where the citizens are voluntary customers. Here, the state is seen as originating in the competition of protective associations to provide the customers with rights-enforced services. Nozick's libertarian utopia renders the state as minimal as possible in which its functions are reduced to the exercise of monopolised violence within a given territorial area. One would expect Nozick's 'ultraminimal state' to only protect those who have purchased its services, but he does actually suggest that protection should also be granted to those residing permanently within the territory. This view on the community suggests inclusion by means of residency and, in the long run, also by birth. From a liberal point of view, the status of citizenship, where the state acknowledges the shift from individual to member of the community, not only implies substantial rights to protection but also the right of non-interference by the state (Bauböck, 1994).

However, as Miller (2000) points out, the common view is more likely to recognise the state as having monopoly to enforce basic personal and property rights in which the citizens are seen as parties to a universal contract. This situation would in turn generate an element of legitimacy. Furthermore, this view stipulates that the individual–state relationship gives individuals the upper hand by means of consumer sovereignty. This can be implemented in two ways. First, by contract – if the provider (the state) fails to provide the appropriate goods, the consumer (the citizen) can take appropriate action in order to reinforce the contract, for example, through legal action. Second, by choice – if the consumer-citizen is not satisfied with what the state-provider supplies, then the former is free to turn to an alternative provider, thereby setting up a quasi-market order. This ideal state of citizenship theory does have certain limitations. The most obvious is that it presupposes that the individual/consumer has full access to information in order to make a rational choice of the alternatives. This will most likely exclude a large proportion of the population and limit the equality aspect of this particular choice of citizenship ideal. It also raises problems of a more practical issue. Most people are not in the position to exercise that option and move to another neighbourhood, municipality, region or country simply because they find the public goods package more attractive there. Several ties – families, employment, house mortgages – bind people to a particular place leaving only the presumably better-off individuals to freely opt for such a choice. Second, if the rights and provisions, or even public goods, are to be provided according to a supply and demand solution, this will make the real distribution dependent on market income and would therefore lose its redistributive character. Although the liberal conception seems to have more negative than positive aspects, Miller identifies that the liberal position does take the notion of pluralism seriously. It assumes, perhaps more so than the republican understanding, that the conceptions of the good life may differ radically amongst people. The argument suggests that in order to come to terms with this diversity, citizenship must be depoliticised and converted into the public realm as a pseudo-version of the market. However, this line of thought can contradict the idea of citizenship as a community-binding concept, if it also assumes that citizenship benefits are rights that are to be accessed on an individual basis only.

In contrast, the idea of civic republicanism stresses that citizenship status is as much a duty as it is a set of rights (Arendt, 1973; Entzioni, 1993). This conception of citizenship connects the individual more closely to the state, aiming to construct a polity characterised by a community of belonging, determined by common interests, mutual respect and social and economic interdependence. It suggests that if the individual is a shareholder in the community, he or she will also strive to entertain this status in order to not lose out on the investment and will hence be more likely to take part in societal activities. The civic conception takes the liberal understanding of citizenship as its starting point and adds a prescriptive dimension of how the citizen ought to be. Implicit in these ideas is an imperative for the citizen to act in a way that he or she displays selfless civic virtue, loyalty and duty to the community. Embedded in the civic republican notion lies a belief that the good society is dependent on the citizen actively taking part in the society by means of discussion or participating, directly or indirectly, in the decision-making process and thereby reaching an agreement. Therefore, this understanding of the citizen might include education in how to benefit from the civic activities that the society provides or enlightenment in terms of what participation means to the status of being a citizen. The relation between the state and the individual is characterised by a notion of impartiality and consensus that differs from the pluralistic competition present in the liberal point of view. It is argued that a citizen body can, through open discussion, reach a substantial degree of consensus on issues of common concern. In order to achieve this, the state must appeal to a strong ideal of impartiality whereby the citizen assumes the role of striving for the common good and sets aside all personal aims and interests and, ideally, reasons from a universal standpoint.

Critics of the civic-republican idea of citizenship argue that impartiality is not only impossible but also goes against the fundamental of principle of equality since it presupposes a homogenous society in which difference is not accounted for. Young (1990) claims that the republican idea of citizenship lacks an understanding of group identity politics. This argument suggests that a certain group or groups dominate public discourse thereby excluding groups categorised as different (being that on ethnic, class or gender grounds) and denying them participation in the public sphere. This area is governed by the idea of reason, that does not give voice to the particular needs and desires of excluded groups. The underlying reason that Young addresses is the claim that consensus can be reached by means of open discussion. This presupposes that groups are prepared to negotiate and, perhaps, stray from their original standpoint. Invoking Miller (2000) again, claims can be primarily made in two ways in a majority–minority negotiation. On the one hand, claims appeal to a common interest of all citizens in a particular society or country – for instance, a wish to safeguard human rights. On the other, claims can be made that apply predominantly to a certain group or groups in the society.

In the former case, one can refer to a normative principle of justice such as equal treatment. This claim is relatively easier to reach a negotiated agreement on since a notion of equality can potentially cut across all cleavage lines. It would be fair to assume that all groups in society would benefit from this principle and would therefore not be a controversial claim to make by disenfranchised groups.

In the latter case, the republican view could be reluctant to acknowledge group-specific claims, not on the basis of being necessarily controversial or contradicting foundational citizenship principles, but on the basis of trying to convince the negotiating partner that the claims are in accordance with the norm to which they refer. The difficulty lies in the inability of the republican dimension, along with other interpretations of citizenship, to fully accommodate everything that passes under the name of 'identity politics'. If one defines the public sphere as a space where various group identities are legitimised by means of recognition, then there will, at least at some point, emerge moments in which different claims will collide. The relative success of achieving a positive outcome for one's claims lies in the ability of the group to portray them in fashion that is compatible with the principles that are generally accepted by the citizen body.

However, Miller concludes that the republican ideal of citizenship is to be preferred over the liberal one since the latter encompasses a conception of, primarily, justice that appears unacceptable to certain groups. A liberal view of citizenship keeps the rights and entitlements to a minimum and thereby limits the opportunities available for citizenry practice, whereas the republican view expands the chances of establishing claims due to a process of negotiation and, ultimately, an agreement between involved parties. However, Miller's argument here starts to become somewhat contradictory. The assumption about the rational position of the individual in the republican definition seems to be very similar to that in the liberal definition, something that Miller criticises the liberal view for. First, the argument assumes that all parties involved enter the negotiation process on an equal basis. That is, he fails to address the difference in the balance of power. Second, parties engaging in a process of negotiation approach the matter with different bargaining strengths. For instance, an ethnic community arguing for enforced discrimination regulations on the labour market holds a different starting position than a trade union arguing for better working conditions even though they both can appeal to the same foundational principle – equality. Second, Miller assumes that this negotiation takes place in an environment where no structural constraints exist. Using the previous example again, a particular society can have few or no opportunities available for mobilisation along ethnic lines and instead be dominated by class division. The level of success for participating parties would then very much depend on the appearance of the overall political system. Furthermore, the role and scope of the state can set limits to the options available for the actors involved.

In addition to these two main strands of what the notion of citizenship should include, one has to distinguish between the formal, or state-based, conception of citizenship and that of citizenship as a sensation or experience. The former entitles the individual to a number of 'on-paper' rights, privileges and stipulated duties in an environment that at least theoretically provides the opportunities for the individual to access these rights. These entitlements could include education and health benefits, a guarantee by the state to secure a minimum living standard or the right to vote in elections. The latter description of the term refers to more subjective understandings of the term in that the relationship between society and the individual becomes the key determinant to whether one actually thinks of oneself as a citizen. Held (1995) argues in a similar vein when emphasising the distinction between citizenship understood as formal and as substantial.

According to this separation, the individual might enjoy the formal political right of standing as candidate for election, but may lack the material (money) and cultural (contacts) resources to successfully pursue this form of action. If citizenship is perceived accordingly, then this relationship expresses a situation of both inclusion and exclusion which challenges the formal aspect of citizenry since this presupposes a notion of equality embedded in the definition of citizenship (Lyon, 1998). In this sense, citizenship is given its importance because people believe it matters (Miller, 1995). Similarly to the idea of an imagined community, this stance argues that the bonds of history, political culture and a common sense of destiny provide the community with a sense of mutual obligation. If the state lacks this communitarian background, which nationality proposes, then the sense of citizenship will be, if not non-existent, at least weak. Naturally, this experience will vary between individuals, a discussion which Miller somehow manages to avoid (see further Faulks, 1998 on this issue), depending on race, gender or class affiliation. Therefore, the settings of citizenship in a given society can influence this experience by being either more inclusive or more exclusive. However, an identity that is linked to a nationality conception of citizenship is most likely challenged when contemporary societies are confronted by increased migration. In contrast to Miller's argument, Oommen (1997) suggests that citizenship must be separated from the close linkage with nationality that it traditionally has had.

Oommen argues against the idea of belonging to a community being based on ethnic origin or blood descent. Instead, an argument is put forward in favour of a residency conception of inclusion, an argument that is not particularly new nor controversial, but continues by stressing the important link between the state and citizenship. This link is necessary, if not crucial, for the understanding of citizenship since, without the state, citizenship becomes an irrelevant concept. Following the economic and bureaucratic expansions, the modern state has opted for more rigorous surveillance and administrative capacities in order to determine who was liable to tax and military duty. This classification deemed it necessary to distinguish the insiders from the outsiders. Consequently, if the state was to maximise tax profits, it therefore required a working population with a sense of unity or cultural homogeneity, stabilising consumer and labour patterns. The sense of belonging was nourished by the elites through providing nationally encompassing education, the use of a single language and rituals in order to create an allegiance with the state. A problem arises when one unreflectively uses these terms. Köchler (1995) argues that 'nationality' as equated with 'citizenship' fails to provide proper legal protection for human rights in the sense of people's ethnic rights since the former relates primarily to imagined concepts of commonality in terms of belonging to a specific group.

Conversely, the latter is related to the relationship between the state and the individual as subject to international law. He continues by suggesting, along the lines of Soysal (1994), that the nation-state needs to reconsider its understanding of citizenship. The distinction made by Köchler is both valid and relevant. However, he seems to be so overwhelmed by the positive traits of a multicultural society in general and the shortcomings of the Germanic conception of citizenship in particular, that he fails to address the fact that the nation-state is still the last outpost in terms of being the decisive actor that determines who is to be considered as a citizen. Naturally, if Köchler is referring solely to the German definition, then the argument that 'a truly democratic system can only be based on socio-cultural self-comprehension along the lines of inter-cultural dialogue' (1995: 45) makes sense. However, this might not necessarily apply to other states which practice and define citizenship according to other principles. The German conception of citizenship as descent or heritage sets out a radically different framework for the relationship between the individual and the political community compared to a state that perceives citizenship as dependent on residence. The residency principle allows naturalisation transitions by placing less emphasis on the uniqueness of the *volk*. Instead, it favours an understanding of citizenry as contributing socially and economically to society. This understanding will furthermore place less emphasis on the conflicting notions of nationality, in the Köchler understanding, and citizenship. The ideas behind citizenship aim at challenging societal injustices within and across states by making the population equal and thereby promoting a social identity rather than other identities such as class, religion or ethnicity (Faulks, 1998).

These identities could potentially divide the state, but abandoning this conception and invoking a shared understanding of citizenship indicates a new situation characterised by inclusion rather than exclusion. Faulks suggests that a too strong emphasis upon the exclusiveness of certain identities might create hazardous consequences of attributing positive or negative characteristics to individuals on the basis of the social group membership. Therefore, group conflict could be kept to a minimum if all citizens were entitled to state provisions in terms of being members of the state rather than perceiving them as members of the working class or a specific ethnic group. However, a matter that is still unresolved remains in the built-in contradiction of the liberal understanding of citizenship. This paradox refers to the simultaneous recognition and suppression of difference. Compared to the more explicit rejection of difference, as in the case of the French republican tradition, where a strong emphasis on equality renders cultural assumptions impossible thereby enforcing assimilation, the liberal conception can accept and even promote difference. However, the liberal understanding has a tendency to perceive difference as a matter of private practice rather than that of public concern as the British example shows. Once again, the state seems to be the main point of reference in order to understand this contradiction. As Balibar (1991) notes, the state is an administrative, policing and judicial apparatus that is primarily designed to protect one part of the population [the majority] at the potential expense of another [the minority/ies] and where the dividing lines between the two groups or populations might be impossible to distinguish or even arbitrarily make.

The liberal state thus faces a mutual dilemma. On the one hand, it must provide the institutional arrangements for its citizens to be able to enjoy the social, political and economic benefits of citizenry on an equal footing. On the other, the state has to create unity and symmetry between its citizens, thereby potentially trading off difference. This suggests that identity and the subsequent process of identification are a complex matter that is structured by different relations of power. Promoting certain types of identity or imposing limits to identification are sites of power fuelled by conceptions of difference which may become potent political and social categories around which individuals and groups can mobilise and construct politics. Dominant representations of difference, as Solomos and Schuster (2000) show, may serve as a way to exclude and exploit as well as to justify unequal access and involvement in institutions. Those with the possibilities of exercising power are thus able to validate and impose their own definitions of normality as well as to define the boundaries for the purpose of excluding or including certain groups. Furthermore, it is suggested that identities expressed through notions of race and ethnicity are intrinsically political resources that can be used by both dominant and subordinate groups for purposes of legitimising and promoting their own social identities and subsequent interests. The ways in which opportunities and constraints are set by the host society are likely to have an impact on both identity construction as well as on the social and political role of migrants and minorities. Seeing that identity formation is formed and transformed in relation to representation, state institutions, understanding of citizenship and host-society's policy towards its new population play crucial roles. By determining the meaning and understanding of a particular identity, the nation-state not only constitutes a political entity but also functions as a system that produces cultural representation and meaning, a symbolic community that one can be more or less part of. The country-specific use of cultural, religious and class manifestations and struggles over hegemony provides the national context in which both the national identity as well as the different types of sub-national identities are constructed and referenced against through time and space. The state is here in a privileged position since it can influence the public discourse and decide on what type of identity or identities are to be supported and which are to be suppressed.

This situation brings us back to the central issue of citizenship and what the concept means since the term sets out the premises of who belongs and who is to be excluded from a particular collective identity. Migrant communities in many of the receiving Western European countries are becoming aware that they might not be fully included in the political process or represented fully by the political institutions. In other words, the discussion of substantive citizenship as contrasted to formal citizenship needs to be more fully explored and evaluated. Important features here are not only citizenship regulations but also how this term is understood and implemented in country-pecific cases as well as relating this to prevailing power relations and struggles over identity and legitimate actors.

## Identification and political participation

As we have seen, different interpretations and practices of citizenship give variance in terms of the scope available for identity expressions. How important is this sense of belonging for migrants when it comes to political participation? Trying to pinpoint the factors that influence levels of political participation has been keeping political scientists busy for years. When dealing with migrants and minorities, scholars have applied a similar framework to that used when explaining political participation in general.

By and large the literature available on this subject falls into two categories. The first one stems from governmental investigations, often commissioned to academics dealing with migrant issues. Such studies tend to be framed in such a way that they serve as policy guidelines (see e.g. the reports published by the Swedish Board of Integration). The second set of literature is more theoretically orientated and attempts to provide general theories or replicate previous studies.

Both types of studies often arrive at very similar conclusions. That is, varying levels of integration are seen as the key explanatory factor as to why migrants tend to engage in politics to a lesser (or greater) degree compared with the majority population. Bäck and Soininen (1993) have approached variations in political participation by invoking Olsen's (1970) ethnic community approach. This asserts that membership in a socially, economically and politically disadvantaged minority reinforces the sense of group belonging and this in turn tends to spill over into increased levels of political participation. Here, political activity is used as a means to improve one's socio-economic status. What Bäck and Soininen emphasise is how integration, both into the migrant's own ethnic group and into the majority society, affects political participation. They conclude by saying that the more integrated the migrant is into society, the more the migrant is affected by political decisions. That is, a fully integrated migrant has more to lose than the non-integrated migrant. The main interest for these authors is thus how migrants perform in different socio-economic arenas. Their focus is to explore education levels, employment and welfare dependency rates (economic integration), housing segregation, racial violence and marriage patterns (social integration), and formal-legal citizenship rights (political integration). In the same vein, Bennulf and Hedberg (1999) suggest that it is the social resources possessed by the individual that determine whether or not one engages in political life. However, they also acknowledge the importance of cultural differences alongside differences in terms of political and electoral systems.

Similarly, a Dutch investigation into ethnic minority political participation has adopted a civic community approach (Fennema and Tillie, 1999). In this study, the relative lower degrees of involvement in different aspects of political life amongst Moroccans and Surinamese compared with the Turkish population are interpreted as the result of the former groups' lack of density in their associational network and lack of trust in local politicians. In this case, the political aspect of integration is the key explanatory factor. Turks tend to participate to a higher degree since their integration has been more 'successful'; Surinamese and Moroccans, on the other hand, participate less since they have 'failed' to integrate in the political sphere. Elsewhere, declining voting levels or lower degrees of political participation have been explained with reference to socio-economic differences but without explicit linkage to integration (Bobo and Gilliam, 1990; Verba and Nie, 1972), or in terms of resources that the individual or group may posses (Petersson *et al.*, 1989). Although these approaches have significant explanatory potential, it only takes the research to a certain point.

Previous studies tend to emphasise the dramatic difference between the native population and the migrant groups in terms of socio-economic inequalities. As Soininen and Bäck (1993: 121) point out, 'class membership has relevance for political attitudes and activities partly because of the deprivation due to lower status, but also because of the greater resources that follow from a higher class position'. They also suggest a correlation between employment and voting levels. Therefore, one would expect a lower socio-economic status to affect political participation negatively.

However, in the surveys I conducted in Malmö and Rotterdam, socio-economic differences between the targeted groups were not dramatic. In Malmö, levels of unemployment amongst the Chilean and Iranian respondents were similar – 15 per cent of the Chileans and 18 per cent of the Iranians. In addition, the proportion of Chileans who claimed to be currently employed was practically identical to the Iranians, 52 per cent compared to 51 per cent. In terms of housing, one-third of the Iranians owned their accommodation compared to one-fifth of the Chileans, but the Iranians were more likely to live with more people in a limited space. Both groups also, by and large, live in areas dominated by people of Swedish origin, but a larger proportion of the Iranians stated they would prefer more people with a Swedish origin to live in their neighbourhood compared to the Chileans. The results stemming from this survey show that socio-economic differences between the various groups are not as dramatic as previous studies have shown. These figures show similar levels to those found in the larger national survey by the Swedish National Board of Health and Welfare (1998), although the survey done here displays somewhat lower averages. However, one should be aware of the possibility that the respondents might want to 'adjust' the answers and give a more positive view of their current status.

The Rotterdam figures, however, display more difference between the three study groups. In terms of unemployment, 5 per cent of the Turkish respondents stated that they were currently unemployed compared to 11 per cent of the Surinamese and 38 per cent of the Iranians. However, when comparing the respondents currently in the workforce, the figures are slightly more even, 49 per cent for the Turks, 48 per cent for the Surinamese and 31 per cent for the Iranians. In addition, the numbers of students were also remarkably high, two-fifths of the Turks were currently undergoing some form of education compared with almost one-third of the Surinamese and one-eighth of the Iranians.

In terms of living conditions, most of the respondents from all groups stated that they were currently renting their accommodation. However, compared to the Malmö respondents, the Rotterdam figures show that a majority of the respondents tend to live in three or four bedroom flats or houses with enough living space. With regard to the ethnic composition of the respondents' neighbourhood, half of the Turks and Surinamese live in fairly mixed areas whereas the Iranians tend to live in predominantly white Dutch areas. All groups seem to prefer the current ethnic composition with the Turks as an exception (with one-third stating that they would like to have more white Dutch neighbours compared to one-tenth of the Surinamese and Iranians).

The communities studied in Malmö seem to be quite similar in terms of socio-economic characteristics, yet they display different levels of engagement and interest in politics. In Rotterdam, the socio-economic differences are greater but levels of political participation and interest in politics are very similar. This suggests that there is a danger of overestimating the importance of these socio-economic traits when it comes to explaining why individuals or groups choose to engage in political life. If the previous predictions were correct, one would expect, for instance, more activity stemming from the Chilean respondents, which my survey findings tend to contradict. Therefore one needs to supplement these previous interpretative efforts with another dimension – identification with the host society – in order to grasp the full complexity of why individuals choose to engage in political life, or not.

## Identification as an explanatory variable

The debate on what exactly constitutes the national identity and who is supposed to be included has had something of a revival in recent years (Hjerm, 1998; Lyon, 1998; Prior *et al.*, 1995). The edges have become blurred in terms of what it means to be Swedish, Dutch and even British, or what is to be included in Swedishness, Dutchness and Britishness (see also Hansen, 2003).

In the literature, a number of scholars have recognised the importance of identity preservation or recognition of minorities' identities in a minority–majority situation (Kymlicka, 1995; Mouffe, 1995; Rath *et al.*, 2001; Taylor, 1994). This recognition is viewed as crucial for the successful relationship between the multitude of communities residing within a given area. In addition to these arguments, one also finds a large body of literature that covers the concept of citizenship, its formal policies, its implications for - citizens as well as non-citizens, and how different nation-states have responded to the emerging presence of newcomers (see e.g. Birch, 1989; Brubaker, 1992; Castles, 1995; Joppke and Morawska, 2003; Oliver and Heater, 1994). The question remaining is how these different types of identities are able to relate to the overarching interpretation of citizenship and national identity, and how they can be accommodated into a new understanding of what it means to be a citizen in a new environment. Apart from being just an academic debate, one can find examples of this re-routing in official policy as well. The Swedish Government Bill on immigration and integration policies (1997; see also 2001) speaks of creating a new environment in which the expression of 'difference' should no longer be perceived as being something substantially deviant or 'outside' in relation to an implicit Swedish 'normality'. In fact, efforts should be made to understand these expressions as internal variations of Swedishness. That is, the meaning of this term needs to be expanded and different types of identities need to be incorporated into the overarching collective identity of 'being Swedish'. It does, however, strongly suggest that sub-group identities need to relate, or identify with, the total collective identity. Similarly, Dutch policy seems to be heading in the same direction. With the introduction of a policy that recognises a number of migrant groups as being ethnic minorities, the intention is that they should be perceived as legitimate members of the overarching Dutch national identity. This process dates back to 1994 when the Dutch government published the policy document *Contourennota integratiebeleid etnische minderheden* which replaced the *Minderhedennota* from 1983. The main goals were no longer to emphasise the promotion and facilitation of multiculturalism but shifted their weight towards integration and participation in the education and labour market sectors. In this document, citizenship became a key concept and it was argued that it should mean something more than merely a change of nationality and obtaining a Dutch passport. More so than previously, an emphasis was made on the need for migrants to be able to identify with the political community and to be part of it (Entzinger, 2003).

Furthermore, this relates to the Dutch post-1980 view on immigration as enriching the country's cultural diversity, rather than identity preservation as a precondition for a successful return. As mentioned previously, this policy echoes the Dutch tradition of institutionalised pluralism. Even though pillarisation has now lost much of its significance in Dutch society, it is still very much present in minority policy, especially in terms of the generous public support directed towards immigrant social and cultural life.

However, the question of identification and its potential importance has by and large only been hinted at in a number of academic texts that deal with the politics of belonging. In addition, there have been few attempts to connect and study identification in relation to political participation. In terms of identification, Castles and Davidson (2000) suggest that ethnic minorities are usually defined according to two premises – a self-definition and an other-definition. The former involves commonalities that are shared by a certain group in terms of language, history, religion and shared experiences. The latter stems from definitions imposed by the dominant on the subordinate group and includes different varieties of stereotyping, discriminatory structures and practices in the legal, economic, social and political arena. Elsewhere, identity and processes of identification are described in terms of individuals forming an objective and a subjective identity (Ahmadi Lewin, 2001). In the former, an individual is either defined and categorised on the basis of what others believe to be his or her characteristics (here labelled, objective personal identity) or with regard to certain social groups to which he or she is ascribed membership by others (here, objective social identity). In terms of subjective personal identity, this requires an individual to ascribe certain attributes to the self without necessarily feeling a sense of belonging to a certain group. However, if the individual perceives certain categorisations as making his or herself a member of a social group, this would indicate a case of subjective social identity (see further Friedman, 1994; Nesdale and Mak, 2000; Tajfel, 1978).

Modood's (2000) study of ethnic group affiliation treads a similar path but suggests that ethnic identification does not necessarily have to include the above-mentioned criteria. Instead Modood suggests that it could be the case of associational identification, which could take the form of pride in one's origins, making a connection with certain group labels; and might not have a strongly present behavioural component (although this comes very close to a mainstream nationalism definition). However, Modood perceives identification along lines of identity, that is, the concept is viewed as being understood solely in terms of identification with one's own ethnic group and not as identification with the host society or the overarching identity of the new community. If ethnic identity and ethnic identification are to be understood as fluid, everchanging and open for negotiation, then the same should also apply in terms of host-identity identification. It will be of interest therefore to examine to what extent different levels of host-society identification affect levels of political participation. Identification is here to be understood as a process in which the individual relates his or her own ethnic group affiliation and belonging as being an acceptable part of the new community's collective identity.

This definition includes self- and other-definition elements, which I here refer to as internal and external levels of identification. Internal identification indicates the extent to which an individual is able to relate linguistic, cultural, social, ritual and political practices in the host society as being part of his or her identity. Relevant questions asked in my survey were related to attitudes towards contributing to and being part of the new society. These were particularly important since this type of identification takes place within the culture of the new society in which specific systems of belief, value systems and life-styles demand a reconstruction of the individual's identity and an ability to match 'old' and 'new' identities with each other (Ahmadi Lewin, 2001). External identification relates to the respondents' experiences when coming in contact with the majority population. Important factors that determine the level of external identification are issues concerning racially induced violence, discrimination in different areas of society, and behaviour and attitudes of members of the majority population towards the minority member.

This leads me to the following hypothesis:

> *Higher levels of identification will yield higher levels of political interest and participation.*

However, much like the concept of identity, identification should not be seen as a process with a clear beginning and an end but rather as an ongoing process in which these identification levels fluctuate and differ both temporally as well as spatially. The findings should hence not be seen as the final proof of Iranian, Chilean, Surinamese and Turkish identification levels but rather as indicative signs of where we can locate these levels as a result of time of stay, exposure to policies directed towards immigrant groups in combination with the internal and external definition of identification.

## The study groups – Sweden and the Netherlands

In Malmö, the Iranian, Chilean and Turkish speaking communities were considered to be suitable groups for comparison.[30] There are three main reasons for this choice. First, all groups have resided in Sweden for a substantial length of time. The Chileans were one of the first refugee groups to arrive in Sweden. Two waves of Chilean migration can be identified – from the early to mid-1970s, and during the early 1980s. The first Chileans came as political refugees after the coup against President Salvador Allende. During these early stages, most arrivals consisted of political activists, students and trade union leaders while at the beginning of the 1980s this composition changed towards more labour-oriented migrants hoping to improve their standard of living, sponsored by friends or family already dwelling in Sweden.[31] During the Allende years, members of the left wing opposition from other Latin American countries sought refuge in Santiago, which in turn meant that people from Argentina, Uruguay, Bolivia, Brazil and Peru also came to Sweden along with the Chileans.

The Iranians, by and large, constitute the largest group from the Middle East (possibly now rivalled by Iraqis). The Iranian communities consist mainly of young urban middle-class families, many of them academics and intellectuals from Tehran. In 1996, Iranians numbered just over 50,000 persons making them one of the largest non-European migrant groups (Westin and Dingu-Kyrklund, 1996). The first wave of Iranians arrived during 1979–81 but the flow of Iranian refugees continued throughout the 1980s (whereas Chilean migration more or less ceased in the latter half of the 1980s). The Iranian population is geographically rather unequally distributed. A majority of the Iranians reside in the Stockholm area, followed by Gothenburg and Malmö and the provinces of Uppland and Östergötland. The ethnic composition of the Iranians can be divided into four sub-groups. A majority of the Swedish-Iranians are of Persian origin (with a smaller proportion being Azeris, Armenians and individuals with Kurdish origin) (Bretschneider, 2001; see also Hosseini-Kaladjahl, 1997). A large number of Iranian migrants stem from the middle or upper classes in Iranian society, which means that they also tend to be well educated. In addition, the vast majority are also secularised and originate from urban areas (Ahamdi Lewin, 2001; Darvishour, 1999).

The Turkish-speaking communities are built up of a variety of nationalities and ethnic groups. During the 1960s, 'Turkish Turks' came to Sweden as labour migrants, with a majority of these stemming from the rural district around Kulu in Anatolia. However, compared to the Netherlands, the Turks destined for Sweden were comparatively small and in the aftermath of the Communist era also became more ethnically diverse. Today, ethnic Turks from Bulgaria and Macedonia alongside Kurdish Turks constitute the main Turkish speaking communities in Sweden. The three groups have thus been residing more or less permanently in Sweden for between ten and twenty-five years.

Second, the three groups are geographically distant, both in terms of each other and in relation to the receiving country. Third, the study groups are also significantly large in terms of quantity although, on a local level, absolute figures are hard to obtain since official statistics only show the number of non-nationals with a legal residency status. Since obtaining Swedish citizenship has not been a major difficulty, most long-term residents are Swedish nationals and hence 'disappear' from local official records (although these are available on a national level). Recent figures show that there are approximately 2800 of Iranian birth, 1300 of Chilean birth and 900 of Turkish birth currently residing in the Malmö area (SCB, 2002). Furthermore, individuals originating from Bulgaria and Macedonia are not registered as Turks even though they might consider themselves to be ethnically Turkish.

What will be presented here are some data obtained from a modest questionnaire survey conducted in Malmö during 2001. A number of Iranian, Chilean and Turkish speaking voluntary associations were approached during the course of this study. The aim was to distribute questionnaires on location in order to get a higher response rate compared to a postal send-out. As pointed out in Chapter 1 the final response rates were not that high. This difference in returns stems by and large from the greater number of Iranian organisations. Iranian associations also have a higher degree of formalisation, more organised activities and associational strength combined with an outward-looking attitude.[32]

In contrast, the Chilean associations displayed a looser structure, fewer scheduled activities and a more informal and non-professional attitude to associational life. I was also told that many Chileans were suspicious of questionnaires and that these were associated with governmental control and monitoring. This situation was even more problematic with the Turkish-speaking associations where a majority of the questionnaires ended up being thrown away. However, the relative lack of quantitative data has been balanced by a decent number of qualitative interviews with Turkish respondents. In terms of gender, the returns were split fairly evenly for the Iranian and Chilean groups – 48 per cent males and 52 per cent females (Iranians) and 52 and 42 per cent (Chileans), but 100 per cent male for the Turkish speaking group.

The Iranians, Surinamese[33] and Turks were chosen as suitable groups for comparison in the Dutch case. Initially, the intent was to keep two groups constant with one additional context-specific group, which unfortunately had to be altered due to insufficient questionnaire material.

Compared to Sweden, Iranians are a fairly new migrant group in the Netherlands, dating back to the early 1990s, and constitute a far smaller percentage of the foreign-born population, so small that they are not accounted for in the statistics (COS, 2003). An estimate would be that Iranians constitute somewhere between five to ten thousand based on the average number of Iranians (1077) who migrated annually to the Netherlands between 1995 and 2000 (Muus and Gerritsma, 2000). However, an increasing quantity of Iranian asylum applicants have been directed towards the Netherlands. Figures for 1994 show that around 30 per cent of the estimated 18,000 Iranian asylum-seekers heading for Europe chose to apply for asylum in the Netherlands, making it the second most important country of destination after Germany (IGC, 1995). This has meant that Iranian asylum seekers in the Netherlands have gained increasingly more attention since the mid-1990s. Prior to 1994, the Dutch government considered Iran to be an unsafe country and rejected asylum applications were not repatriated but granted a tolerated status, the so-called gedoogdenstatus. However, this policy changed after 1994 with the publication of a report from the Ministry of Foreign Affairs which stated that in some cases Iranians could be sent back to Iran without fearing that their human rights would be violated (Koser, 1997). A smaller survey conducted by Koser shows that a majority of the Iranians who claimed asylum in the Netherlands primarily chose the country based on their knowledge about Dutch asylum policy and not, as in Sweden, primarily due to family connections.

The Surinamese community constitutes around 9 per cent (52,000) of the Rotterdam population and is the largest ethnic minority in the city. A significant majority of the Surinamese in Rotterdam (97 per cent as of 1997) are Dutch citizens, given the colonial link, but two-thirds were not born in Rotterdam, which suggests that Surinamese residents in the city are a fairly new phenomenon. In addition, the Surinamese community is relatively young, with just over two-thirds under the age of 35. In comparison to the native population, more Surinamese tend to live in the newer suburbs of Rotterdam and are also more likely to inhabit high-rise buildings rather than family homes. In terms of participation in the labour force, this group participates slightly less than the national average (66 per cent for men and 49 per cent for women compared to 69 and 45 per cent respectively) (Anderiesse *et al.*, 1997).

Turks constitute the second largest ethnic minority, around 7 per cent of the total Rotterdam population. This group consists mainly of individuals who migrated for labour reasons, especially Turkish men over 36, but with a significant number who came due to family reunification. Many Turks have tended to settle in the old urban renewal areas in the first and second ring of the city. As with the Surinamese, the Turks are a predominantly young group with 77 per cent under the age of 35. Attitudes towards naturalisation amongst the Turkish community have changed rapidly: from being a virtual taboo and something considered to be disloyal to the Turkish group to becoming more and more frequent. This is most likely the cause of a change in Dutch citizenship policy which now allows dual nationalities. Almost 60 per cent of the Turkish community now have Dutch nationality (CBS, 1998).[34]

The data obtained on the respondents in respect of their socio-economic position show that, the Turkish and Surinamese respondents are quite similar in terms of individuals currently in the workforce, with 49 and 48 per cent respectively, but only 31 per cent of the Iranians were currently in some form of employment. However, if one compares unemployment levels, these show more significant differences, with 38 per cent of the Iranians currently unemployed compared to 5 per cent for the Turks and 11 per cent for the Surinamese. With regard to housing, an overwhelming majority from all groups are renting their accommodation rather than being home-owners (around 80 per cent) and also seem to live more crowded (one-third of the respondents live with 5 or more people in one or two bedroom places). The ethnographic composition of the respondents' neighbourhood reveals some interesting figures. Over half of the Iranians stated that they live in areas which are predominantly inhabited by white Dutch compared to one-third of the Turkish and one quarter of the Surinamese, who tend to live in more ethnically mixed areas. On the question regarding their satisfaction with the ethnic composition, over half the Iranians were satisfied with the current composition compared to almost half of the Turks and Surinamese. However, one-third of the Turkish respondents stated that they would prefer more white Dutch to live in their area compared to only one-tenth of the Surinamese and Iranians respondents.[35]

As in Malmö, a number of ethnic associations were approached in order to distribute the questionnaire, either through intermediaries or directly on location. However, given that the Iranian population in Rotterdam is fairly new, the number of voluntary associations was low compared to the Surinamese and Turkish associations. In addition, the Iranian associations were characterised less by cultural and social activities compared with the latter, and dealt more with interpretation and consultancy for newly arrived Iranians (similiary to the refugee help organisations in Britain). However, in contrast with the Malmö Turks, the Rotterdam Turks seemed to be more open to answering questionnaires and participating in surveys. Instead the main obstacle lay in finding English-speaking respondents.

The gender division was weighted towards slightly more female respondents in the Iranian sample (40 per cent men and 60 per cent women) but with a more even spread amongst the Surinamese (47 per cent men and 53 per cent women) and the reverse for the Turkish sample (62 per cent men and 38 per cent women). Again, the gender division is related to the associational structure which displays a similar type of dominant male presence as found in the Swedish case.

## Identification levels – Malmö and Rotterdam

A key purpose of the questionnaire survey was to establish three sets of identification scales; internal, external and total. A total of seven questions were posed in which the respondent was asked to grade a number of statements. Some of the questions referred to internal identification, others pertained to external identification. Questions were set up using a Likert scale and given a grade (1–5) with 1 being the lowest (disagree strongly) and 5 being the highest (agree strongly).

Each variable was then added together and given an average to indicate an identification level ranging from a theoretical minimum (7) to a theoretical maximum (35). The questions attempted to establish how strong the respondent's attachment was to the new community. A number of statements were made, ranging from more general queries: I should always obey the law (internal), I think Malmö/Rotterdam is a safe city for immigrants (external); to more specific: I am Swedish/Dutch (internal), Other Swedes/Dutch treat me as a Swede/Dutch (external).

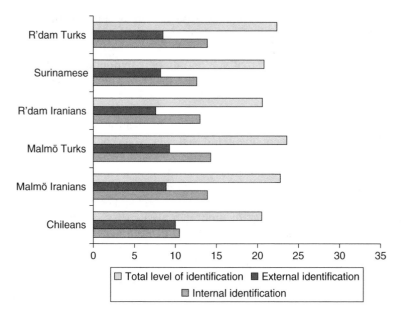

*Figure 4.1*  Levels of identification

Figure 4.1 displays the aggregated internal and external levels of identification for the Chilean Surinamese, the Malmö and Rotterdam Iranians and the Malmö and Rotterdam Turkish respondents; while Table A.1 and A.2 (see Appendix) set out the scores for the six groups on the individual seven questions relating to identification. Again, it is important to point out that the reader should bear in mind that these figures are to be interpreted as a guide sheet for comparison due to the low rate of returns.

Figure 4.1 shows that the Malmö Iranians score higher on the internal identification scale but lower on the external scale. Combining the two scales shows a slightly higher level of total identification for the Malmö Iranian respondents compared to the Chilean sample. Worthy of note is that the more recently established Iranian respondents show higher levels of internal identification compared to the earlier-settled Chileans. One explanation for this can be found in the respondents' views regarding their duration of stay in Sweden. A number of Chileans still hold a firm belief that their presence in the new society is still of a temporary character and that they will soon be able to return to Chile, once the political climate makes this possible (see also Lindqvist, 1991; Lundberg, 1989). The following quote highlights a fairly typical attitude expressed by the Chilean respondents regarding their stay in Sweden.

My dream is to return to Chile, I don't know when it will happen but I hope to do it one day. (Male, mid-50s, 2001)

However, some of the interviewees expressed more ambivalent attitudes regarding the myth of return as shown in the following quote.

> It's a big burden, to feel that you're only here temporary and I felt that way too, it took me ten years to realise that I was never going back and that I had to start living here. (Male, late-30s, 2001)

In contrast, the Iranians have by and large realised that their stay in Sweden is likely to be permanent and that they would be highly unlikely to return to Iran. As a consequence of this realisation, Bretschneider (2001) points out that many Iranians have tried hard to adapt to life in Swedish society and their basic attitude seems to be sympathetic rather than condemning. Bretschneider also suggests that Iranians tend to perceive themselves as different from other immigrant groups in Sweden, especially in terms of their readiness to adapt to a new cultural environment. Many have tried to escape from segregation in the less desirable high-rise estates and moved to predominantly 'Swedish' areas. These factors help to explain why they display higher levels of internal identification than external identification. The following quotes show the contrast of the Iranian conception of staying in Sweden compared with the Chilean.

> I could never go back to Iran, I can't live there, I mean, I didn't even like it there in the first place. (Female, mid-30s, 2001)

> It would be very difficult to go back, because my children have grown up here and that bond is stronger even though you're unemployed and lack contact with the natives but you can't leave it, you get used to living in a certain way. (Male, early-30s, 2001)

In terms of differences in external identification, one could assume that the time factor would influence these levels, in that a longer exposure to 'difference' generates more familiarity and perhaps also affects attitudes towards migrants who are more physically visible. In addition, many Iranians are of Islamic belief, a majority of them Shia affiliated, although it is unclear how many are actually practising their faith (Hosseini–Kaladjahi, 1997). Their Muslim faith may give rise to certain stereotypes of and prejudice against Iranians by the majority population. Consider the following quote in which an Iranian male describes how he thinks Iranians are perceived in Sweden.

> What they think of when they hear the word 'Iranian' is that movie, 'Not without my daughter', an Iranian is a Muslim man who beats his wife, kidnaps the children and shouldn't be trusted. (Male, early-30s, 2001)

Another explanatory factor can be found in terms of the difference in state reception that the groups got upon arriving. In the Chilean case, they arrived during a time when Swedish refugee policy was at its most generous level. Sweden was at the time also very much engaged in different countries' struggles for democracy and especially so in Chile. The Chilean refugees thus received a very positive welcome and were perceived as 'freedom fighters' for democracy (see further Lindqvist, 1991). In contrast, the Iranians, who came almost ten years later, arrived when refugee policy had come under heavy criticism and also during a time when anti-immigrant sentiments had started to become more openly displayed (Pred, 2000; Westin and Dingu-Kyrklund, 1996). This could in turn affect the levels of external identification in a negative way.

With regard to the Rotterdam groups, we find relatively similar levels of internal identification between the three groups with the Turkish respondents displaying a somewhat higher level. As with the Malmö respondents, the levels of external identification are lower compared to the internal levels for all three groups although the Turks, again, display a slightly higher level compared with the Iranians and Surinamese. In addition, when these two categories are combined the differences are not very drastic and show very similar differences to those found in the Swedish case. The total levels of identification for Surinamese and Iranians are virtually identical but with the Turks showing a slightly higher total score. Of interest is also that the ratio between internal and external identification in relation to the total level of identification seems to run along similar lines in both the Malmö and Rotterdam case (approximately 40–60) with the Chilean sample being the main exception, with equal levels.[36]

As with the Malmö Iranians, the Rotterdam sample displays similar characteristics with regard to how they perceive their stay, ways of adapting and reaction from the majority population. For instance, the following quote shows the difficult relationship between internal and external identification as expressed by an Iranian male.

> After twelve years here I am still a stranger, I get the feeling of not belonging here every time I interact with the Dutch even though I am as Dutch as they are. (Male, late-50s, 2001)

However, the Rotterdam respondents display slightly more ambiguity in their responses regarding which identity they wanted to emphasise, as shown in the following quote.

> I'm not 100% Iranian and 100% Dutch either. If I say 'I'm only Iranian', I'd be lying. Iranians must accept this and Dutch people too of course. (Female, late-30s, 2002)

This uncertainty seems to be a more common feature amongst the female respondents whereas the male interviewees seemed to be more firm about their national identification. Compare the above quote with how a Chilean female respondent describes herself in a similar fashion.

> I'm not Chilean and not Swedish, it's very difficult, I can't say I'm one or the other. (Female, early-30s, 2001)

The Surinamese samples display even more conflicting attitudes towards who they perceive themselves to be. As noted previously, Surinam was a Dutch colony in which the inhabitants were subjected to Dutch education, language and society and were perceived as Dutch up until 1975 when they were transformed into Surinamese. In addition, the Surinamese identity is encouraged by official legislation through recognition as an ethnic minority. This could affect the way in which the respondents chose to answer the questions. The conflicting relationship between the Surinamese and the Dutch identity is highlighted by the following quote.

> I have a passport, so officially I'm Dutch but I feel more Surinamese. It's difficult when you have been under a colonial rule to know who you are because until 1975 we were Dutch and after that we were not. (Creole male, late-40s, 2002)

Also, one should take into account intra-group differences between the Creoles and Hindustanis. Generally the former have been characterised as tending to associate more with the white Dutch than with the latter (van Niekerk, 2000). Witness the following quote:

> I come in contact with a lot of white Dutch people through my associational work, but I don't have any close Dutch friends but it doesn't bother me because where I live there's a lot of Hindustani Surinamese so I don't really feel the need to have any white Dutch friends. (Hindustani male, late-30s, 2001)

These differences also shine through in terms of which identity the Surinamese respondents want to affiliate with. In the following example, the interviewee discusses the difficulties of being accepted as Dutch when coming in contact with the majority population.

> They still see me as a foreigner even though I was born a Dutch citizen but that's how they see us all, we are Surinamese, not Dutch, that's what they think, you know, that we are foreigners. (Hindustani male, mid-50s, 2001)

Whereas the Hindustani interviewee discusses difference with reference to being a foreigner, the next Creole interviewee frames it in more specific terms relating to country of origin and the perceived confusion that the Dutch migrant management has given rise to.

> I mean, when I'm sitting here talking to you, I'm Dutch, when I talk to Dutch people I'm an African-Surinamese. The government is making everyone confused with who they are because of this multiculturalism. (Creole male, late-40s, 2002)

In addition, the Rotterdam quotes also show similar types of arguments regarding external identification to those found amongst the Malmö interviewees. That is, the internal identification experienced by the respondents does not match the external levels and creates a certain amount of friction.

According to my guiding hypothesis, the Malmö Iranians and the Rotterdam Turks, who have a slightly higher level of overall identification, will also be more likely to engage in participatory acts. They would tend to show higher degree of political interest, compared to the Chilean and Surinamese respondents, who are assumed to show lower levels.

The following section contains a number of graphs constructed from the collected data. However, due to the small number of returned questionnaires, more serious statistical calculations have been difficult to make and even the basic correlation analysis has to be interpreted with some caution. Therefore, the figures should be taken as indicative rather than as hard, empirical proof.

## Satisfaction with performance of local politicians

A second purpose of the questionnaire was to relate identification to the level of satisfaction with the performance of local politicians in six areas that could be considered relevant to individuals with a non-Swedish and non-Dutch origin. In the Swedish case, there has been a long tradition of local self-governance in which the state, traditionally, has provided the specialised knowledge and implemented this through strategic decision-making and policies. The local municipality, on the other hand, has provided area- or region-specific knowledge that has been used to adjust the state's welfare programmes to the local context. Furthermore, some larger urban localities have been divided into sub-sections in order to deal more effectively with the demands of its citizens (Gidlund, 1994). This process of decentralisation was, as Dahlstedt (1998) observes, primarily a question of democracy and a way of bringing decisions closer to the citizen, to increase the opportunities for citizens to participate in local municipality issues and improve the relationship between the voter and the politicians. In addition, the aim was to make it more manageable to create local solutions to local problems. The local municipalities in Sweden are said to constitute the foundations of society by having responsibility for the most crucial tasks that directly affect the everyday life of individuals. Given that the local municipalities are also responsible for implementing decisions received from the state level, the local authorities are thus responsible for providing certain goods and services that apply to immigrants specifically as well as generally.

Therefore, the questionnaire sets out to establish the respondents' satisfaction with a number of policies that were directly related to their immigrant status with three questions corresponding to the prime directives in Swedish integration policy. First, introductory courses about Swedish society are part of the 'welcome pack' provided to newly arrived migrants and are thus an important initial action.

Second, migrant organisations are considered as equal to ethnically Swedish associations and should thus be eligible for the same type of funding assuming that they conform to certain criteria.

Third, knowledge of one's mother tongue was considered essential for an individual's personality and for the social, emotional and intellectual development and would also facilitate migrant children in achieving more in education (Municio, 1987).

The remaining questions related to the experience of settling and how the respondent feels the receiving society has dealt with issues concerning their immigrant status. In terms of unemployment levels this is of particular importance since many immigrants suffered more than the native population during the crisis of the early 1990s. During this era, employment levels dropped by 33 per cent amongst migrants who had been in Sweden ten years or less (compared to 8 per cent amongst native Swedes) (Vogel and Hjerm, 2002). Similarly, in the Dutch context, the main goals of the inclusion policy were to overcome problems of social deprivation by providing instruments for individuals in a disadvantaged position. This particular policy was later expanded to include both immigrants as well as the majority population. This objective was framed to encompass four major areas: (1) youth, including education and delinquency; (2) combating unemployment among older as well as more recent immigrants; (3) preventing and combating prejudice; and (4) facilitating communication between 'partners of integration'. However, what is interesting to note is that a number of the measures introduced in order to institutionalise the promotion of migrants' interests, on both local and national levels, have primarily been initiatives originating from authorities justifying their policies rather than at the migrants' own request (Entzinger, 2003).

Figure 4.2 displays the satisfaction of the various target groups with their local politicians.[37]

In the Swedish case, the Malmö Iranians show overall higher levels of satisfaction with the performance of their local politicians compared with the Chileans. This relationship corresponds with the proposed hypothesis. The Iranians display higher levels on three of the six questions (Qs 1, 4 and 5) but with minor differences on two (Qs 2 and 3) and very similar levels on one (Q 6). However, it should be pointed out that very rarely do the Iranian levels surpass a score of 3 or higher (i.e. Neither Satisfied nor Dissatisfied)

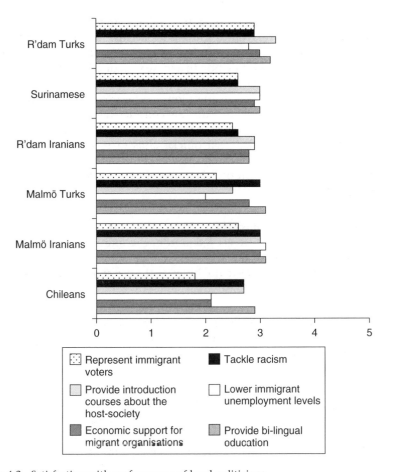

*Figure 4.2*  Satisfaction with performance of local politicians

*Note*: Correlation coefficient: R'dam Turks 0.03, Surinamese 0.35, R'dam Iranians −0.05, Malmö Turks 0.9, Malmö Iranians 0.9, Chileans 0.36.

which in a way could be interpreted as the respondents not having thought the issues to be of major importance. In the Chilean case, half of the questions seem to cluster around a score of 2 (Dissatisfied).

First, as mentioned above, bi-lingual or mother-tongue education has been a fundamental cornerstone in Swedish integration policy since the 1970s, and has been offered alongside 'normal' school classes or as extra-curricular activities and is considered a right. However, whether or not a child receives this type of education depends on the parents applying for this at the particular school. In addition, an evaluation is made in order to consider which is the main language that is spoken at home (Tema Modersmål, 2003).

Second, governmental funding for migrant organisations is of crucial importance for the survival of these associations. As shown, the Chileans score lower compared to the Iranians. As mentioned previously, many of the Iranian organisations function in a more structured way compared to the Chileans and are also relatively more outward reaching. In addition, governmental support for migrant organisations can be a way for the receiving state to signal that new types of identities are considered legitimate.

However, monetary worries are of concern for both groups, which creates a strained relationship between official aims of promoting diversity and monetary constraints preventing these from becoming fully implemented. The following quotes from the chairmen of two associations highlight this relationship.

> This place we have, it costs 60,000 [around £4,000, *author's note*] Swedish crowns per year and we get 8,000 from the municipality. The 8,000 are supposed to go to all the activities that we want to do, so a lot of work goes into getting money to do things ... the economy of the association is a big burden for us. (Chilean male, mid-50s)

> We have some minor activities here but we can't really do anything large-scale because we don't get a lot of funding ... we always need stuff to keep this place going, that's where the money goes and to pay the rent. (Iranian male, mid-40s, 2001)

It is, of course, in the interest of the interviewees that their associations receive as much monetary support as possible. However, what is interesting with the satisfaction scores is that the Iranians, with their lower level of external identification, seem to be, on average, more satisfied with the funding they receive from the local governments and hence the type of recognition this entails. Similarly, lower scores with regard to unemployment measures and tackling racism amongst the Chilean respondents are interesting to find since these issues were not expressed as being of equal importance as among the Iranians. The latter group expressed – both during interview sessions as well as during more informal talks – that these areas needed to be dealt with more thoroughly by the local authorities. In addition, the question regarding representation, where both groups state some dissatisfaction, was not an issue which was brought up during interview sessions. However, it does point to some form of political awareness in that the respondents had noticed that there were few political representatives with a non-Swedish heritage in local politics.

In the Rotterdam case, it was assumed that the Turkish respondents would display higher levels of satisfaction with the performance of the local politicians. This is true for four of the six categories (Qs 1, 2, 3 and 6). However, the Turks score slightly lower on one question (Q 4) and the scores are the same for the Turkish and Surinamese respondents on one question (Q 5).

As in the Malmö sample, differences between groups are not striking and the total scores cluster around the 'neither satisfied nor dissatisfied' category. It is also worth pointing out that the scores for the Turks are not lower in the first category since 20 per cent of the Turkish voters cast their vote for parties set up by Turkish migrants in the 1998 election. However, most migrants cast their votes for the established Dutch political parties, predominately those on the left, and not for immigrant or ethnic parties (Tillie, 2000). Even though the Dutch electoral system is organised in such a way that a vote is cast primarily for a party list and not for a specific candidate, many parties have started to place candidates of immigrant origin on their list. This has meant that in the Rotterdam case 20 per cent of the local councillors (9 out of 45) are of immigrant origin whereas the local council in Malmö has 13 per cent (8 out of 61) (Malmö and Rotterdam local council homepages, 2003). Therefore, the presence of ethnic councillors, in the former case from the ethnic minorities, could potentially produce candidates that represent, or are perceived as representing, their 'own' community and thus link with levels of identification. In the Malmö case, only one councillor was of Chilean origin with no representatives coming from either Iran or Turkey.

In terms of the Surinamese and Iranian respondents, their scores are virtually the same, with slightly higher overall scores for the Surinamese. However, with the Surinamese, given their historical position in Dutch society, some of the questions might have been interpreted as referring to migrants in general and not to their own group, especially questions relating to bi-lingual education and providing introduction courses about Dutch society. In addition, the correlation is very weak and in the case of the Iranians, even negative, whereas in the Malmö case, the Iranians showed a much stronger connection between the two variables.

## Likelihood of participating

The respondents were asked to grade four questions regarding their likelihood of engaging in acts which concerned their immediate surroundings and the city they live in. These questions were replicated from a study done by Fennema and Tillie (1999) in which the same questions were asked to a number of ethnic minorities in Amsterdam. These authors refer to political trust as being crucial for the legitimacy of institutions since the civic community relies on voluntary co-operation among its citizens to enhance a common goal. This wider definition of political participation is important since it suggests a less elitist focus on who the participants are, and also that these additional acts are crucial mechanisms for democracy itself (Putnam *et al.*, 1993). The Dutch study shows that the Turkish sample not only tends to participate to a higher degree but also has higher levels of political trust and political interest compared to the Moroccan, Surinamese and Antillean

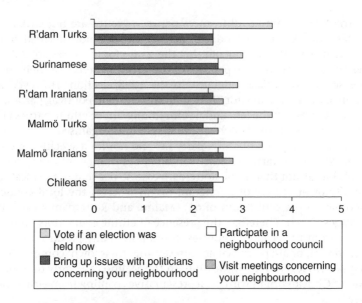

*Figure 4.3*  Likelihood of participating

*Note*: Correlation coefficient: R'dam Turks −0.07, Surinamese 0.6, R'dam Iranians −0.008, Malmö Turks −0.12, Malmö Iranians 0.58, Chileans 0.48.

samples. The explanation put forward by the authors is that the Turks in Amsterdam have more links within their ethnic community in terms of a denser inter-organisational structure compared to other groups. This density generates higher levels of social trust within the community which in turn creates opportunities for a civic culture to develop where organisations provide channels of communication and opportunities for joint action for the members of the ethnic group.

Figure 4.3 displays the likelihood of the various target groups participating in four domains of political activity. Although the differences are rather slight, Figure 4.3 shows a slightly higher overall probability for the Malmö Iranians to engage in activities that are related to their immediate concerns or surroundings compared with the Chileans. This is consistent with the previously stated hypothesis. However, the differences are not dramatic and the Chileans actually score slightly higher on the second question, relating to neighbourhood councils. This could be explained by the habitational space that many of the Chilean respondents occupy; multi-storey buildings where neighbourhood councils are more frequent, compared to the single-storey houses that many Iranians live in which might lack such a forum. Interesting to note is also the quite significant gap between the Iranians and Chileans on Q.1. Recalling our earlier discussion on the differences between the groups in terms of internal and external identification, respondents having a stronger attachment to a community would be more likely to have something to lose by not participating. Despite showing relatively higher levels of likelihood of participating, the scores are not high and in fact show slightly lower levels compared with the scores in Figure 4.2. As one might expect, activities that are less time consuming – for example voting – are also overall more likely to happen compared to more costly activities such as attending meetings which require preparation and getting information.

According to the guiding hypothesis, we were expecting the Turkish sample to display higher levels of participation. This only goes for Q.1, whereas the Surinamese score slightly higher on the last three questions and the Rotterdam Iranians display slightly higher levels on the last question. All three groups also display very similar scores as the Chileans and again cluster around the 'unlikely' category. As with the previous analysis, the correlations are rather weak although the Chilean and Surinamese levels of identification and likelihood to participate correlate slightly better compared with identification and satisfaction with local politicians. The Rotterdam Iranians and Rotterdam Turks display a slight negative correlation, similar to the scores achieved in the previous figure.

## Intensity of participation

The third part of the survey tried to establish the intensity of a wider set of participatory acts, as well as respondents' interest in Swedish and Dutch politics in general and local politics in particular. Most of the Iranian and Chilean associations in Malmö have a specific agenda directed at the situation in their country of origin. Especially in the former case, this has led to a process of fragmentation in some of the associations and sometimes to the exit of key members, who have set up alternative, less politicised associations. The Chilean associations do still have very strong attachments to the 'Chilean cause' but also display more first-generation members than the Iranian. Similarly, Iranian organisations in Rotterdam were primarily a supportive framework for newly arrived refugees and were engaged in the situation in Iran. The Surinamese and Turkish associations, on the other hand, displayed a mix of religious, social and political associations, with the latter having a number of organisations with strong links with both Turkey and Turkish organisations in Germany, as well as more socially and culturally orientated organisations. As with the previous phases of the questionnaire analysis, the results are presented graphically in Figure 4.4.

The most significant difference can be found in the last two questions. Interestingly, the items where Iranians score higher than the Chileans are also areas which require relatively less individual input, and are also associated with less personal cost compared to the first three. This could also explain why all groups have higher scores on the last question as compared to the more time-consuming ones. Also, the last question could

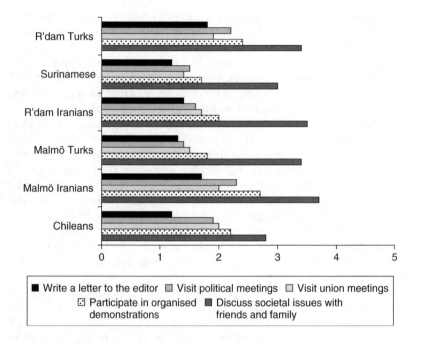

*Figure 4.4* Intensity of participation

*Note*: Correlation coefficient: R'dam Turks 0.14, Surinamese −0.07, R'dam Iranians −0.7, Malmö Turks 0.4, Malmö Iranians 0.62, Chileans −0.02.

have been interpreted as relating to current events happening elsewhere and not just in the domestic arena. This yields an interpretation problem since the respondents could have understood this question as referring to events occurring in their country of origin, which does seem to play a major role for both groups. Worthy of note are also the very low levels of attendance at political and union meetings which was stated as one of the major concerns in the latest Governmental Proposition (2001/02: 129) as well as the extremely low levels of expressing opinions through published media.

However, compared to the Rotterdam figures, the Malmö scores are relatively high. Apart from the last question, the intensity levels of the Rotterdam groups cluster around 'rarely' but the rank order does correspond to the guiding hypothesis with the Turks performing certain acts more frequently compared with the Surinamese and the Iranians, who both show similar levels. Compared to the previous figures, this analysis shows the weakest correlation. There seems to be an internal ranking between the questions that is consistent amongst three groups (Chileans, Rotterdam Iranians and Malmö Turks), with only slight variation amongst the remaining three.

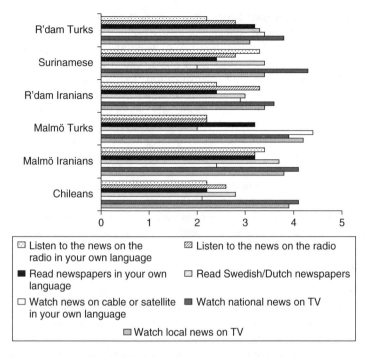

*Figure 4.5*  Interest in Swedish/Dutch politics versus country of origin

*Note*: Correlation coefficient: R'dam Turks 0.03, Surinamese 0.3, R'dam Iranians 0.57, Malmö Turks 0.46, Malmö Iranians 0.46, Chileans −0.29.

Again, the more time-consuming the participatory act is, the less frequent it is performed.

## Interest in Swedish/Dutch politics versus country of origin

All six groups display an overall higher degree of political interest when it comes to domestic events. Figure 4.5 shows where the responding groups put the emphasis with regard to their interest in political events in Sweden and the Netherlands compared to the respondents' country or origin.

Both the Malmö Iranian and Chilean respondents seem to keep up with current events to a similar degree, although the latter tend to watch local news slightly more often. However, this could be interpreted as the Chilean group simply having a higher frequency of watching TV in general rather than displaying an interest in the news *per se*. The most remarkable differences can be found in the questions relating to the respondents' reception of broadcasts in their own language or coming from their country of origin. Here, the Malmö Iranians score significantly higher than the Chileans on all three issues. One would expect the Chilean respondents to show greater interest in home-country events since their levels of identification are lower; conversely, the higher levels of identification found amongst the Iranian respondents would be expected to yield higher interest in political events in general. Similarly, the Rotterdam groups also seem to follow both local and national TV news but with the Rotterdam Turks viewing home-country news less often compared to the Swedish sample. Of interest is also the difference in reading Dutch newspapers and country-of-origin newspapers, in which the former category shows higher levels. The Surinamese sample is problematic here since the posed questions concerning home country could be confusing to interpret given the unclear relationship between the Surinamese and Dutch identity. All groups apart from the Chileans also display a positive correlation with regard to these questions, although not particularly strong coefficients.

## Conclusion

This chapter has discussed the relationship between identity, citizenship and host society identification. The starting premise of this chapter was to compare levels of political participation for Chilean, Iranian and Turkish migrants in Malmö and Iranian, Surinamese and Turkish migrants in Rotterdam, and provide an explanation as to why these levels differ when compared with each other. In contrast to previous studies, this research has not opted for a purely socio-economic or resource-based approach, but instead has introduced the concept of identification as a key variable. Seeing that the target groups share similar socio-economic profiles but exhibit different levels of political participation, we need an additional variable in order to explain these discrepancies. It was argued that a higher level of internal and external identification would yield higher levels of political participation, satisfaction with the performance of local politicians and political interest. The empirical findings seem to support this statement, but only to some extent. There seems to be a connection, although it is often rather weak, between higher levels of identification and higher levels of political participation. The Malmö Iranians, who displayed the highest level of identification, followed by the Rotterdam Turks, were by and large more satisfied with their local politicians, more likely to participate, showed more political interest and engaged more frequently, compared to the other groups who displayed somewhat lower levels of participation.

Although the sample size cannot be said to be fully satisfactory in terms of statistical representation, the results presented in this analysis can still be used as a guide for future research. Above all, I have demonstrated the potential relevance of the identification variable and its ability to yield complementary evidence in addition to socio-economic traits.

# 5
# Civil Society, Migrant Organisations and Political Parties

## Introduction

This chapter deals with the role of migrant associations in civil society and their relationship with the political parties. First, the ideas and rationale behind civil society are discussed. An ideal model of types and purposes of organisations is elaborated, and migrant associations, with reference to the five case countries, are then compared within this context. Second, the role and relevance of these associations are discussed with reference to the structural opportunities and constraints that exist within the Swedish and Dutch political environment. In the former, the intention is that migrant organisations should serve as partners in the integration process, functioning as bridges between the Swedish society and the new population. In the latter, organisations are founded under the label of ethnic minorities and are encouraged to do so under the Dutch policy of cultural pluralistic policies (Vermeulen, 2002). This suggests that migrant associations should be involved in the political process to some extent. Although official policy seems to encourage mobilisation according to ethnic belonging, structural conditions determine to what extent this is feasible. Therefore, the chapter will examine in more detail to what degree migrant organisations have been utilised as channels for claims-making and what type of relationship they have with the political parties.

## Civil society

The essential ideas behind civil society suggest that the quality of societal life depends on the fruitful interaction between individuals and between the individual and society. Traditional civil society has been conceptualised as being a crucial condition for a healthy democracy in that the civil society and the state are mutually dependent on each other. Despite much disagreement concerning the exact nature of civil society, most scholars in the field seem to agree with a view of civil society as an arena of friendships, clubs, churches, business associations, unions and other voluntary associations that mediate the vast expanse of social life between the household and the state. This associational sphere is seen as the place where citizens learn habits of free assembly, dialogue and social initiative. If handled in a proper manner, it is suggested, civil society can also help to bring about the delicate balance of private interests and public concern vital for a vibrant democracy (Hefner, 1998).

From a liberal standpoint, Held (1987) conceives the unique feature of civil society to be the extent to which it constitutes different areas of social life. Held suggests that these components are made up of domains such as the domestic and economic world, cultural activities and political interaction. However, civil society is at the same time separate from these areas in that it is organised, primarily, by voluntary arrangements between individuals and/or groups outside the direct control of the state. A healthy civil society, liberal democrats insist, can counterbalance the power of the state. In contrast to this liberal definition, a more communitarian view argues that the position of civil society should be strengthened at the expense of the state. This should be implemented either by emphasising legality, private property and interest groups, or by promoting the empowerment of groups on the basis of equality with their fellow citizens. Here, civil society acts as a measure against the state becoming too powerful.[38]

This reciprocal relationship makes it difficult to conceive civil society as functioning successfully without the existence of a state. The state provides civil society with an integrative framework that allows it to operate under a number of rules. These rules include settings which allow political contest to be played out in such a fashion that outcomes must be accepted and valid for participants as well as consistent with the shared culture of the society in question. Therefore it is necessary to position civil society in relation to the state or, at least, utilise the state as the ultimate point of reference. The modern democratic state is not only the sole legitimate user of violence but is also the provider, and guarantor, of socially valued goods. In other words, the state is simultaneously target, sponsor and opponent to the actors in civil society (Jenkins and Klandermans, 1995). The dispersion of powers and the balancing of forces associated with self-organisation also provide important supports for civility and participation. On their own, these structural conditions would most likely create no more than partial freedoms, enjoyed by only a portion of the populace. The broader achievement of citizen equality requires at least two other things – the incorporation of civic values into a certain kind of state and a broadly based civic culture. Civil society requires a state that is both strong and self-limiting. It must be self-limiting in the sense that it does not monopolise society's powers, drawing all vital personnel, services and enterprise back into itself. But civil society must also be strong, in the sense that it is capable of safeguarding the freedoms of association and initiative on which vigorous public life depends. Thus, civil society needs a civil state, because public life can be threatened by societal forces as much as the state (Hefner, 1998).

The rule of law and the state's ability to create a certain degree of coherence prevent civil society from becoming too 'uncivil' and eventually to decline (Schopflin, 2000). At the same time, however, civil society must remain free to challenge the state in order to prohibit or restrain the bureaucratic apparatus of state action from becoming too dominant. The presence of the state raises a number of problems in terms of what Walzer (1998) describes as civil society's need for political agency. That is, the state can never be fully neutral – as liberal theory suggests – since the state, by its mere presence, is an instrument of the struggle in that it is used to give shape to a particular common life. Liberal theorists would argue that the state could never impose this type of system on its citizens since universally shared rules are not feasible to implement. Instead, they opt for a system with abstract, formal rules and procedures to govern civil society. However, this type of argument omits the point that, regardless of societal settings, the prevailing state and its institutions help to shape the nature of civil society in that particular context. That is, a society with a lesser degree of state intervention, where civil society is governed only by formal rules, will display different types of involvement and action by actors compared to a society characterised by extensive state influence, support and control. Consider, for instance, the different types of civil society and their relative success found in the West, Latin America, Central and Eastern Europe. Or, as Cohen and Arato (1995: 16) point out, '[m]ovements rooted in civil society have learned from the revolutionary tradition that these fundamentalist projects led to the breakdown of societal steering and productivity and the suppression of social plurality, all of which are then reconstituted by the forces of order only by dramatically authoritarian means'. As these authors go on to argue: 'collective action involves forms of association and strategies specific to context ... [which] includes public spaces, social institutions (mass media), rights (to associate, to speak, to assemble), representative political institutions, and an autonomous legal system, all of which are targets for social movements seeking to influence policy or initiate change' (1995: 496–7).

Therefore, the important issue to consider is how the societal-specific settings in terms of institutional frameworks influence the way in which voluntary associations function, and hence what type of relationship they can or cannot have with the political actors. This means that, depending on the institutional settings, societies will tend to differ in their relation to Tocqueville's (1972) ideal conception of civil society which states that the democratic character of the political culture or of the social and political institutions is dependent on active participation on the part of citizens in egalitarian institutions.

The presence of civil society suggests that there is a precarious balance between individual – voluntary – participation and social obligations; in other words, a middle way between private interests and that of society at large. Scholars of democracy have long argued for the importance of a well functioning civil society in which voluntary organisations can play an important and crucial part.[39] Participation through voluntary associations could thus be considered to be one of the key features of a vital, modern, civil society and an important form of citizen participation in public life. Voluntary associations, much like social movements, function as a supplement to the institutional arrangements of representative democracy and thus renew and refresh the democratic culture by bringing in new values and issues to the public sphere and contributing to reproduce public consensus.

Putnam *et al.* (1993) famously notes that the norms and values of the civic community are embodied in and reinforced by the distinctive social structures and practices of the voluntary organisations, making these the key actors. These civil associations contribute to the effectiveness and stability of democracy both due to their internal effects on the individual member and because of the external effects on the wider polity. Building on the seminal work of Toqueville (1972), Putnam argues that voluntary associations provide their members with the habits of co-operation, solidarity and public-spiritedness. Thus, participating in civic organisations includes skills of working together as well as a shared sense of collective responsibilities. These spill-over effects, created by social capital accumulation, are those of a more tightly knit community. The latter refers not only to a geographical location but also to a social system in which strong social relationships take place within a given locality (Vasta, 2000). Trust, co-operation and reciprocity are social resources that increase with use in that high levels of trust generate high levels of co-operation and vice versa.

Furthermore, it is argued that, when individuals become part of groups with diverse goals and members, which in turn are connected to the wider range of collectives, their attitudes could potentially become more moderated and the risk of conflict could decrease. In terms of the external benefit, it is suggested that interest articulation and aggregation will be enhanced if there is a dense network of associations. These associations are located in a sphere that is not only separate from the coercion of the state but also distinct from the sphere of the family and the economy (Fennema and Tillie, 2002). These authors point out that civil society mirrors the public sphere in that it is simultaneously separate from the state, the economic and private sphere. The central feature in civil society, they argue, is that here, the citizen reigns rather than the administrator, the bourgeoisie or the family. The citizen is here not only the locus of a bundle of rights but also constitutes a set of roles that relate the individual to other individuals and to the state. The difference in relationship between individual citizens and between citizens and the state is that the former emphasises equality and respect rather than the individual rights and accountability of the latter.

Civil society in this sense can thus be defined as the totality of social institutions and associations, formal as well as informal, that are not strictly orientated towards production, and are not governmental or familial in character (Rueschmeyer *et al.*, 1992). Thus, civil society occupies a middle ground between the private and the public sphere in its detachment from the political society and the state (Fine, 1997). More specifically Schmitter (1979; see also Whitehead, 1997) defines civil society as a set or system of self-organised intermediary groups that are

1. relatively independent of both public authorities and private units of production and reproduction (firms and families);
2. capable of deliberating about and taking collective actions in defence and/or promotion of their interests;
3. not prepared, however, to seek to replace either state agents or private (re)producers or to accept responsibility for governing the polity as a whole; and
4. willing to act within pre-established rules of a 'civil' or legal nature.

In this view, the idea of civil society serves as a counterweight to the above-mentioned types of institutional arrangements in which the voluntary organisations play a key role. These organisations become part of the civil society definition if they display low thresholds for entry and the right to exit is guaranteed. However, as Ahrne (1998) points out, the term does not denote a new kind of society in the sense that it is not a new type of social system but is rather presented as an alternative social sphere. This sphere is characterised by its means of organisation, which distinguishes it from other forms of institutional arrangements.

An important feature here is that this sphere remains autonomous by protection of the rule of law enabling individuals and collectives – whose values diverge – to co-exist peacefully (Gray, 1993), since the rule of law provides the framework for conflict resolution. This suggests that voluntary associations can be more or less part of the civil society judging by the degree to which they are considered voluntary and their scope for being autonomous. Interest organisations, for instance, are voluntary but have limited autonomy. A business organisation, on the other hand, displays the opposite characteristics, with high autonomy but less of a voluntary character. These criteria also apply to the source of organisational funding. If funding is received from one source and tied to a number of conditions, the autonomy of the organisation is limited. Furthermore, if the organisation is heavily dependent on state subsidisation and sponsorship, the line around organisational autonomy becomes blurred since the organisation's contribution to civil society could be questioned – especially if the mission of such a state-sponsored association is formulated by policy concerns. If these associations are too dependent on the state then this could potentially clash with the very notion of civil society (Fennema and Tillie, 2002).

Furthermore, civic organisations also differ in terms of professionalisation, which determines the amount of direct ties between members. The more professionalised the association is (e.g. a consumer organisation or new social movement associations such as Amnesty), the less individual participation is needed. According to Fennema and Tillie (2002), such organisations provide less input to civil society since the prevailing vertical relations offer few services for its members but instead act as representatives for the political cause that the members believe in. Since the members of professional social movements contract out their political participation by joining a so-called cheque-book organisation, few direct ties are created between the members since there exist few or no joint activities. Although contributing less to civil society, these organisations do contribute to the working of liberal democracy by providing a counterweight to governmental power (Newton, 1999). That is, membership in voluntary organisations implies a notion of democracy and equality since all members, in principle, have equal rights to take part in decisions. This gives a precondition for democratic dialogue since the voluntary organisations combine freedom with equality.

In addition, there needs to be a minimum amount of voluntary organisations in order to speak of a civil society. If citizens can exercise power in terms of joining or leaving an association, then their degree of freedom and autonomy increases. This suggests that entry and exit barriers become less influential on individual freedom if there is a possibility to join or set up new organisations. The ideal model of civil society posits further that there needs to be some form of contact between the associations. If no such contacts exist, it becomes difficult to talk of a civil society since trust and co-operation are minimal. A higher frequency in the number of contacts not only facilitates the spread of information and trust but it also contributes to dampen conflicts and bridge cleavages. Some studies have pointed out that particularly political trust seems to be higher for members of associations which in turn yields positive results for levels of political participation (Fennema and Tillie, 2001).

Migrant organisations are both similar and different with regard to these criteria. Immigrant organisations are social movements like other organisations are; what distinguishes them from others is that they do not (only) take a shared interest as their starting point, but (also) a shared ethnicity. This shared ethnicity is what binds immigrants together despite differences in class and interest (Schrover, 2003).

In terms of organisational aims, migrant associations can be said to serve four characteristic purposes that separate them from other types of voluntary organisation. First, migrant organisations can act as a link between the sending country and the receiving one in that they can provide advisory services for future migrants. This means that the organisation could potentially act as an intermediary or an alternative for the complex bureaucracy in that it can offer first-hand experience of the migration process in the host country. In addition, they can also have a cushioning function, that is, they can 'soften' the shock of transition by offering a setting in which immigrants could meet fellow-nationals and speak their own language. The organisation can also maintain the interaction among immigrants. This is especially relevant for migrants who lack informal ties, therefore they attempt to forge formal ties so as to retain some form of bonding.

Second, the organisation can function as an alternative or complement to the state in terms of integration and adaptation to the new society. If an organisation or a number of them are able to set up well-functioning relationships with authorities responsible for integration policies, migrant associations can potentially facilitate integration. This could include providing information about the host country in the native language, or acting as a link between migrants and different socio-economic areas of society and/or the political world. In this way, organisations allow migrants to practice the ways of the host society in an ethnic setting. As such, they can thus be used as a 'training school' for participation in the host society.

Third, migrant associations, if part of an established network, can serve as a unified voice for their particular ethnic group in relation to the host society. Organisations can be used to translate the group's consensus on certain subjects. The extent to which immigrants cluster in organisations is also an important indicator in order to measure the extent of a collective (or collectively expressed) identity. The character, number and size of organisations indicate the extent to which immigrants intend to profile themselves as different, or are seen by others as different. Organisations can thus be viewed as an expression of the collectively felt identity of their members. They can be defensive (as a response to exclusion) or offensive (stemming from a choice of immigrants to set themselves apart from others). Furthermore, one should make a distinction between organisations that aim at enforcing or encouraging integration, and those aiming to keep an identity. Offensive organisations will often have as their goal the retaining of an identity, whereas defensive organisations have strategy rather than identity as their main goal, where strategy can either be stressing or eliminating difference. The concentration of migrants and their home-country-based social networks are viewed as crucial to their organising on the basis of ethnic attributes. Finally, migrant organisations can play an important role for the maintenance of a linkage between the ethnic group and the country or region of origin, especially in a diaspora type of situation. Also, they can serve as contact points between ethnic communities in different settler countries. This last characteristic has been particularly dominant amongst for example Turkish communities residing in different European countries (Vermeulen, 2002: see also Breton, 1964; Cordero-Guzman, 2001; Schrover, 2003). The above-mentioned criteria can be summarised by the scheme set out in Figure 5.1.

| | | DEGREE | |
|---|---|---|---|
| | | **Low** | **High** |
| | **Voluntary** | Involvement of state regarding purpose or running of association | Opportunities to set up organisations. Minimum threshold for entry/exit |
| **TYPE** | **Autonomous** | Degree of control and steering by other bodies apart from association board and members | Participation and ability to influence feasible and desirable. Independent in terms of financing |
| | **Professional** | Number of board members on salary. Association should not be orientated towards profit | Volunteers play greater part in governance. Ability to influence desirable and feasible |
| | **Contacts** | Level of isolation or exclusion from society | Cross-cutting memberships and relationship with other actors |

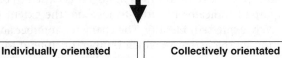

| | **Individually orientated** | **Collectively orientated** |
|---|---|---|
| **PURPOSE** | Serve as a counterweight to state intervention on individual freedom and rights. | Serve to empower excluded groups in society. |

*Figure 5.1*   Ideal conceptualisation of organisations in civil society

## Structure and organisation

Even though migrants arrive with a set of organisational modes and history, interaction with the host society through its political and bureaucratic institutions will most likely reshape these forms and characteristics. Migrant organisations can also take on a new appearance and function depending on, and as a response to, changes in the international arena. Increasing emphasis on human rights and new multicultural/pluralistic discourses on identity serve as incentives for social movements which in turn can be adopted by migrant associations in their negotiation process with the host state (Soysal, 1994). However, to create a well-functioning civic community is most likely not the prime objective when an organisation is initiated. In general, voluntary associations are set up since there exists a belief that the organisational forum better serves the actors' needs compared to the prevailing social arrangements. They believe that the organisation will remain effective and that benefits will exceed costs. Castles and Davidson (2000) suggest that ethnic mobilisation within the realms of the organisational structure could be an important factor for the incorporation of minorities as citizens. This type of mobilisation may facilitate the conditions for societal participation of minorities since groups based on common ethnic identification perform them within the mainstream structures.

Therefore, as Vermeulen (2002) proposes, one must pay attention to demand and supply factors in order to understand why migrant organisations are set up. On the demand side one finds group identification and the perceived need for a specific organisation; on the supply side, resources in terms of wealth, power, legitimacy and the existence of intra-organisational competition. Demand-side factors are dependent on the characteristics of the particular migrant group in terms of its size, demographic composition, socio-economic position, linguistic and religious features. Supply-side characteristics are however more dependent on the institutional context and the POS that prevail (as described in Chapter 3).

The emphasis on mobilisation as a response to the political environment provides a different focus compared to the two previously dominating paradigms regarding the relationship between migrants/minorities and collective action. The first suggests a class-based approach where the underprivileged structural and socio-economic position of migrants has a direct consequence for their degree of mobilisation and underlying motives. According to this line of thought, economic divisions within the working class are seen as racialised under the structural crisis of advanced industrial capitalism which transforms a common race or ethnicity into a class of its own and serves as a common identity for political participation and as a form of emerging, but false, class consciousness. This precarious situation can only be overcome by co-operating with the indigenous working class through trade unions and labour parties, where the race category becomes subordinate to the more general class category. The second explanation – the ethnicity/race paradigm – takes an opposite stance, advocating that the ethnic class is not so much a display of false consciousness but rather a continuous form of collective action independent from class. Here, shared experiences, such as racism and discrimination, distinguish migrants from the host society's population. However, the ultimate causes of behaviour – class and ethnicity – are taken as given and not related to the political specifics of the differing country contexts. Both approaches assume that migrants will tend to behave in a similar fashion regardless of the political institutional framework (Koopmans and Statham, 2000; see also Castles and Kosack, 1974; Rex *et al.*, 1979).

In contrast, the POS approach suggests that collective action is determined by external events, the availability of resources and opportunities made available by changes in the institutional setting. The key issue here is that the opportunity approach places group mobilisation in a political context and provides an explanation as to why mobilisation takes a certain appearance rather than why it originally emerges. Furthermore, this model also predicts that the amount and type of group formation are a direct outcome of the particular structure of political institutions and the construction of political power in a given society. Thus, it is when changes occur in the external opportunities that we are more likely to find change in group action and formation. If powerful groups change their attitudes against politically marginal groups, these groups should respond to this opening by increasing group action, founding new organisations and using these as channels for mobilisation. This perspective originally builds on the resource mobilisation theory of collective action as based on the perceived cost and benefits of alternative strategies and the need for resource mobilisation prior to mobilisation. However, as proposed above, it also places social movement actors more concretely in their political context. The impact stemming from the shift from local to national power structures on organisational forms and types of collective action makes an important addition to the understanding of the social and political terrain that forms the condition for the emergence and success of modern movements.

This stance helps to explain why migrant organisations take on different appearances when one compares mobilisation across different countries. As Soysal (1994) shows, organisational variables and modes of incorporation are crucial elements in order to understand why different organisational patterns emerge amongst different migrant communities. Host societies have an important influence and contribute to the collective organisation of migrants by the provision – or non-provision – of resources for and models of organisation. As Soysal's account tells us, the receiving Western European countries display remarkable differences in this regard. Some host societies provide explicit channels for the participation and organisation of migrant populations, thereby shaping the means and appearance of self-organisation, whereas others put constraints on migrant mobilisation. The way in which the host society's institutions and policies encourage or discourage collective identity and organisation by means of officially sanctioned categories and availability of resources, sets the type of overarching unity around which mobilisation can take place (Tilly, 1978). At the other end of the scale, migrant organisations define their goals, strategies, functions and level of operation according to the prevailing policies and resources available. They put forward demands and claims as well as attempting to set the agenda in relation to state policy and discourse by exploiting institutional opportunities. Ultimately, the expression and organisation of migrant collective identity are facilitated or constrained by particular institutional forms and choices of incorporation patterns.

However, as Cohen and Arato (1995) point out, Tilly's framework displays two main problems. First, his resource-mobilisation stance (organisation, interests, resources, opportunities, and strategies account for large-scale mobilisation) merely describes the emergence of the action repertoire and the types of associations predicted by the resource-mobilisation theory.

Cohen and Arato argue that Tilly's historical comparison both situates and transcends the framework by providing examples of group life that do not fit into his analytic scheme of resource-mobilisation. Furthermore, his model allows civil society (as being distinct from the state and the economy) to serve as the terrain but not as the target of collective action. It is somewhat difficult to see the validity of this criticism (especially the latter claim). If civil society is characterised as being essentially different from the state then civil society would logically not display the same characteristics as the state and would conversely not be the target for movements in order to induce change. The ideal conceptualisation of civil society suggests that it serves as a counterweight or complement to the state and not as an internal enemy. This becomes more apparent considering that civil society lacks many of the necessary means to implement political decisions, a feature which is unique for state apparatus. Modern collective action presupposes that the development of autonomous social and political spaces within civil and political society is seen as legitimate and is thus guaranteed by rights and supported by the democratic political culture underlying the formal representative political institutions.

In addition, Tilly (1978) proposes that it is by means of transition from 'community' to 'society' that the character of conflict is transformed. Here, the locus and mode of work, neighbourhood structure and residential areas have changed, which in turn steers organisations away from communal solidarity in favour of voluntary associations. The analysis implies that two main types of collective action came to be prominent – reactive and proactive. The former indicates collective action as induced from an external threat by the state to attempt to gain control over the general population and its resources. Here, a group reacts to the claims made by another group over a resource currently under its control. The latter relates to group-claims to power, privileges or resources that have not previously existed. In this case, instead of resisting to external pressure, the collective assumes a more agency-based role in its attempts to gain control. Tilly's explanation for the increase of non-parliamentary activities – such as demonstrations – is related to the growth of general elections and the beginning of popular participation in national politics which promotes these types of activities.

Anheier (2002) argues in a similar vein when he explores the rapid expansion of the 'third sector' over the last decades. He suggests that this is the cumulative outcome of economic and demographic reasons but, more importantly, is also due to political and ideological factors. Existing demands are channelled to and through civil society in accordance with the prevailing political frameworks and legislation. In addition, countries that have experienced the highest growth of voluntary organisation formation are also the countries that have policies in place that facilitate not only formation but also working partnerships between the government and the voluntary associations.

However, change in dynamics can also take place within groups of organisations relating to the total number of similar-type organisations. Labelled the 'organisational ecology model' by Hannan and Freeman (1989), it proposes that fewer organisations will tend to monopolise a given space and new organisations will experience resistance both from existing organisations as well as from the host society (due to unfamiliarity with these types of associations). This approach suggests that increase in the number of similar organisations will increase intra-group competition over the same public space. However, this view seems to be applied to specific categories of organisations, under specific circumstances and also primarily to highly politicised migrant groups. Naturally, if Hannan and Freeman refer to migrant organisations that are formed around homeland political affiliation, competition and rivalry seems more likely to occur. Implicit in their argument is that organisations exist in the context of minimal state intervention, that is, few restrictions are found with regard to the nature and purpose of the organisation's *modus vivendi*. Furthermore, it seems to neglect the influence of the prevailing institutional environment. If organisational life is regulated and controlled by the state then this will most likely affect the type of organisation that is set up. If politicised migrant associations are not sanctioned by the state then it is probable that we will see less of these types of organisations in favour of others. Naturally, conflicting political and ideological claims might still exist but the point is that these claims will not be part of the founding principles of the organisation but will rather be a spin-off effect.

## Migrant organisations in France, Germany, the Netherlands, Sweden and Britain

Since officially being labelled a multicultural society in 1975, the Swedish state has provided institutional sanctions facilitating the formal organisation of migrant organisations. Similarly, since 1980 the Dutch authorities have actively encouraged immigrants to integrate while simultaneously supporting their identity. This has been done by teaching migrant children their own language, actively supporting mono-ethnic organisations and establishing a target group policy to combat social and economic inequality (Berger and Vermeulen, 2001).

Sweden and the Netherlands are somewhat unique compared to other west European countries in that they display such a high degree and variety of both voluntary migrant and non-migrant organisations. Migrant groups and religious minorities have a constitutional right to express and develop their cultural heritage. This right – which corresponds to one of the main principles in Swedish integration policy, freedom of choice – also entails the right to mother-tongue education for children of non-native-speaking parents as well as support for ethnic radio and occasional television space such as news programmes. In addition, a number of migrant-language newspapers and periodicals receive monetary support from the central government. The German situation shows a quite different development. Immigrants have traditionally been under more pressure to assimilate and adjust culturally than in Sweden and the Netherlands and official policy in Germany does not recognise immigrants as being minorities. Consequently, no special provision is granted towards these on a national level but as pointed out in previous chapters, individual states differ remarkably in relation to how they support and fund migrant organisations (Vermeulen, 2005). Similarly, migrant (as well as non-migrant) associations in France have a weaker civil society position where the French state is prone to advocate and fund general organisations that cater for a cross-section of the population. Voluntary organisations have become more involved in local and regional level decision-making as equal partners but are at the same time in a weak position in that they are subject to local authorities or government agencies to 'ok' them and then admitting them within their orbit (Cole, 1998). However, the British case provides a comparatively different approach to migrant organisational patterns with regard to professionalisation and purposes. First, these organisations are more formally run compared to the Swedish, Dutch and German ones with a number of full-time staff funded for welfare services to pay administrative, social and legal advice workers with an annual income between £50,000 and £250,000. Second, a majority of these organisations deal primarily with issues of racial discrimination and legal matters or are community care groups aimed at specific ethnic communities or ethnic minorities with particular needs (McLeod *et al.*, 2001, see also Soysal, 1994).

In contrast, then, migrant associations in Sweden and the Netherlands are intended to function as natural channels for the incorporation of different migrant groups. In Sweden, by having the same status as ethnically Swedish associations, they are to a certain extent recognised as formal partners and expected to maintain the link between migrants and Swedish institutions (Odmalm, 2004a). Furthermore, migrant associations are part of the central plan that supports and subsidises other Swedish organisations. The Swedish model stipulates that different societal organisations are viewed as representatives of different segments of the population and are to be given a significant role as the state's formal partners. Migrant associations are thus supposed to represent the interests of their particular ethnic group, region or multi-country federation. On the national level, umbrella organisations are provided with opportunities through consultative bodies and advisory councils. Each category is represented by its federation as councils attached to ministries and funding arrangements which in turn gives them the same status as other Swedish umbrella organisations in accordance with the policy goal of equality (Soysal, 1994).

Ålund and Schierup (1991) point out that the flourishing Swedish civil society was enabled through the successful control and transformation of radical claims and by disciplining and institutionalising spontaneous organisation through incorporation and co-option. Migrant associations were built on the same foundation that had previously proved successful at the turn of the twentieth century when the labour movement was initiated. Modern associational life stems from the traditional vehicle of political socialisation and moral supervision known as the popular social movement (folkrörelser) which has encompassed, most famously, the trade unions but also education movements of women, youth and workers. Migrant associations were thus considered to be able to function in a similar way where emphasis was put on education and acculturation in areas deemed necessary in order to achieve the integration goals of equality, partnership and freedom of choice. A similar idea, but perhaps less related to migrant organisations, is echoed in New Labour's re-emphasis on the role of the voluntary sector as an equal partner alongside the state and the market in which its contribution to community and civil life supersedes ideas of economic efficiency having taken onboard the suggestions put forward in the Deakin Commission's report (Lewis, 1999).

In the Netherlands, similar emphasis is put upon the right and importance of migrants to organise in voluntary organisations but based on a different rationale. As pointed out previously, Dutch society was organised around state-supported social and religious pillars. The pillars were vertically structured social and ecclesiastical organisations, each headed by a non-clerical administrative board. Today, the pillars administer funds provided by the state for religious education and social services.

Originally, the pillars were social emancipators and considered equal vis-à-vis each other – at least inasmuch as it provided Roman Catholic and orthodox Protestant minorities with protection from the majoritarian liberal Protestants. In practice, the structure was managed by pillar leaders in a rather authoritarian and elitist way, even though it allowed a remarkable social and political pacification (Hefner, 1998). The relation between Dutch society and its immigrants is still firmly rooted in its pillar tradition. Government policy in this area provided a large degree of autonomy for ethnic minorities in the cultural sphere and has also incorporated minority elites into the policy process (Koopmans, 2001). This has been enabled through subsidisation of representative organisations, similar to the national umbrella organisations in Sweden, but has gone one step further by also including them in the policy deliberation and implementation processes (Koopmans and Statham, 2003).

Dutch policy has thus managed to establish collective categories and support for migrant organisations under the guiding terms of integration and emancipation. This type of support, much like in Sweden, fosters scope for an assertion of collective identity. The number of organisations is also similarly high.[40] A majority of these organisations are federated at the national level under roughly 25 umbrella organisations. The goals or aims of these nationality-based organisations fall under either community development or emancipation activities heading. As in the Swedish case, Dutch migrant organisations are tightly structured and co-ordinated by a number of advisory boards and as such are linked with and incorporated into the state apparatus. On the national level, the LAO (National Advisory Council for Ethnic Minorities) brings together a number of politically and functionally diverse organisations and provides migrant groups with a channel for participation. In addition, the recognised ethnic groups have a number of sub-councils attached to them. This situation filters down to the local level as well. In the early 1980s, the city of Rotterdam established an overarching forum for its organisations, the so-called Platform Buitenlanders Rijnmond (PBR). The main purpose of the PBR is to 'support and guide migrant self-organisations in their efforts to participate and integrate in Dutch society. PBR also maintains contact and co-operates with organisations, institutions and municipal services … advice on starting an organisation, administrative problems, financial business and fund raising. PBR also helps with annual reports, plans of action and the development of activities and projects. PBR also organises cadre education, helps to develop networks and mediates to political parties' (PBR webpage 2003). In short, the PBR forum deals with most areas of self-organisational life.

In addition, the criteria for funding are very similar to those found in Sweden. Migrant organisations must form federations and assume the task of interest representation. Funding is dependent on the organisation functioning on the national level and performing certain tasks – providing informational, cultural and emancipatory activities aimed primarily at migrant women and youth, training volunteers as professional organisational leaders (Soysal, 1994). As in Sweden, the state is the major source of funding.

In the Swedish and Dutch cases, a majority of the ethnic organisations can be said to have a high degree of voluntariness since entrance and exit thresholds are low. The relevant authorities exercise few restrictions on the type of organisation that can be set up as long as it does not contradict fundamental democratic values or have an anti-social purpose. Similarly, in France following the abolishment of legal restrictions on migrant associations in 1981, the opportunities for starting up migrant organisations have increased but are rather local than national (as in Britain) and do not represent a united front (as in Germany).

Professionalised ethnic organisations in Sweden are virtually non-existent (as opposed to the UK) and seem to be more frequent in terms of general non-ethnic organisations such as Greenpeace and Amnesty. Nevertheless, some large-scale organisations do have full-time staff specifically employed to deal with organisational administration and are usually part of local unemployment schemes. In the Netherlands, more professionally run organisations can be found amongst those associations which have the umbrella-tag. These organisations also have a special status vis-à-vis the local authorities as the advisor for social and economic affairs in Rotterdam explains.

> The city decided to subsidise a number of professional organisations and today we have about 10 or 12 of these and they have specific tasks in terms of the integration policy. They work and co-operate with the municipal department but they also have a separate function, they are umbrella organisations and their work is to support the volunteer and grass-root organisations. They are a very important part of the city because they are intermediaries for the communication processes. (Advisor of Social and Economic Affairs A, 2001)

In relation to the intra-group competition argument above, migrant organisations in Sweden rarely seem to compete over the same territory. This is partly due to the non-dominance of one or a few ethnic groups but also due to the monitoring system of the local authorities – there should be as little overlap between organisations as possible in terms of similar purpose and activities. In the Netherlands, the situation is similar. In her study on Turkish associations, van Heelsum (2005) finds that despite political and religious cleavages, a significant number of Turkish associations are in fact interconnected with each other through a cohesive network of interlocking board members, thus suggesting that intra-group competition might be low. In addition, due to the existence of numerous platforms, advisory boards and co-ordinating agencies, overlapping organisations would most likely be discouraged at an early stage when registering the organisation.

Migrants are organised in a number of parallel associations defined according to a vague national or ethnic definition. One of the most concrete forms of organisational steering can be found in the ways of funding. In Sweden, and to some extent in the Netherlands, authorities have been very keen on emphasising the term 'voluntary' and any sign of privatisation or profit-making has been effectively banned from Swedish associational life, and organisations are to a large extent dependent on grants and subsidies from the state for their survival. Associations that serve as umbrella organisations on a national level are eligible for funding if they comply with a number of criteria. Sweden and the Netherlands have a comprehensive funding scheme that aims at strengthening migrant self-organisation and to further contact and co-operation between migrants and the authorities. The Swedish guidelines for funding on a national level (SFS 2000:216) state that organisations must have at least 1000 members, a geographical spread that is representative of its members, be involved in activities that promote integration for at least two years, and provide some of the costs for its activities in order to receive monetary support. Funding is divided into three types: organisational, project and activity based relating to the above criteria. In the Netherlands, funding is also dependent on a number of criteria which are evaluated by both the local city council as well as a different city sub-council. The following quote shows the somewhat difficult process.

> Funding for grass-root associations is up to the sub-council in which that particular association operates, the city has a number of urban social programmes so the umbrella organisations are funded by the city, but the smaller ones have to apply to neighbourhood authorities. There are a number of formal requirements, credibility, budget, type of activities and so on and if they don't comply with them then it's very difficult ... in general they value self-organisation initiatives, but I have to admit that a lot of the people only look at the formal requirements so if it doesn't fit, they don't pass it. (Advisor of Social and Economic Affairs A, 2001)

In Sweden, organisations must to a larger extent comply with the goals set out by the governmental directives compared to the more loosely defined regulations in the Netherlands.[41] First, following the goal of partnership, newly arrived immigrants should be given better opportunities for self-support and participation in society; therefore national organisations should develop their involvement in performing activities that stimulate the spread of information regarding democratic values. In addition, such organisations should also make co-operation with local authorities more effective when it comes to their participation during this introduction. Second, the goal of equality presupposes that equal rights, obligations and opportunities for all citizens regardless of ethnic background should be promoted; while discrimination, racism and xenophobia should be prevented. National organisations must thus try and work actively to increase equality within their organisation, develop their achievements in terms of encouraging members to become self-funding, and strive to bring signs of ethnic discrimination into public light. Finally, in accordance with the goal of freedom of choice, national organisations must supply knowledge about living conditions for youngsters with a foreign heritage. On a local level, two types of monetary aid are available: first, associational aid, which is based on the number of fee-paying members; and second for registered activities that are aimed at promoting integration. However, the activity-based money is calculated according to an evaluation of how well the association has achieved these goals and the amount of active local-branch associations (Odmalm, 2004b).

Since associations are formed according to ethnicity or nationality this generates a limited number of members and consequently a limited amount of funds compared to the more generally aimed organisations such as sports clubs. This, in turn, makes associations focus primarily on increasing membership numbers rather than concentrating on their own activities. The emphasis on organisation formation according to ethnicity is also encouraged by the Swedish state. As Vermeulen (2002) shows, host societies play an important role in terms of influencing the type of identity that is deemed to be legitimate in the new environment. Here, the state can steer the expression of a particular type of collective identity by offering and promoting categories of identification. This could in turn generate the emergence of an unprivileged ethnic community, characterised by their marginalised position and being defined as different (or 'other') by the dominant groups, and thus likely to form their own social groups or communities as a response to this. However, as Koopmans and Statham (1999) suggest, depending on what category the host society adopts, this will also have an impact on what claims are made and where they are directed. For example, in Britain and the Netherlands, the labelling of migrants as 'ethnic minorities' yields more participation relating to the situation of one's 'own' group in the country of residence than towards the country of origin. Whereas in Germany, the label of 'foreigners' prompts more homeland-based participation.

In the Swedish (and French) case, the category of 'immigrant' has been promoted over the 'ethnic minority' category. Two main reasons can be found for this choice of action. First, the use of the latter term has been firmly resisted and predominantly absent in Swedish public policy partly due to the late start of immigration and partly because of the general conception of the Swedish ethnic make-up whereas in France the term relates to a stage prior to becoming French and adopting the republican values connected with being a citizen. The general conception was that Sweden was a predominantly mono-ethnic society with little need for a minority policy similar to that found in say Canada. Similarly to Vasta's (2000) account of Australia's Anglo-dominance at the local and central levels of power, the political and legal institutions are still dominated by ethnically Swedish personnel. Seeing that Swedish national identity is officially constructed through Swedish culture and institutions, the dominant 'white Swedish' perception is perceived to have the power to articulate and construct the prevailing ethnic categories. Furthermore, this classification occurs as soon as the migrant enters the country, as the manager for the Department of Ethnic Relations points out:

> People are informed that they are immigrants as soon as they get here –
> that's an identity that they have never had before – and when they
> come here they are branded as 'immigrants' and their 'Turkish' or
> 'Iranian' identity is taken away from them and that's a very strange
> identity because there's nothing that unites 'immigrants' with each
> other ... their children haven't migrated but they are still immigrants and

that identity is becoming more confirmed, you get people who say 'I'm an immigrant' ... they have stopped saying 'I'm Chilean'. (Manager of Ethnic Relations A, 2001)

The previously dominating attitude towards Sweden's indigenous minorities follows a similar path. Despite the presence of linguistic minorities (Saami, Tornedal-Finns), these were not considered to be numerous enough to have a unique infrastructure and cultural tradition in order to qualify under the heading of an ethnic minority. That is, these groups were not deemed to differ sufficiently from the stipulated Swedish national identity. Second, the migrant who showed a willingness to adapt to the new society could not at the same time be granted the status of an ethnic minority, which echoes the French approach to integration. However, this was not entirely clear in the guidelines for integration set out in the 1980s. Even though the key sentence 'it is only the individual who can decide to what extent he is to adopt another cultural identity' (SOU 1984:58) suggests less emphasis on assimilation, it nevertheless points to the adoption of a specific type of national identity which seems to be mutually exclusive. In addition, the freedom of choice goal (in its 1980s understanding) prompted the numerically large Finnish communities to lobby for an ethnic minority status and the official definition of the term was re-drafted (Soininen, 1999).

Furthermore, the goal of freedom of choice has peculiar effects on the cultural identity that migrant organisations choose to emphasise. Although one can find specific ethnic labels in the name of the organisation (e.g. the Iranian-Swedish Association), the latest development shows that more and more associations are likely to include the 'culture' or 'sport' tag to their ethnic name. These types of associations are referred to as 'migrant' associations in public policy and not as 'ethnic'. Thus, the Swedish state here seems to send out somewhat contradictory signals. The state encourages organisation according to ethnicity but is at the same time not inclined to sponsor ethnic identities over the 'immigrant' status.

This becomes clearer if we consider the relationship migrant organisations have with the authorities on a local level. Here, migrant associations are primarily responsible to the municipal recreational board which administers, registers and monitors new and old associations. Several of the migrant associations are also members of a central organisation or national alliance, and these in turn are closely connected to the state bureaucracy, with the Swedish state being the ultimate source of finance. Local-level associations play a limited part in the relationship between the state institutions and the central organisations, and function primarily as distributors of informational material received from the two.

In addition, migrant organisations are strictly regulated in terms of what type of activities they are allowed to undertake in order to get funding. The formal regulations issued by the Malmö recreational board state that migrant associations are only liable for municipal funding if they perform activities directed towards children and youth as well as engage in activities that promote integration. As one of the NGO co-ordinators puts it, '[a]ctivities for adults should be financed by themselves' (2001). A majority of the association representatives who were interviewed stated that lack of money was a major obstacle for the future survival of their particular association. The way in which the prevailing regulations are structured thus effectively manages to steer the organisations into performing activities that are perceived as acceptable by the recreational board. As pointed out by Ålund and Schierup (1991), the original role of migrant associations as bridge-builders between immigrant communities and the new Swedish environment seems to have become less and less significant since the mid-1970s. Rather than contributing to ethnic pluralism in the public sphere, migrant culture has become, according to the authors, increasingly more subjected to a Swedish institutional ideology and practice where emphasis is primarily put on cultural differences. That is, despite the attempt to perceive 'new' cultural manifestations as internal differences of 'Swedishness', the way in which migrant organisations function and their supposed role in Swedish society does rather seem to widen the gap between 'Swedish' and 'non-Swedish'.

In the Netherlands, however, the view on 'Dutchness' is not as clear-cut as in the Swedish case. Dutch cultural pluralism has not, officially at least, provided its immigrant subjects with a 'racialised' straightjacket for minority identities. Rather than requiring resident, primarily colonial migrants to become racial minorities to achieve rights, the Dutch view integration as best accomplished through recognised and confident subcultures and as such make the preservation of minority cultures an essential part of incorporation (Koopmans and Statham, 2003). This view thus provides migrant organisations with different sets of opportunities compared to their Swedish equivalents in that minority identities are to a larger extent incorporated into the Dutch public sphere. Similarly, in Britain the understanding of 'Britishness' was for a long time very fluid, which on the one hand suggests a more flexible and inclusive definition of belonging (e.g. British-Asian) but on the other has recently been the subject of governmental debate as to what should be included in this definition given the British state's concern with societal fragmentation (BBC, 2001).

The proposed contradiction inherent in Swedish multiculturalism becomes more explicit when one looks at the way that migrant organisations function in practice. On the one hand, migrant associations are intended to be a forum through which difference could and should be expressed by means of public support according to the goals outlined in the 1975 proposition. On the other, the goal of partnership runs the risk of slipping over into monitoring and control when these associations are subjected to the rationalisation of the general organisational framework. Here, an emphasis is placed on acquaintance with Swedish norms and values and Swedish cultural life in a positive way. A number of associations expressed concern about their cultural activities being 'Swedicised', in that the meeting procedures and ways of conducting their associations were tightly controlled and organised from a top-down perspective. This situation seems to emphasise the distinctive stereotype of 'the spontaneous immigrant' versus 'the rule-driven Swede', where the former needs to be controlled and accustomed to ways of running an association.

This problem stems from the paradox created by the particular Swedish multicultural policies, in that although a main framework of 'cultural preservation' and co-existence was the aim, the actual outcome corresponds more to that of an assimilationist policy. Immigrants were, in other words, free to practice and engage in culture-specific activities, as long as they performed these in a 'Swedish' way. The effects of the top-down model and the abolition of associations formed on a political or religious basis have been that immigrant organisations are solely based on country or region of origin. The following quote highlights the tight control put on the associations by the local municipality.

> [A]t the beginning of last year we appointed an association advisor whose sole purpose is to visit associations, primarily to help them with something because it's not the easiest thing to run an association, to understand what we want from them, that they have to have democratic elections, annual meetings and annual financial reports, account for their activities because they get paid according to the number of activities that involve [at least] five youths and one leader and you can only have one activity per day and so forth so it's quite a lot of complicated rules which everyone might not understand. And they might be sloppy or they might not understand or they might deliberately try to misappropriate means … because [associations] have an educational and fostering dimension to them, they are a prerequisite for democracy. That you learn the rules of the game, to take other people's views into consideration, that you respect the will of the majority. (Director of Malmö Board of Recreation A, 2001)

The intention was to enable the 'old' culture to survive in, and according to the rules of, the 'new' environment. In combination with a number of compulsory courses such as association knowledge (föreningskunskap), the formalised way of conducting an association and the strict ruling hand of the responsible bodies, cultural survival and partnership on an equal basis appears to be somewhat difficult. This suggests that the formal institutions – laws regulating organisational life – effectively hinder migrant organisations from becoming influential political actors as well as constraining their scope of actions. The views from the Recreational Board, responsible for the allocation of funding, suggest that immigrants' 'unruly and spontaneous' behaviour presents a normative threat to Swedish society, with its impressive institutional mobilisation for the production of consensus, and needs to be controlled. Thus, if immigrants are permitted to play their role in Swedish society – as stipulated in Swedish immigration policies – then related norms must not only be explicit and predictable but also followed (Fred, 1983). The threat of the uncontrollable and spontaneous becomes increasingly problematic if the society is based around mutual understanding and conflict avoidance (Berntson, 1983). This could provide an opportunity and opening if a shift in the configuration of institutional power would come about, although much of Swedish political culture has been characterised by its consensual democratic appearance and its long-term stability. In turn, a problem is generated for migrant associations who wish to put ethnic-specific issues on the agenda, since they have to convince the potential adherents that collective action is a necessary and potentially successful means to an end and mobilise a consensus around these issues (Klandermans, 1988). Mobilising such public constituencies can prove to be very difficult since migrant associations face competition from other actors who might be more established and/or perceived as more legitimate, and who offer alternative definitions and solutions for the contentious issue. In addition, the structure of the public sphere is such that it favours access to elites over movements and attempts to change the dominating political discourse that itself defines a contentious issue. Hence, interpretations of almost any issue are likely to be biased towards the view of the established elite.

In contrast, the Netherlands displays a number of alternative channels for closer co-operation with the decision-making bodies. As Rath *et al.* (2001) show in their analysis of the Dutch Muslims' relationship with the local authorities, by treating and viewing Muslim organisations as social partners in the immigrant policy, the Rotterdam City Council managed to initiate a dialogue with these groups and in a sense attempted to defuse the potential threat of a Muslim party. The option taken here was to create a secretariat modelled after the PBR which would serve as a co-ordinating body for Muslim organisations, able to react appropriately to the policies of the municipal authorities in areas such as employment, family reunification, accommodation and discrimination. This type of action is remarkably different from the Swedish type of migrant management and places, at least Muslims, in a more favourable negotiation position compared to the migrant communities in Sweden. The British categorisation of 'Asian' provides a similar dilemma to that experienced in Sweden in that this category appears less likely to be the source of self-identification which has created problems for British Muslims to successfully put forward claims that relate to religion (Koopmans and Statham, 1999).

In Sweden, the corporatist way of handling conflict leaves non-recognised actors, without a substantial grass-root support, facing severe difficulty gaining entrance to the negotiating arena. Here, the more informal dimension of political opportunities and elite strategy is manifested through the social rules and procedures that have developed through the course of Swedish history in terms of how to manage and resolve conflict as well as how to deal with political challengers. If there is a lack of a particular cleavage structure, conflicts are handled through a mix of more inclusive and consensual political traditions. Here, the way in which conflicts have been previously approached and handled by the governing elite helps to shape the official reaction to future challengers. Analogous to what Rex and Drury (1994) discuss in the case of the politics of British race relations, Swedish measures to incorporate migrants into society have been dealt with according to the goals of equality, partnership and freedom of choice. These have been implemented with the same instruments and policies that affected the native population, that is, by the mechanisms of the welfare state. This means that opportunities for political participation have been more or less limited to involvement through the mainstream parties, which have been strongly defined according to class politics. This is particularly evident in the case of the Socialdemocrats who have successfully managed to neutralise and pacify strong currents of class conflict by incorporating the working class into the welfare state apparatus. Furthermore, resident, non-naturalised, migrants also enjoy the same type of citizenry benefits as the native population, which in turn could make it difficult to mobilise around issues which might not be as concrete as lack of certain types of rights. For instance, the right to naturalise in Germany was for many years impossible due to the *jus sanguini* principle, which therefore could serve as a mobilising incentive for long-term resident migrants.

The particular characteristics of Swedish civil society, in combination with a strong regulatory framework regarding what actions and activities are permitted for migrant organisations, seems to constrain their scope as channels for different types of claims-making. In the Netherlands, as we have seen, civil society is based around the concept of pillars and as such provides greater scope for migrant organisations to engage in and have access to the political arena. Despite similar types of regulations regarding migrant organisation activities, the Dutch situation does seem to have a more lenient attitude towards the role of migrant organisations in public life and thus seem to correspond to a higher degree to the proposed matrix (see Figure 5.1).

Institutional frameworks and norms of behaviour are thus key variables in order to understand the role and impact of migrant organisations. The next section will look more closely at how the prevailing structures affect migrant associations.

## Migrant organisations in Malmö and Rotterdam

The idea of collective organisations as a way of organising and structuring influence has been an integral part of Swedish public life since the mid-nineteenth century. The initial thought was that migrants should be given the possibility to organise in the same manner as any other mainstream organisation. As mentioned previously, migrant organisations very rarely function as pressure groups but instead seem to act as ethnic institutions or social clubs (Freyne-Lindgren, 2000). In this section, my focus will be on three ethnic associations in Malmö: the Turkish Association, the Iranian-Swedish Association and the Chilean 'Victor Jara' Association; and four in Rotterdam: Wimasanga 1st July (Creole-Surinamese); Stichting Krosbe (Surinamese umbrella organisation); Iranian-Kurdish Refugee Council (IRC) and HADD (Turkish). All organisations are relatively large in size and well established in terms of longevity and reputation, apart from the IRC which is slightly 'younger'. However, they do also display a high degree of internal difference in the way that they function and their relationship with local parties and authorities. The Rotterdam organisations seem to have a more explicit focus on the Rotterdam situation and are more politically orientated towards the 'new' country compared to the Malmö case. The Iranian and Chilean associations could be characterised as politicised in the sense that both associations are concerned with the political situation in their respective country of origin. This is particularly evident with the Chileans. The Chilean Association's name clearly indicates that the association was set up with a specific goal in mind – to continue fighting for the Chilean 'cause'. In contrast, the Iranian Association, with its more general orientation, is more concerned with preserving Iranian culture in the new society while at the same time stimulating contacts with the host society. However, some of the Iranian members stated that a number of informally scheduled meetings occurred in which the Iranian situation was discussed, but this was not part of the official agenda. The representatives from the Turkish Association, both current and former, show few signs of political interest, either towards Turkey or towards Sweden. This is an interesting feature since Turkish associations elsewhere in Europe display a rather opposite stance (Östergaard-Nielsen, 2000; Rath *et al.*, 2001). This association also appeared to have a more strained relationship with the local funding body – the Recreational Board – from which they had been suspended after fraud allegedly had been committed. Some of the former Turkish members stated that the association as such would most likely cease to exist within the near future due to this increasingly difficult relationship, which the following quote shows.

> One time we disagreed on something and she says 'In this country we do it like this' so I asked 'What do you mean in this country? We live in this country too. Do you mean that you're one type of person and I'm another? I'm from the outside and have to adjust to what you tell me? How long have you worked with this?' And she said that she had worked with it for three years; which is nothing, I have done it for thirty. So I told her that she couldn't teach me anything. Everything I did was done

correctly but she found all these petty things to complain about. It was the Recreational Board that screwed it up for the association, they withdrew all forms of economic aid to the association. (Male, mid-50s, 2001)

On the other hand, the Iranian and Chilean associations seemed to display a more harmonious relationship, although contacts were brief and limited to once a year, apart from a random check-up performed by an official from the Recreational Board. However, all three associations shared the trait of having few or no contacts with local political parties. All three stated that local politicians had been present on the association premises during previous elections but did not seem to be very interested in the associations post-election. The Iranian-Swedish association differs significantly from the two others in terms of organisational structure and scheduled activities, which makes the association quite similar to other ethnically Swedish associations. This association also maintained that it had more continuity in their contacts with the local parties, although this was primarily with parties on the left (Socialdemocrats, Left Party and the Greens). None of the associations had made extensive use of their organisation as a platform in order to raise questions relating to their particular group.

Well, it has happened ... we contacted the Socialdemocrats because they are in power, not just because I happen to be a Socialdemocrat ... but I mean it's the board that decides what we do. But we want to remain independent ... . If we did that then those issues should be very general and apply to all immigrants, not just Iranians. (Iranian-Swedish Association Representative, 2001)

This quote highlights, to some extent, the fear expressed by Ålund and Schierup (1991) that migrant associations eventually become 'Swedicised' in the way that they operate. Key phrases here are 'the board decides' and 'should be very general and apply to all immigrants'. What the interviewee describes is the democratic schooling and Swedish emphasis on equality that manages to block out any discourse of raising ethnic-specific claims. Furthermore, this particular relationship becomes more evident in the following quote in which the interviewee discusses the aim of another Iranian association.

The main purpose is to make life here possible for Iranians ... partly we try to educate the Iranians in the sort of Swedish way. We have had study courses about Sweden, the EU, the different 'folkrörelser'. We had some courses about why you shouldn't work in the informal market and we invited people from the unions. (Iranian male, late-20s, 2001)

However, compare this to the quote by a representative from the Turkish Association:

> [Y]ou also have people who come from Yugoslavia ... they're Turkish-Yugoslavs, you have Turkish-Bulgarians. All in all we are 5000–6000 so I mean we have that possibility, we can show the way but we don't pursue that kind of politics. The board doesn't have that type of politics. They said that before they only voted for the Socialdemocrats, but people have changed now [and] we don't have any contact at all. A lot here think that the party is the party of the labourers and that was why. That generation were only labourers. (Male, late-30s, 2001)

This quote suggests that the difficulty lies not so much in the institutional structure but rather in the difficulty of uniting Turks originating from different places. However, the interviewee stresses that the board as such does not want to pursue any ethnic-specific goals, which correspond to the democracy schooling objective of the organisations. A similar view came from a representative of the Chilean Association:

> Not as Chileans, but as immigrants yes. When we invited the parties to come and visit us we were of course interested in their views on immigrants and immigration, and we asked questions and made claims, like any other voter. But we don't always do it as an association because it's sensitive, it has to be made as a general claim from a group of immigrants that are active in the Swedish society, you know that are working, paying taxes, voting and so forth. (Male, mid-50s, 2001)

Again, the interviewee emphasises the equality aspect and does not seem to be very keen on advocating an ethnic-specific approach. In addition, the quote also highlights how national perceptions of citizenship and belonging ('immigrants') influence the interviewees self-definition. These quotes have tried to show how the organisational structure of Swedish society effectively manages to steer the migrant associations away from the fringes of ethnicity towards a more general mainstream. The three representatives stress that these types of issues are difficult to raise – for internal as well as external reasons – and favour either a more inactive stance, like the Turkish Association, or a more generally applicable approach like the Iranian and Chilean associations.

The examples quoted not only focus attention on the way in which migrant organisations are influenced by the dominating Swedish discourse but also point out the next difficulty – the lack of an ethnic cleavage. The presence of cleavage structures define the political space that is available to introduce new lines of conflict into a polity. These quotes support the assumption underpinning the political opportunity structure approach in that the national cleavage structure sets out to define the political space available for challengers to introduce new issues for debate into a polity, such as conflicts surrounding national identity, class, centre-periphery or materialist issues. If a polity lacks a substantial cleavage with regard to a certain issue, in this case ethnicity, then the space available for these types of claims remains minimal. As a result, the main vehicle for mobilisation – migrant associations – become less useful and mobilisation forces are directed elsewhere or diminish. One alternative is to use the association as a means of creating alliances with strategic political partners. This requires a precondition of the elite actors being divided and having conflicting opinions, thereby enabling the challengers to mobilise both established and potentially extra-parliamentary actors and thereby shift the balance of power in their favour. Issues such as immigration can be the source of internal division and open up space for migrant groups to exploit (of course this applies to xenophobic actors as well).

However, the creation of successful alliances is closely connected to the formal institutional or legal structures that are in place. These refer to the set of institutional actors in a polity and the legal arrangements which define their relationship and competencies and are characterised by the degree of centralisation of the political institutions, the type of electoral system and the separation of powers between executive, legislative and judiciary. Thus, the institutional dimension defines the available channels of access for challengers which can be relatively open or closed – a majority type of voting system is more closed than for instance a proportional representation system since the former provides less opportunities for non-mainstream actors to gain access. In the same vein, alliance formation is more likely and competition will be more fierce in a majority-type environment. Here, greater benefits for the alliance partners will be generated.

In the Swedish case, alliance formation has traditionally been done between migrant associations with leftist sympathies and the Sociademocrats, but increasingly more contact has been made with the Left Party. However, the close contact between these parties and the associations does not so much concern the local situation in Malmö but is more related to matters that occur on the international arena and more specifically under the banner of 'solidarity' and 'human rights'. In comparison, local parties and the migrant associations have few contacts as regards domestic issues or on issues with regard to ethnicity. A Left Party member describes this situation as problematic since,

> [I]n the Left Party, international solidarity has always been one of our strengths ... this has been easier for us than integration issues because questions of integration force you to take a stand on issues that might not be obvious in our party, it means that you have to discuss the issue of religious freedom. How free should it be? Religion is not a top priority within our party. (Left Party A, 2001)

Here, the interviewee highlights two problems that face migrant associations. First, that international issues seem to supersede local issues, and second, that issues relating to immigration and integration are both sensitive and difficult since it is not clear which cleavage they arise from. In addition, co-operation with specific ethnic groups or a limited number of associations comes into conflict with the deeper societal value of equality. Ethnicity thus has a limited space within Swedish political life since it becomes difficult to combine with equality unless it is framed more generally in order to be applicable to the more loosely defined group of 'immigrants'. The resistance to invoking the ethnic variable in political discourse is described as a major obstacle by a representative from the Iranian–Swedish association.

> They can't fit those things into their party manifestos, my proposition is that you should get ethnic associations to come together and form national organisations, regardless of what party you are in, it's difficult to raise these issues ... they have a lot of power, the old ones don't want to let the new people come in and the new ones that manage to get in continue in the same old paths ... there are structural constraints as well, the civil servants working within it have to interpret decisions in a certain way and then you have institutional problems like adjusting to these activities. (Male, early-30s, 2001)

In the Rotterdam case, as mentioned, the Wimasanga displays more signs of having another agenda apart from providing a social and cultural function. The name of the association (Wimasanga July 1st) indicates a commemoration of the emancipation from slavery and as such organises a number of activities raising awareness of the Dutch slavery history, as a representative from the association explains.

> We organise lectures, we invite people to talk about our story, not his-story but our story, about slavery. One guy gave a lecture about the different faces of Africa in the world. We do workshops, try to tell people about their past, to give them more power, try to raise their black consciousness. We try and tell them about the system. (Creole Male, late-40s, 2002)

Compare this quote to what the respective representatives from the Iranian and Turkish associations describe as their main priorities.

> We set up seminars and do activities for anti-racism and anti-discrimination and we talk about the situation in Iran and we are a forum for modern and radical people. During the Rushdie Affair we supported him because we thought that he should be free to express what he thought and we support all forms of pro-democratic movements, we thought that the Shah

regime was a dictatorship but the new regime is even worse. (Male, late-50s, 2001)

Integrating the Turks into the Dutch society is our main priority because that's not proceeding well at the moment, they have problems with their identity ... we try to give them an identity by organising lectures and conferences, telling them about their history, about democracy, human rights. We want to give them some tools to find their own identity so they can become confident and participate on an equal basis in this society. (Male, mid-40s, 2001)

The Rotterdam organisations differ from their Malmö counterparts with regard to their main objectives. Whereas the latter emphasise working according to a non-ethnicised principle of equality, the former seem to be more focused on improving or basing their work amongst their own ethnic group. The IRC shows signs of deviating from this and is also more similar to Swedish-Iranian organisations in that they have a more general focus (anti-racism/anti-discrimination) and are also very much engaged in the present Iranian situation. In contrast, the Turkish and Surinamese representatives express clearer views on working solely on behalf of their own communities. As elaborated earlier, this mode of action fits in with the opportunities available for this type of mobilisation within the Dutch context. However, even though the space for ethnic-specific claims-making seems to be wider compared to Sweden, the regulatory framework can in fact put a number of constraints on issues perceived as illicit. The Surinamese and Turkish respondents expressed concern about too-close involvement[42] and monitoring[43] by the Dutch authorities in terms of their activities and goings-on within the association premises. Therefore, despite the possibility of mobilising according to an ethnic cleavage, this opportunity seems to be directed away from the political arena and more towards advisory and consulting bodies. As in Sweden, the organisations interviewed stated that there was a minimal amount of contact between their organisation and the political parties, as well as with other ethnic organisations. The Wimsanga, for instance, stated that they in fact had no wish to co-operate with other ethnic organisations apart from black organisations since

[O]ur organisation started for Surinamese and we just try to connect the other Surinamese organisations with ours. We don't want to connect with the Turkish, Moroccan or Indian associations at the moment because they are already grouped as Muslims. (Creole male, late-40s, 2002)

The Turkish representative argued along similar lines when stating there was no direct point or need to engage with other organisations apart from the Turkish. The IRC, on the other hand, was more open to the idea of co-operation with other ethnic organisations but, mostly relating to the

Kurdish situation or internationally orientated issues such as refugee legislation.

As with the Malmö organisations, contacts with political parties seemed to be kept at a minimum and more related to informal contacts with ethnic councillors. However, as the Turkish representative suggests, having a Turkish councillor does not necessarily mean that they represent the Turkish community, 'if the political parties are taking the Turkish voters seriously, then they should listen to the needs of the Turkish people. The elected Turk should then be a link between them. But there is this paradox because they say they will do something for us and then they change their mind so there's no trust' (Turkish Male, mid-40s, 2001). However, the Surinamese respondent described this relationship in more positive terms but also characterised the situation as being on an informal basis and did not want to specify further the nature of the relationship.

The next section will discuss the relationship between migrant organisations and political parties from the latter's point of view.

## The relationship between migrant organisations and political parties in Malmö and Rotterdam

Swedish political life has managed to display a long-lasting and stable type of electoral environment, with few dramatic shifts or damaging conflicts, which has taken the appearance of a consensual democracy with limited competition and disagreement. The Netherlands, on the other hand, has been characterised by minority government including multi-party coalitions.

As pointed out previously, five parties have dominated the Swedish parliament since 1932, with a clear-cut left-to-right division, although two additional parties, the Greens and the Christian Democrats, have entered the arena in the last thirty years. The traditional parties have tended to represent different social classes, or more specifically different labour categories. The Dutch case has seen a multitude of parties which includes variants of the Swedish parties (PvDA-Socialdemocrats; VVD-Conservatives; CDA-Christian Democrats) as well as parties developed through break-aways from existing parties (D66), city-specific parties (Leefbaar Rotterdam) and numerous smaller, often one-issue based parties (Party for the Animals; Free Indonesian Party; Frisian National Party).

This political space has traditionally been evolving around class-based issues (Sweden) and class and religious issues (the Netherlands). In the former, this has over time juxtaposed the two dominant parties, the Socialdemocrats and the Conservatives, during which the different trade unions became key players, especially the blue-collar unions. The reason why the federation of labour organisations managed to exercise influence through and on the Socialdemocrat Party relates, on the one hand, to a general and all-inclusive claim of improving conditions for the labour class, and on the other, to the fact that it was recognised as a legitimate partner for co-operation. Similarly, trade unions in the Netherlands were part of the pillars and as such closely connected to the particular party representing the pillar. Challengers who are not part of this highly institutionalised and encompassing arrangement of policy negotiation thus find the system inaccessible and difficult to influence. Corporatist arrangements hinder certain types of new challengers, especially those not based on social class. In the Swedish Socialdemocratic Party, for instance, decisions have to be anchored in one of the party's many sub-branches such as the labour union or labour communes. The situation experienced by many immigrants is that they are not perceived to be representing any social class or organisation (Westin, 1998). In contrast, a Dutch Socialdemocratic representative considers the issue of ethnic claims-making to be a problem in terms of uncertain outcomes and diverting from main priorities of the parties and as such these initiatives have limited support within the party (Socialdemocrat F, 2002).

However, the Socialdemocrats have tried to establish links with the different immigrant organisations in order to gain their electoral support since a majority of the Swedish and Dutch immigrants have been part of the 'working class' and the voting pattern for immigrants corresponds to that of the native population; in that they tend to vote according to their social background, education and labour situation. A majority of the immigrant communities, especially the old labour migrants, work in unskilled or semi-skilled sectors, and many of the political refugees originating from right-wing regimes have therefore tended to vote in favour of the leftist-orientated parties, such as the Socialdemocrats or the Left Party (Widgren, 1982). In fact, it is somewhat surprising that there has not been more fierce competition for the migrant vote. A Swedish Socialdemocrat suggests that,

> [O]ver the last years the party has more or less taken the migrant groups for granted ... during the 60s and 70s, a lot of them were labourers and it was natural that the trade unions incorporated them and then Socialdemocracy came in, so they became Socialdemocrats. Then we got the political refugees during the 70s and 80s and there you also had groups who either went to the Socialdemocrats or the Left party, so it was quite natural that you got Latin Americans coming from dictatorship regimes who joined us and the same goes for Iranians. (Socialdemocrat A, 2001)

However, an explicit attempt was made by the Conservative Party in 1999 to challenge the left's dominance over the immigrants' votes (Friborg, 1999). A report put forward at the annual Conservative congress in June 1999 suggested that the growing entrepreneurship among many immigrants was hindered by the Socialdemocratic type of welfare state which created a situation of benefit dependence and social exclusion. The solution, according to the Conservatives, was to de-regulate and facilitate the immigrants' individual choice on the labour market. It was argued that this new deal would create 'a new solidarity' and 'a freedom of choice revolution' (Rojas, 1999). What is interesting here is the lack of an explicit ethnic orientation. The proposed policy does not suggest that migrants experience any form of difficulties that are different from those faced by the native population; references to discriminatory structures within the labour sector are kept to a minimum. Instead the authors opt for more traditional Conservative rhetoric in which the focus lies on the individual and the constraints put on him or her by a too-extensive state.

Similarly in the Dutch case, competition over 'the migrant vote' does not seem to be a main priority, which a number of the Dutch interviews[44] admitted to. However, the Green Party, much like their Swedish equivalents, considered the different migrant communities to be important sources not only of votes but also with regard to bringing in different experiences. A Green Party representative claimed that:

> [T]he Groen Links was the first party to realise that immigration to the Netherlands was permanent. Early on, we had immigrants in important positions in the party, we have attracted a lot of voters from the different ethnic groups because we had appointed people from these groups in different positions. Our policy is that everyone is welcome, the other parties are much more 'We are all the same and just be like us and you'll be fine' whereas we are saying that 'No, everyone's different' and we have to take that into account in local politics'. (Green Party A, 2001)

If ethnicity does not appear to be a 'legitimate' way to approach potential voters, religion and class seems to be more of a winning tactic, especially for the CDA and PvdA, and to a lesser extent the VVD and the D66. The VVD, for instance, have also tried to attract votes from the growing number of ethnic entrepreneurs, which echoes the attempts made by the Swedish Conservatives.

The absence of race or ethnicity in Swedish public discourse can be explained by the relative inexperience of dealing with cultural and religious difference which, in contrast, has had a longer tradition in the Netherlands. However, the outcomes are in both places very similar. Historically, Sweden has been largely homogenous in terms of ethnicity and religion and the change in the demographic composition did not occur until the late 1960s, and even then only on a relatively small scale. As Micheletti (1995) points out, the Swedish structure has been relatively open to non-governmentally sanctioned groups' demands if they can be successfully incorporated into the goal structures of the established, legitimised groups. This suggests that ideas and values are received more generously than new political actors.

Nevertheless, non-class and non-labour market collective action have faced difficulties when attempting to gain public attention. This is the consequence of both a highly interventionist corporatist state as well as a historically stable Socialdemocratic hegemony.

In the Netherlands, migrant groups have in a similar fashion been incorporated into the state apparatus through a variety of policies and strategies. The end results are various consultative bodies that on the one hand create a favourable position in terms of access to decision-making procedures and a certain degree of influence. However, this type of arrangement also shows certain limitations in that class and religious cleavages supersede ethnicity, although not to the same extent as in Sweden, and thus migrant groups end up playing a limited role in political life.

The strong ties that these organisations and intermediary bodies have with the state does in turn create a limited space for manoeuvre and consequently display a similar dilemma in practice to that found in the Australian experience of multiculturalism. Here, the ruling authorities attempt to co-opt minority and migrant movements and their leadership into the state apparatus (Castles and Davidson, 2000). The implementation of multicultural policies has led to the inclusion of many community activists in government bureaucracies and consultative processes. Seeing that minority organisations are dependent on governmental blessing in terms of grants to provide services for their communities, in the long run this could mean an over-dependence on official goodwill rather than a means by which to improve the community's position. Prominent community activists may be offered positions within the welfare bureaucracy which could give them the opportunity to represent the interests of their community, although this will have to be made within the rules and structures set from above. Therefore, minority groups must decide to what extent this 'within'-organisation strategy will achieve their goals rather than working outside the normal political structures. To opt for the former will benefit minorities only if their claims at least to some extent correspond with host-society imperatives. This begs the question that migrant mobilisation is most likely to succeed if such mobilisation is made when there is a high level of independence amongst the civil society actors (Dryzek, 1996). However, given the corporatist structure of migrant management in the two case-studies, ethnic lobby groups could come to play an important role through their representation on governmental consultative bodies, although this is highly dependent on at what stage of the policy-making process these bodies are able to exercise influence. These organisations have not used this channel to introduce their demands as much as one might have expected. On the whole, these organisations have not functioned primarily as mouthpieces for the immigrants' social, political or cultural interests but have rather been preoccupied with sports and traditional cultural activities. Since voting rights for denizens and certain linguistic rights have already been implemented, specific immigrant interests have been subordinated (Koopmans and Statham, 2003; Soininen, 1999). The opportunity available for the individual migrant or organisation is then to affiliate with a certain party or an interest group. The difficulty with this approach is that the corporatist model of representation is primarily based around class and religious interest that hinders, for instance, labour unions from recognising interests stemming from other causes.[45] This situation makes it problematic for voluntary organisations to gain access to the political arena as well as attempting to exercise influence.

> They make associations and councils of everything. And that's also a way of neutralising them, 'Well, alright you can have an association or we'll give you a representative', but not on the actual issue which concerns them. They are so concerned with the process of political decision-making ... and they can handle that very well, but it does also create a structure which can be very difficult to gain entrance to. (Christian Democrat C, 2001)

Here, the interviewee discusses the difficulties involved for both the migrant organisations as well as the umbrella organisations when it comes to influencing the political process due to the long history of Socialdemocratic dominance. The Socialdemocratic possession of power for more than forty years meant that the party has had considerable time and opportunity to implement and ground their particular *modus operandi* into Swedish politics. As pointed out by Micheletti (1995), one of the main reasons for the success of Swedish Socialdemocracy has been its ability to prevent and foresee potentially damaging ideological conflict by introducing division of power and to share this with other political actors. This way of handling conflict made way for a particular political style in which certain norms developed which tended to emphasise consensus and thorough pre-decision discussion of events and proposals, thereby reaching agreement and reflection beforehand (Ruin, 1981).

Although highly effective as regards preventing political crises and hastily considered decisions, the basis for Swedish cross-class co-operation implies a POS that only gives certain types of collective organisations a share of the political power. Similarly, the Dutch multi-party coalition experience has traditionally been a compromise between labour and religions' interest, thus providing preferential treatment to a certain and limited type of actor.

Despite being categorised as relatively open (Kitschelt, 1986), the corporatist state often limits the number of relevant interest groups, in which there is basically one single group for each interest sector, such as labour, employers or farmers. To gain entry to the political arena is constrained by the state through requirements (such as those mentioned earlier) and requirement for the organisation to be 'representative' of its members, which in turn forces the association to accumulate a large number of members.

The structure is thus selective and open primarily to labour market organisations since they are given a central role, while other, non-class-based organisations are kept at a distance. The discriminatory structure of Swedish policy-making, in other words, effectively filters out other competing actors who in turn are not able to place issues on the political agenda either through informal discussions or in negotiation with public agencies and parliamentary advisory bodies. In the Dutch case, this filtering mechanism does not seem to be as extensive as in Sweden; many of the councillors interviewed stated that their parties as well as the local council had been approached by ethnic communities and also that minority claims stand a possibility of being brought onto the political agenda, albeit subject to certain preconditions.[46] In contrast to the Dutch case, the ethnic issue seemed to have been covered and thus made a non-issue by the new directive for integration, the so-called Action Plan to promote integration in Malmö, taken in 1999.

This is not to say that attempts can not be made – all types of organisations can use the same general methods of influence – but the selectively open character of Swedish government is underscored by the importance corporatist organisations have been given through confidential contacts with government. This also helps to explain why the process of lobbying has never been able to establish itself as a political tool for these important organisations and why a space available for ethnic-specific claims has not been able to get established since it neither corresponds to class nor fits in within the overall framework – equality for leftist-orientated parties and individual freedom for conservatives. The following quotes highlight this situation:

[I]t depends if you adopt the strategy to follow temporary opinions or if you have a more long-term plan … it depends on what claims are made, if they are according to what the party stands for and believes in. (Socialdemocrat A, 2001)

[W]e just try to approach people in general … we found that there were similar types of deficits in both the Swedish group and the immigrant group and so we wanted to find out how to come to terms with these problems. (Socialdemocrat C, 2001)

I guess you could do that but it presupposes that it doesn't go against the basic ideological principles of the party … you can't collide with the values of the party because then it's not a party anymore but more of a lobby group. I wouldn't see that as a problem as long as it doesn't clash with the values of the party. (Liberal Democrat A, 2001)

We never deviate from our ideology or compromise our basic assumptions in order to adjust and buy votes from a specific group. (Conservative Party B, 2001)

## Conclusion

This chapter has discussed the role of voluntary associations within a general civil society framework, how migrant associations function within the French, German, Dutch, Swedish and British contexts and more specifically the relationship between migrant organisations and political parties on a local level in Malmö and Rotterdam. The civil society typology suggests that voluntary organisations can serve as a counterweight to the state and/or as a means to empower excluded groups in society. Migrant associations can thus attempt to use this platform as a way to either bring attention to issues which concern their particular ethnic group or nationality or attempt to bring about change in the political environment. However, depending on societal settings and structural conditions, migrant associations can potentially face a number of difficulties when attempting to raise such issues. This problematic situation has been explored through analysing the relationship that migrant organisations have with the political parties on a local level in the cities of Malmö and Rotterdam. First, the degree of autonomy, in terms of action and financing enjoyed by associations, vis-à-vis the state seems to play an important role. If the state is able to exercise influence on the associations with regard to activities and funding, this will tend to steer migrant associations towards a particular field which runs in accordance with the host-society's goals.

Second, the appearance of the state also influences the type of POS that are available. In the Swedish and Dutch case, displaying strong corporatist elements, the prevailing structures favour certain types of actors and certain types of cleavage over others. Issues related to ethnicity lack a natural mobilising ground, especially in the Swedish political environment, but seem to have more potential in the Dutch case; whereas issues concerning class (Sweden and the Netherlands) and religion (the Netherlands) have a higher potential to become politically relevant and thus enable mobilisation. As shown by the interview material, this situation is recognised both by association representatives as well as by the party candidates. The statements also show the influence of the prevailing structural conditions on the actors' choices and to what extent they are prepared to pursue questions and issues that seem to be difficult to either resolve or contest in the political arena.

# 6
# Summary and Conclusions

## Introduction

This book has explored factors that influence political participation amongst migrant communities. The research has adopted two comparative perspectives and first, examined how institutions provide opportunities and constraints for migrant actors in five Western European countries and, second to what extent three migrant groups on a city level in Malmö, Sweden and Rotterdam, the Netherlands have engaged in political life. Theoretically, the explanatory framework has involved the use of the historical institutionalist approach and applied these ideas to the French, German, Dutch, Swedish and British contexts. Relevant institutions have been introduced and discussed alongside the outcomes in the form of POS which in turn serve as constraints or facilitators for certain types of action.

The main findings suggest two things. First, prevailing institutions do matter and play a crucial role in determining the access, potential and success of organised migrant interests to function as influential actors in the political arena. In addition, the specific POS that these institutions give rise to are important explanatory tools in order to understand how new challengers act, what strategies they adopt and why certain issues, in this case relating to ethnicity, face difficulties gaining political support. Furthermore, by grounding the concept of POS within neo-institutional theory this research contributes to a less developed aspect in the field and serves as a blueprint for future research utilising other countries' case-studies.

Second, there is a connection, albeit a statistically weak one, between higher levels of host-society identification and higher levels of political participation. The studied groups who displayed a stronger attachment to the host society were also more likely to engage in various types of political participatory acts. This finding suggests that there is a need to explore this connection further, utilising a larger scale survey, in order to more firmly establish the explanatory potential of this variable.

Thematically, the research has been structured around three areas where institutions have had an impact:

1. Strategies adopted by organised migrant interests as a consequence of context-specific POS.
2. Effects of institutions on identity and identification with the host society and the potential relevance of these concepts as an explanatory factor for variance in political participation.
3. Effects of institutions on the relationship between migrant organisations and political parties within a civil society environment.

This chapter will briefly summarise the main outline of the book, encompassing the principal research question, the case-studies, the theoretical framework adopted and what the empirical findings suggest. In addition, the theoretical positions set out in Chapters 3, 4 and 5 will be examined in conjunction with the empirical data gathered during the fieldwork. In synthesis, the aims of this chapter are threefold.

First, with reference to Chapter 3, to reflect upon the relevance and utility of the neo-institutional historical approach and how it has been operationalised through the adoption of Tarrow's (1994) analytical tool of POS in the five cases. This aim is exemplified with a discussion of how migrants have responded to the institutional environment and how differences in the political structure have generated different types of responses.

Second, with reference to Chapter 4, the focus on institutions and their effects on political behaviour have been explored in relation to how these structures influence levels of host-society identification. These levels have then been used in conjunction with intensity and likelihood of participation as well as interest in political life. The aim here, in other words, has been to test the explanatory value of identification in relation to variance in levels of political participation.

Third, Chapter 5 covered the interaction between migrant organisations and political parties. The focal point here has been the role and impact that these organisations have had within a civil society context and how prevailing structures and institutions provide opportunities and constraints for these actors to pursue issues related to ethnicity. The findings suggest that the institutional set-up matters to a high degree for the political participation of migrants and for the extent to which they are able to utilise the channels provided to them by the host societies. This seems especially true for societies characterised by corporatist negotiation and strong state involvement.

## Explaining political participation amongst migrants

The starting point of this book has been – what factors influence relative levels of political participation amongst migrant groups? In other words, if we want to explain why a certain group or groups differ in relation to each other in terms of their degree of participation, what indicators can be used?

This research has challenged the socio-economic paradigm invoked by previous studies (Bäck and Soininen, 1993; Bennulf and Hedberg, 1999; Bobo and Gilliam, 1990; Fennema and Tillie, 1999; Olsen, 1970; Petersson *et al.*, 1989; Verba and Nie, 1972) and introduced the concept of identification (Ahmadi Lewin, 2001; Castles and Davidson, 2000; Friedman, 1994; Modood, 2000; Nesdale and Mak, 2000; Tajfel, 1978) as a complement to relying on socio-economic variables.

The rationale behind using identification as an additional tool refers to what this research considers to be a 'missing link' between, on the one hand, literature on migration and identity, and on the other, migration and political participation. As I will discuss more thoroughly in a later section, this area has by and large not received much attention by scholars and this book thus attempts to fill this gap.

Identity and identification are, however, difficult concepts to operationalise, which has generated problems for the research in terms of how to create reliable ways of measuring these variables. In order to potentially overcome these pitfalls, the research opted for a number of different methods in order to fully grasp and cover these areas in a satisfactory way, as well as to create a concrete tool of measurement. This enabled the research to locate total levels of identification given time of residence, exposure to integration policies and interaction with members of the majority population.

This was approached in two ways. First, a questionnaire was created which, on the one hand, covered the socio-economic background of the respondents and on the other, asked a series of questions relating to the more 'psychological' relationship between the respondent and the new society. A total of seven questions were posed in which four related to internal identification (subjective) and three to external identification (objective). The framing of the questions ranged from general and more abstract statements (I feel part of a Swedish/Dutch community) to more concrete and specific (I am Swedish/Dutch). An average for the separate scores was then calculated and summed to get a total level of identification. This overall average was then used in comparison with the respondents' stated satisfaction with performance of local politicians, likelihood and intensity of participating and political interest.

As pointed out above, identity and identification are problematic concepts, especially in terms of finding satisfactory ways of measurement.

Therefore, the questions asked were the result of a compromise developed through a number of draft questionnaires.

Since the questionnaire distribution was limited to on-location handouts and relied heavily on the help of intermediaries, the total return was not large enough to enable more serious statistical analysis. Therefore, this part of the research has been constrained to a correlation analysis between total levels of identification and the various aspects of political participation. The reader should in other words view these figures with healthy scepticism since the data has been used primarily for indicative purposes to highlight certain relationships.

As a complementary methodology, and in order to compensate for the rather small size of the survey data, a series of in-depth, semi-structured interviews were conducted with respondents from political parties, policy practitioners and migrant organisations. The choice of interview subjects served a number of purposes. First, in terms of the elite interviews, these were intended to unravel how different types of institutions and norms of behaviour influence levels of identification as well as how the institutions facilitate and constrain certain types of political issues. Second, in terms of the non-elite interviews, these aimed at understanding how the respondent perceives him/herself in relation to the host society's national identity as well as describing the interaction that did or did not exist with members of the majority population. Here, concepts of identity and identification were explored more fully and it was also made clear that there exists an inherent contradiction between different types of identities, especially when these are challenged or reflected upon. These interviews also aimed at showing how the dominant discourse of identity within the host society, integration policies, and a particular understanding of belonging, affected the respondent's view of him/herself.

In addition, the in-depth interviews also covered areas that were of importance for Chapters 3 and 5. In the former, the Malmö interviewees were asked to give an account of their party's interaction or non-interaction with the Rainbow Party during the 1998 election. In addition, they were asked to evaluate to what extent an ethnic cleavage exists in the Swedish context and the reasons for certain cleavages dominating the political agenda over others. In Rotterdam, the interviewees were asked to speculate (seeing that a similar party did not exist) on the same issues and what type of impact such a party would have. In fact, this proved to generate insignificant data since the concept was primarily of a hypothetical nature. However, as described in more detail in a subsequent section, the role and impact of institutions played an important part for the success of new challengers to mobilise around ethnicity.

In Chapter 5, the aim was to establish the relationship between political parties and migrant organisations. This relationship was framed around a discussion and conceptualisation of civil society. The end result was an ideal-type matrix which was then compared to, primarily, the Swedish and Dutch understanding of civil society. Using this matrix, the aim was to explore the role and impact that migrant organisations have had within particular contexts. The interviewees were asked to describe what type of relationship and interaction existed between political parties and migrant organisations, covering both actors' point of view. The overall picture that materialised through these conversations was the significance of the corporatist style of arrangements prevailing in Sweden and the Netherlands. This situation privileges certain types of recognised interests and also centres on specific cleavages (class in Sweden; class and religion in the Netherlands). This hinders new challengers who wish to mobilise around other type of cleavages, such as those based on migrant status or ethnicity, from gaining access to the political arena.

## Strategies adopted by migrants as a response to the institutional environment

Chapter 3 comprised two parts. First, a literature review of theories and ideas behind the neo-institutionalist school of thought was elaborated upon and its various sub-branches were discussed. The key purpose of this chapter was to explore the role and importance of institutions in terms of how they shape and structure the political environment. My key argument in this chapter suggests that institutions play a very important role. The particularities of the context-specific institutional make-up, their impact on the options, actions and strategies of political actors and how they create modes of conduct and dominating discourses, are key factors that need to be taken into consideration if we want to understand and explain how political parties and migrant organisations react to ethnicity as a potential source for mobilisation.

Furthermore, the chapter argued that formal institutions serve as either constraints or facilitators for specific types of policies and priorities and as such manage to filter out certain questions and issues in favour of others. Having discussed and contrasted the various sub-disciplines of neo-institutionalist theory, the research subsequently argued in favour of a historical-institutionalist approach. Here, the emphasis lies on the role of institutional choices made early on for the development of political systems and policy areas (Peters, 1999). In other words, the initial structural and normative base will have persistent effects on future public choices. As shown in this chapter, institutions will in this understanding determine the number of legitimate actors, the sequence of action and the amount of information available for the actors regarding their intentions and agenda. This institutional organisation of a polity becomes the main factor for the way in which collective behaviour is structured.

This generates distinctive outcomes in which the institutional arrangements determine the opportunities available as well as the level of acting risk (Hall and Taylor, 1996). In addition, the historical development and emergence of prevailing institutions will also point to whether competition will take place in an environment which is either more plural or more corporatist in character.

The chapter then set out to explore the particularities of the Swedish and Dutch political structure, paying closer attention to the reasons behind the development and introduction of certain types of institutions and societal structures. As we saw, both countries display a number of corporatist traits such as interest representation through units that are organised into a limited number of singular, compulsory, non-competitive, hierarchically ordered and functionally differentiated categories. Another key feature is that these interests are not only recognised or licensed but are also sometimes created by the state. In turn, these interests are granted a deliberate monopoly on representation within their particular domain, where the trade-off is state influence with regard to the control of leader selection and articulation of demands and supports (Schmitter, 1979). We also found similar institutional constraints in the additional case countries. In France, prevailing understandings of citizenship excludes ethnic interests from the public arena in combination with a poorly developed civil society. However, due to the particular POS present in French society, this has created specific types of reactions in response to these settings in terms of mobilisation around issues of religion (primarily Islamic identities). Similarly, in Germany, the exclusive nature of German citizenship has also prompted participation from migrant groups through alternative channels for increased rights, significant variance in the degrees of opportunities present in more liberal states as well as most claims being directed at the country of origin. The British case provides both differences and similarities. First, the lack of an ethnic cleavage on a national level has been explained with reference to the dominating cleavage structure of class and the north–south divide as well as the appearance of the political institutions which favours well-established class-based parties with significant local support. However, these political institutions work in favour of organised migrant interests on a local level given the high concentration of certain ethnic groups in parts of the United Kingdom.

The institutional set-up is thus an important factor for the understanding of why certain societies tend to lean more towards a pluralistic or a corporatist arrangement of interest access. This arrangement gives certain groups substantial opportunities to exercise influence on decision-makers while at the same time limiting the number of interest groups through the process of selective dispersal of power. In addition, as I as made clear in Chapter 3, these licensed groups also tend to be based or mobilised around class

(Sweden, France and Britain) or class and religion (the Netherlands, Germany).

In combination with an integration policy that emphasises equality, Swedish discourses of ethnicity have been effectively steered away from the public sphere towards the realms of more 'private' associational life. Since ethnic-specific issues or claims are perceived to clash with the overarching goal of equality, migrants' claims must be framed in such a way that make them compatible with political mobilisation around the class cleavage.

In contrast, the Dutch case displays a polity shaped by the early twentieth century pillarisation process which managed to accommodate potential ideological conflict by assigning separate spheres for each pillar, and negotiation on an elite level. The integration of migrants was conducted within this structure which created a number of ethnic minority categories with a variety of consultation and intermediary bodies attached to them. This institutional set-up was meant to channel demands made by these recognised groups into the decision-making process.

In countries such as France and the United Kingdom where migrants are integrated as individuals, efforts have been made to incorporate these groups through facilitating labour market participation and enforcing anti-discrimination legislation (United Kingdom) and through access to general welfare institutions and inclusive but assimilationist citizenship policies (France). Consequently, one finds ethnic mobilisation around issues of discrimination in the former through formal channels whereas in the latter migrant mobilisation tends to be framed around recognition for their collective identity. In Germany, on the other hand, mobilisation is significantly less likely to relate to the situation in the host society, thus reflecting their lack of full citizenship rights and the symbolic exclusion of migrants as 'foreigners' from the political community.

Having established the particular institutional framework for the five countries, the chapter then set out to explore how collectives of migrants have responded to the POS that the institutional surroundings gave rise to. This was done by invoking the example of the Rainbow Party in Malmö but whose counterpart was not present in the Netherlands or in any of the other countries. The chapter further suggested that the Rainbow Party would be better understood as a strategy adopted by a social movement rather than as a traditional party. The reasons for this particular view could be found in the party's many similarities with a social movement. In order to explore in more detail the reasons and conditions as to why a party with an explicit ethnic agenda emerged in Sweden, a more thorough discussion was made in relation to the prevailing POS. The Swedish context seemed to offer more favourable conditions for this type of mobilisation than the Dutch, although structural arrangements and dominating cleavage lines influence the type of success this type of option has in the long run.

Chapter 3 demonstrated two effects of institutions and subsequent responses. First, it showed how the historical development of particular institutions shapes the political environment and provides certain structural settings in which competition takes place. With regard to the case-studies, I argued that successful influence is dependent on being able to comply with the prevailing cleavage lines and gaining the recognition of being a 'legitimate' partner in this process. In addition, the institutional settings also give rise to certain windows of opportunity which can be exploited by non-conventional actors. Second, these effects were exemplified with reference to an ethnic social movement and the lack of success was explained by the dominance of certain types of cleavages over others.

I summarise the key findings of this part of my analysis under the following list of points:

1. Depending on what type of institutions are in place, societies will lean more towards a pluralistic or corporatist type of system, both of which favour certain types of actors and issues over others.

My analysis shows that, as Consensus-type democracies, in combination with high levels of state involvement, Sweden and the Netherlands share a number of corporatist features. They display a system of interest representation with a limited number of recognised or licensed groups, which are granted representational monopoly within their respective categories. Groups which are not part of this selective system encounter a number of thresholds in gaining access to the political sphere, unless they frame their claims in a way that matches those of the recognised groups. This is particularly problematic for migrant actors in Sweden, but less so in the Netherlands, since raising questions relating to ethnicity clashes with the overarching notion of equality. Furthermore, ethnicity is not as compatible with this notion as the class paradigm.

2. Development and presence of institutions, and the norms created over time through these structures, set the parameters for how conflict is managed.

I pointed out that the long-term Socialdemocratic dominance in Sweden has created a particular type of conflict resolution characterised by consensual agreements and close co-operation with recognised interests. The main source of conflict has revolved around class-based issues which puts constraints on other types of interests, such as ethnicity, from becoming issues on the political agenda. Non-recognised interests are steered towards the private sphere of society.

On the other hand, the Dutch pillar legacy and negotiations on an elite level have led to a situation of political accommodation. Through these mechanisms, potential conflicts around the two major cleavages – class and religion – have by and large been absent from national-level politics. By recognising certain migrant groups as 'ethnic minorities', and as such being part of the pillar system, claims relating to ethnicity are neutralised due to the inclusive nature of the minorities' position.

3. Context-specific institutions create POS that determine the strategy adopted by social movements.

My empirical data support the theoretical assumption that migrant organisations rarely function as key actors in the public sphere. This is recognised by both political parties and migrant organisations as shown by the interview material. Institutional settings in Sweden facilitate party formation as a strategy for migrant interests but are most likely to be short-lived if they do not conform with dominating norms and cleavage lines (see also Odmalm and Lees, 2005).

Alternative channels for migrants' participation in the Dutch case, through advisory and consultative bodies alongside the special status enjoyed by ethnic minorities, facilitates access to decision-makers and thus limits the need for party formation by migrant interests.

## Institutional influences on identification

Chapter 4 covered the key research area of identity and identification. I argue that these concepts need to be taken into account in addition to socio-economic factors in order to more fully understand variance in levels of political participation amongst migrants. This line of thought originated from what has been identified as an overlooked aspect in the literature. In order to address the current views within these fields, Chapter 4 set out to cover existing debates by means of a thorough literature review.

The body of literature on identity and migration has been mainly concerned with establishing the nature of identity, how specific types of identity emerge and the importance for receiving states to acknowledge and give recognition to these identities, especially in a majority–minority situation (Kymlicka, 1995; Mouffe, 1995; Rath *et al.*, 2001; Taylor, 1994). According to this literature, and which I am in full agreement with, identity is considered to be of a fluid and changing nature, depending on time and space and the interaction with other members of society. Identity in this sense only becomes relevant when challenged either by other collective identities and/or the state.

However, the main area of concern is of a normative nature: that is, why states should give recognition to minority identities, and the different ways of achieving this. Less attention has been paid to the interaction and co-existence between different types of sub-collective identities and the overarching national identity of the receiving state. In addition, there seems to be an underlying assumption that different types of identities are mutually exclusive, which this research has challenged. In contrast to the more vertical understanding of identity, this research has opted for a more horizontal understanding of identity. Accordingly, movement between identities can be either facilitated or constrained according to types of responses and prevailing understandings of inclusion that the receiving state has put in effect. In other words, the way in which state policy, primarily in the area of integration, is constructed will have an impact on what type of identity expressions are considered to be legitimate or accepted.

This argument leads into the key feature – identification – which in turn is closely linked to notions of citizenship. If the receiving state opts for a wide, inclusive definition of citizenship in which sub-collective identities are considered as natural elements of the national identity, then the process of identification would, theoretically, be facilitated. And the two national case-studies display a number of traits that would indeed facilitate this process. Citizenship regulations are liberal and based on residence rather than descent. The state in both countries actively supports the maintenance of 'old' identities through a number of mechanisms. Therefore, my research set out to establish the extent to which the target migrant groups were able to relate to their 'old' identity, and how compatible it is, with the 'new' identity of the host society. That is, to what extent they identified themselves as being part of the receiving state's national identity.

The literature on political participation and migration has, likewise, not explored the concept of identification to a great extent (see Bäck and Soininen, 1993; Bennulf and Hedberg, 1999; Bobo and Gilliam, 1990; Fennema and Tillie, 1999; Olsen, 1970; Petersson *et al.*, 1989; Verba and Nie, 1972). Instead, these studies have opted for a more socio-economically orientated analysis in which a 'failure' to integrate politically, economically and socially has been the main explanatory reason for relatively lesser involvement in political life. Given that identity and identity preservation has been perceived as being a crucial element in terms of the relationship between migrants and the receiving state, it is somewhat surprising that identity and identification have not been studied in relation to political activity. Therefore, Chapter 4 argued that, in addition to the socio-economic variables, one needs to complement these indicators with a more 'psychological' understanding of belonging. The purpose, in other words, was to bridge the gap between the two types of literature and to analyse to what extent host-society identification has an impact on political participation. In order to establish levels of identification, two types of research methods were used.

First, a questionnaire survey was constructed. This survey encompassed both original questions as well as questions replicated from a previous study (Fennema and Tillie, 1999). These aimed to establish comparable data framing responses according to a Likert scale. The findings suggest rather similar levels of total identification amongst the migrant groups. In addition, the ratio between internal and external identification in relation to the total level of identification was virtually identical, with a 60 (internal)/40 (external) division for all groups apart from the Chilean sample (50/50).

However, there does seem to be a certain connection between levels of identification and the various forms of political participation, as well as a fairly consistent rank order between the groups.

Second, in order to get a fuller account of the migrant groups' relationship and attachment to the new society, a series of in-depth interviews were conducted. This was seen as highly necessary since it was anticipated that the low questionnaire return could be a potential problem. The research thus tried to safeguard the deficit of quantitative data by triangulating the survey material with more detailed interview material.

The interviews brought out the complexity of identity and processes of identification, that were difficult to establish through the survey material. The respondents' statements showed how different types of identities fluctuate and overlap in addition to being highly dependent on context. However, more importantly, the interview material shows how prevailing structures and dominating discourses of what constitutes national identity influence the extent to which new types of identities are able to fit in and relate to this overarching structure.

As pointed out by the quotes, the Malmö interviewees did by large adopt the existing dichotomising rhetoric of 'Swedish'/'immigrant', which has been a key discourse in Swedish integration policy. They rarely referred to nationality or ethnicity, instead choosing the more general and 'equality-compatible' category of 'immigrant'. In contrast, the Rotterdam interviewees were more inclined to refer to an ethnic group or nationality, which corresponds to the prevailing space available in the Netherlands for this type of identity expression.

The findings suggest two things. First, that identification is important when migrants choose whether to participate or not in the new environment. Responding groups that displayed a stronger sense of compatibility with the national identity of the receiving society were also more likely to be interested and concerned about political issues. The research conducted here points to the need to complement socio-economic migrant surveys with questions related to host-society identification in order to achieve a more encompassing picture regarding the reasons for engaging in political activities. Second, the process of conducting this research also points to the problematic task of operationalising such a highly abstract concept as identity and identification.

Hence my key findings are:

1. A socio-economic analysis of migrants' political behaviour needs to be complemented with an understanding of the influence that host-society identification has on political participation.

Analyses that focus mainly on socio-economic traits may tend to overestimate the importance of these features. My research has highlighted that the migrant groups studied did not differ significantly in socio-economic terms but showed differences in their levels of political participation. Therefore one needs to supplement these previous interpretative efforts with another dimension – identification with the host society – in order to grasp the full complexity of why individuals choose to engage in political life, or not.

These conclusions are not fully supported by the quantitative material but rather point out an interesting, although weak, relationship. In the qualitative material, this connection is made more explicit with several examples from respondents claiming that lower levels of identification are the reasons for not participating politically.

2.  In order to determine why levels of identification differ, one has to take into account the way in which prevailing institutions determine the space available and what type of channels are available for identity expression.

Both countries have extensive institutional arrangements – in terms of citizenship legislation and integration policies – which facilitate expression of difference. However, this expression is in the Swedish case steered towards the private associational sphere. In addition, public discourse favours the more equality-compatible term of 'immigrant' over nationality or ethnicity, which in turn affects levels of host-society identification. In the Dutch case, similar institutional arrangements exist but differ in that identification is facilitated through a more inclusive public discourse. This involves official recognition of 'ethnic minority' categories that are said to be compatible with an overarching Dutch national identity.

3. Measuring levels of identification needs to involve several research methods in order to grasp the complexity of the concept.

As pointed out, identification is a difficult concept to measure given its highly subjective nature. The questionnaire was constructed in such a way as to cover both general and more specific aspects of the term, but my research has also triangulated these findings with a number of in-depth interviews. In combination, these approaches provide my research with data firmly suggesting a link between political participation and identification.

## Institutional effects on the relationship between organisations and political parties

The final theme of the book – the subject of Chapter 5 – concerned migrant associations in civil society and their relationship with local political parties. More specifically, this chapter aimed to determine the role and impact of migrant voluntary organisations within a civil society framework and to what extent these have been used as channels for ethnic claims-making. Again, the purpose was to establish how institutional arrangements impact on the opportunities available for migrant organisations to raise such issues and as such, how they can either facilitate or constrain this type of action.

The starting point for this chapter was to contextualise the relationship between organisations and political parties by, first, invoking a general civil society framework and second, comparing this framework with the Swedish and Dutch way of arranging voluntary life. This was executed by a discussion emanating from existing literature on civil society. The chapter covered ideas and rationales behind civil society and its various interpretations (liberal versus communitarian understandings). This literature review served as the basis for the creation of an ideal-type conceptualisation of organisations in civil society. The matrix suggested four characteristic features that distinguish these types of organisations from others (voluntary-high, autonomous-high, professional-low and contacts-high). In addition, such organisations can have two different purposes, either individually or collectively orientated. My civil society matrix pointed out that voluntary organisations might also serve as a counterweight to the state and/or as a means to empower excluded groups in society. This situation provides migrant associations with opportunities and particular platforms that can be used to bring attention to issues concerning their ethnic group or nationality or attempt to bring about change in the political environment.

Within this matrix, the types and purposes of organisations were elaborated upon and migrant associations in the Swedish and Dutch contexts were compared in order to establish the extent to which they correspond to this ideal-type categorisation. The end result suggested that Swedish migrant organisations fulfilled the 'high voluntary and low professional' criteria but displayed low degrees of autonomy and inter-organisational contacts. Dutch migrant organisations displayed similar features but scored higher on the cross-cutting contacts criteria. As argued in Chapter 5, the particular appearance of Swedish and Dutch civil society is explained by the level of state involvement and support for these organisations as well as how integration policy has defined the role and goals of migrant organisations.

Second, the effects of structural opportunities and constraints on migrant organisations (which in turn determine their role and relevance) were discussed in more detail. In Sweden, migrant organisations are intended to serve as partners in the integration process and with the more specific function of acting as bridges between the host-society and the new population. In the Netherlands, organisations are founded under the label of ethnic minorities and are encouraged to do so under Dutch policies of cultural pluralism. In other words, Dutch official policy seems to encourage mobilisation according to ethnic belonging. This suggests that migrant associations should, at least to some extent, be involved in the political process. However, structural conditions and dominating cleavage lines are influential factors that determine to what extent this is feasible.

Furthermore, Chapter 5 aimed to establish what type of relationship prevailed between migrant organisations and political parties in Malmö and Rotterdam by deploying interview material from representatives of both groups. As argued in the chapter, societal settings and structural conditions create a number of difficulties for migrant organisations to initiate co-operation with parties on issues relating to ethnicity. These obstacles were, in the Swedish case, directly related to the paradigms of class and equality which have effectively eliminated any natural mobilisation ground around ethnicity. In the Dutch case, however, ethnic mobilising has a higher potential given the presence of an ethnic minority discourse and also through the advisory body channels that are available. However, such mobilisation has, in many respects, been neutralised by the structure created through the pillar-type integration regime that exists.

As shown by the interview material, this situation is recognised by both association and political party representatives. The statements also show the influence of prevailing structural conditions on actors' choices and to what extent they are prepared to pursue questions and issues that seem to be difficult to either change or bring up on the political agenda.

In addition, the intimate relationship that migrant organisations have with local and national authorities and the type of control exercised by these, affect the scope of action available for migrant organisations. This is most evident in terms of the degree of autonomy that organisations have. In both countries, the state is able to exercise influence on the associations with regard to activities and funding. This steers migrant associations into a particular direction that runs in accordance with the host-society's goals.

To sum up, the key findings from this final part of analysis are:

1. The nature of civil society is determined by the overarching institutional structures.

Based on the literature discussed on civil society, a matrix was designed which conceptualised organisations in civil society. This matrix displayed a number of features which organisations would display in a situation with no, or little, state involvement. The institutional settings in Sweden provide favourable opportunities to set up organisations with low degrees of professionalisation but are at the same time highly dependent on the state with few cross-cutting links with other associations. The Dutch case displays a similar scenario but intra-organisational contacts seem to be more frequent due to inter-locking board membership and co-ordinating advisory bodies.

2. The more dependent civil society actors are on the state, the greater the state influence will be in determining the role and influence of these actors.

My interview material shows that migrant organisations in Sweden are closely dependent on the local authorities in terms of funding, which in turn is conditional on performing certain tasks. The scope of action is thus limited for migrant associations if their activities are not in accordance with the goals of the host-society. Therefore, migrant associations have rarely functioned as channels for migrants' claims-making. In the Netherlands, certain organisations – such as the foundations – are less dependent on the state in terms of financing but monitoring of activities appears to be high. However, migrant organisations are to a greater extent involved in policy-making due to the more inclusive institutional arrangements.

3. Co-operation between migrant organisations and political parties is infrequent if ethnic claims are not compatible with dominating cleavage lines.

This was pointed out by a majority of the party representatives in Malmö. Emphasis was placed on conforming to party ideology, which by and large in Sweden would have to be based around class interests. Issues relating to ethnicity seemed more difficult to accommodate in political discourse, especially if they were perceived to clash with the overarching norm of equality. In Rotterdam, political respondents were less hesitant towards such specific interests but, in the long-term, these would have to be accommodated within the more general class and religious cleavages. Similarly, respondents from migrant organisations also recognised these institutional hurdles and as such were reluctant to pursue ethnic-related issues through the channels provided by the associations.

# Appendix: Questionnaire

This questionnaire is part of a research project at the University of Sussex (GB), which looks at political participation amongst different migrant groups in Malmö, Sweden and Rotterdam, the Netherlands.

The purpose of this questionnaire is to look at the relationship you have with the society you live in. It will not take more than 15 minutes to complete.
**These questions will be treated confidentially and you will remain anonymous.**

YOU AND YOUR NEIGHBOURHOOD

Some say that where you live can be important for the relationship you have with the town and society you live in. The following questions concern your place of residence and its surroundings.

1. How long have you been living in S/NL?                    ——

2. How long have you been living Malmö/R'dam?            ——

3. Where in Malmö/R'dam do you live?                          ——
   (e.g. Centrum/Bernisse)

4. What type of accommodation best describes your
   residence? (Please tick one box in each column)

   ☐ Self-owned accommodation          ☐ Villa or small house
   ☐ Rented accommodation              ☐ Small block of flats (up to 5 stories)
   ☐ Other (please specify): ————      ☐ Large block of flats (more than 5 stories)

5. How many bedrooms does your accomodation          ——
   have? (Don't include bathrooom or livingroom)

6. How many people are there in your household?       ——
   (including yourself)

7. Which of the following descriptions does          ☐ More of S/NL origin
   best correspond to the people living in your       ☐ More of non-S/NL origin
   neighbourhood?                                      ☐ Both of S/NL and non-S/NL origin
                                                       ☐ Don't know

8. Would you prefer it if there lived more people of  ☐ More of S/NL origin
   S/NL origin or more of non-S/NL origin in your      ☐ More of non-S/NL origin
   area, compared to now?                              ☐ Don't know
                                                       ☐ Satisfied as it is now

# YOU AND SOCIETY

To feel part of a community, it might be important to be able to identify with the area you live in and that other people see you as part of that community.
The following questions concern the relationship between you and the society you live in.

---

9. What's your opinion on the following statements?
   (Please tick one box only.)

|  | Agree Strongly | Agree | Neither agree nor disagree | Disagree | Disagree strongly |
|---|---|---|---|---|---|
| I should always obey the law. |  |  |  |  |  |
| Since people see me as S/NL, it was easy to get a job. |  |  |  |  |  |
| Paying taxes is a duty. |  |  |  |  |  |
| Malmö/R'dam is a safe city for immigrants. |  |  |  |  |  |
| Other S/NL treat me as a S/NL |  |  |  |  |  |
| I feel part of the S/NL community |  |  |  |  |  |
| I am S/NL |  |  |  |  |  |

---

10. How would you rate your local council's performance on the following issues?
    (1=Excellent, 2=Very good, 3=Neither good nor bad, 4=Bad, and 5=Very bad)

Provided bi-lingual education for pupils with another mother-tongue than S/NL. ———

Provided introduction courses about the S/NL society ———

Funding for ethnic associations. ———

Tackled racism. ———

Lowered unemployment levels amongst people of a non-S/NL origin. ———

Represented voters with a foreign heritage. ———

# POLITICAL PARTICIPATION

Some people say that to be part of a society involves a certain amount of political participation. This is not limited to the act of voting, but could also include membership of a political party, visiting associational meetings, taking part in a demonstration or discussing political issues. The following questions concern the extent to which you take part in different political activities.

11. Score each of the following in accordance to how likely or unlikely you would be to do them.
(1=Not at all likely, 2=Somewhat likely, 3=Neither likely nor unlikely, 4=Likely, 5=Very likely)

___ To attend meetings where matters concerning the neighbourhood one lives in are discussed
___ To raise issues with politicians which refer to your neighbourhood or city.

___ To particpate in a so called 'neighbourhood council'.
___ To vote in a local election, 'if they were held now'.

12. Did you vote in the last **local** election?

☐ Did not have the right to vote    ☐ Don't know
☐ Yes                                ☐ No

13. Did you vote in the last **national** election?
If you tick 'No' or 'Did not, have the right to vote' please go to question 15.

☐ Yes                                          ☐ No
☐ Did not have the right to vote ☐ Don't know

14. What party did you vote for?

| | Local | National |
|---|---|---|
| PvdA/SAP | | |
| VVD/M | | |
| CDA/KDS | | |
| D66/FP | | |
| Groen Links/MP | | |
| Other party (state which) | | |
| Don't know | | |
| Didn't vote | | |

15. How important are the following sources for you when you want to get information on social and political issues?
*(1=Very important, 2=Important, 3=Somewhat important 4=Less important and, 5=Not at all important.*

___ Television        ___ S/NL friends
___ Radio             ___ Friends of my own nationality
___ Newspapers        ___ Other sources (please specify) ——

16. How often do you do the following activities?

| | Very often | Fairly often | Sometimes | Almost never | Never |
|---|---|---|---|---|---|
| Watch the local news on TV | | | | | |
| Watch the national news on TV | | | | | |
| Watch news on satellite TV from your 'home country' | | | | | |
| Read S/NL newspapers | | | | | |
| Read newspapers from your 'homecountry' | | | | | |
| Listen to the news on the radio | | | | | |
| Listen to radio programmes in your language | | | | | |
| Discuss societal issues with friends and family | | | | | |
| Participate in organised demonstrations | | | | | |
| Attend union meetings | | | | | |
| Attend political meetings | | | | | |
| Write a letter to the editor | | | | | |

17. Are you a member of a union, association or club?

☐ Yes  ☐ No If you tick 'Yes', please state the name of the union, association or club.  ——

18. Are you a member of a political party?

☐ Yes  ☐ No If you tick 'Yes', which party are you a member of ?——
If you tick 'Yes', do you participate actively in party activities?  ☐ Yes ☐ No

## YOUR BACKGROUND

| | |
|---|---|
| 19. Please state your gender | ☐ Man        ☐ Woman |

| | |
|---|---|
| 20. In what year were you born? | 19____ |

| | |
|---|---|
| 21. To which of these groups do you belong? (Please tick one box only) | ☐ Married or cohabiting    ☐ Widowed<br>☐ Divorced or separated    ☐ Single |

If you are (or were) married or cohabiting, what country is your partner from? _____

| | |
|---|---|
| 22. To which of these groups do you belong? (Please tick one box only) | ☐ Employed    ☐ Self-employed    ☐ Retired<br>☐ Student    ☐ Unemployed    ☐ Employment scheme<br>☐ Other (please specify) _____ |

| | |
|---|---|
| 23. What country were you born in? | _____ |

| | |
|---|---|
| 24. What country were your parents born in? | _____ |

| | Occupation before moving | Current occupation |
|---|---|---|
| 25. What was your occupation prior to moving to S/NL and what is your current occupation? | _____ | _____ |

| | |
|---|---|
| 26. Do you have a permanent residency permit in S/NL? | ☐ Yes        ☐ No |

| | |
|---|---|
| 27. What nationality are you? | ☐ S/NL citizen<br>☐ Double citizenship (please state both) _____<br>☐ Other (please specify) _____ |

| | |
|---|---|
| 28. What is the highest education you have completed? | _____ |

| | |
|---|---|
| 29. How old were you when you stopped your full-time education? | _____ |

| | |
|---|---|
| 30. Which of the following statements best corresponds with how you see yourself? (Please tick one box only) | ☐ I am S/NL.<br>☐ I am more (your cultural group/country of origin) than S/NL.<br>☐ I am both (your cultural group/country of origin) and S/NL. |

| | |
|---|---|
| 31. If there was a party that primarily represented immigrants and their interests, would you vote for it? | ☐ Yes        ☐ No |

| | |
|---|---|
| 32. What would make you vote for such a party? | _____<br>_____<br>_____ |

Would you be prepared to be interviewed by the researcher?    ☐ Yes        ☐ No

If so, could you please provide contact details (e.g. address, phone, email) _____

Best time to reach you _____

### Thank you very much for completing this questionnaire!

*Table A.1*  Average identification scores for Iranians, Chileans and Turks on seven questions

| Question (i = internal identification; e = external identification) | Iranians | Chileans | Turks |
|---|---|---|---|
| I should always obey the law (i) | 4.1 | 3.2 | 3.9 |
| Since people see me as Swedish, it was easy to get a job (e) | 3.2 | 3.5 | 3.2 |
| Paying taxes is a duty (i) | 4.2 | 3.4 | 4.1 |
| I think Malmö is a safe city for immigrants (e) | 3.1 | 3.6 | 3.5 |
| Other Swedes treat me as a Swede (e) | 2.6 | 2.9 | 2.6 |
| I feel part of the Swedish community (i) | 3.3 | 2.4 | 3.3 |
| I am Swedish (i) | 2.3 | 1.5 | 3 |

*Source*: Author's questionnaire survey, Malmö, 2001.

*Table A.2*  Average identification scores for Iranians, Surinamese and Turks on seven questions

| Question (i = internal identification; e = external identification) | Iranians | Surinamese | Turks |
|---|---|---|---|
| I should always obey the law (i) | 3.4 | 3.7 | 3.6 |
| Since people see me as Dutch, it was easy to get a job (e) | 2.5 | 3.4 | 2.9 |
| Paying taxes is a duty (i) | 3.6 | 3.8 | 3.9 |
| I think Rotterdam is a safe city for immigrants (e) | 2.6 | 2.5 | 3 |
| Other Dutch treat as me a Dutch (e) | 2.5 | 2.3 | 2.6 |
| I feel part of the Dutch community (i) | 3.4 | 3 | 3.6 |
| I am Dutch (i) | 2.6 | 2.1 | 2.8 |

*Source*: Author's questionnaire survey, Rotterdam, 2001; 2002.

# Notes

## 1 Introduction

1. The implicit assumption running through the course of this book is that higher levels of political participation are perceived as beneficial for the society as a whole in accordance with the ideal of 'the active citizen' (Held, 1987). As suggested by Mill (1976: 217), despite his views on public opinion and mass ignorance, '... the only government that can fully satisfy all the exigencies of the social state is one in which the whole population participate; that any participation, even in the smallest public function is useful; that the participation should everywhere be as great as the general degree of improvement of the community will allow'. However, this idea is not uncontested especially since political participation is generally viewed as a right which entails that there is also a right to freedom from democracy (Arendt, 1973). Also, lower degrees of participation could be a sign of the population being content with the present situation and there is no need to participate because that would interrupt the status quo. Elsewhere, writers like Schumpeter (1943) and Lippmann (1956) argue that mass participation is in fact a threat to liberal democracy and that the only justified act of participation is the act of voting. This research will not focus on this particular area for reasons of scope. Instead, I assume that relatively lower degrees of participation constitute, at least, a concern for governing bodies and present a legitimacy problem. However, I am aware that this is not necessarily the general consensus.
2. Consider for instance Kitschelt's (1986: 63) point regarding the factors which determine the relative openness of a political system, '[t]he number of political parties, factions, and groups that effectively articulate different demands in electoral politics influences openness'. However, this number is a consequence of the political institutional arrangement which is left implicit.
3. Although the term 'integration' is a widely used and popular concept, it does present certain drawbacks when used in actual empirical research. First, integration is not a unitary concept but can refer to different societal areas in which integration can occur (e.g. economic, social and/or political integration), thus rendering its explanatory potential unclear. If one were to opt to use relative levels of integration in order to explain low levels of political participation, it could equally be used as a point of reference for when a migrant crosses the line from being a burden to society to an asset. In order words, a migrant could hypothetically be categorised as being fully integrated but still lack the sensation of being part of the system or the new society. Equally, the term 'integration' can be used as a means to measure or check when an ethnic group starts to operate on the same economic, social and political level as the native population – so that, for example, someone who is fully integrated participates politically to the same extent as a member of the indigenous group. The problem arising from this usage is that it effectively blurs the distinction between the generally more positively valued 'integration' and the arguably more negative connoting 'assimilation' and does not take into consideration conflicting and/or simultaneous identity possessions or levels of identification. Furthermore, the term also obscures cause and effect. That is, measuring levels of

political participation by means of political integration could easily be reversed. To clarify, political participation could induce a higher level of political integration seeing that a formerly inactive group now starts acting politically at the same rates as the native population. Conversely, there needs to be a minimum amount of political integration in order to be able to participate politically. This also entails the problematics of what constitutes the dependent and independent variable.

4. However, this definition includes children born abroad but with Swedish or Dutch-born parents and children born to mixed couples in the Netherlands and, naturalised migrants as well. In other words, there are several problems involved when trying to measure the amount of migrants in the two cases and, more importantly, how to distinguish them from the so-called majority population. In the Dutch case, with its significant number of migrant groups and colonial ties, the term 'ethnic minority' has been introduced. 'Ethnic minority' in the Dutch case refers to an ethnic group with a low socio-economic position over a number of generations (Vermeulen and Penninx, 2000). This usage of the term relates to the Dutch government's wish to monitor the socio-economic progress of the migrants in the areas of labour, education and housing. National policy defines which migrant groups are to be considered as 'ethnic minorities' and target groups of this policy. Dutch policy does not further define the specifics of what an ethnic minority or group is, but does relate it to country of origin (place of birth of self and/or parents), religion and language. The adoption of the term 'ethnic minority' is however primarily used as a practical tool for policy purposes. In the Swedish case, no concept of ethnic minorities exists, as far as official policy goes. Instead one finds the categories of 'Swedish' or 'foreign national', depending on whether there has been a naturalisation process or not. This entails that the number of individuals that constitute the category of 'immigrants' is unusually large and includes everyone who is either foreign-born or has both parents born abroad. Officially, this means that no distinction is made between Danish and Botswanian migrants in terms of their status, both belong to the group 'immigrants', but they are subjected to different citizenship regulations and conditions. In everyday language and in the media, the term 'immigrant' is sometimes used to refer to migrants primarily from outside Western Europe and sometimes even as a derogatory way of referring to individuals perceived as not being Swedish. However, certain policies are aimed specifically at certain migrants which could facilitate the definition problem and some migrants are not officially perceived as being migrants. In the Swedish case, governmental policy does not consider migrants from the Nordic countries to be significantly different from the majority population in terms of cultural, linguistic (although the Finns are an exception) and social characteristics, and Nordic migrants are hence not affected by immigration policies. In the Dutch case, certain policies apply specifically to certain groups especially during their initial period of stay. The groups in question are primarily those who fall under the 'refugee' category; in addition to this there are also certain religious and linguistic rights that affect certain groups more than others. Migrants from within the European Union constitute another category, that are not affected by official policy since their rights and obligations are regulated by EU prerogatives. Also, these migrants could be considered to inhabit a relatively more favourable socio-economic position and would hence not be seen to be problematic by the state.

5. Liberal/Conservative Party (VVD), Liberal Party (D66), Green-Left Party (Groen Links), Christian Democrats (CDA), Socialdemocratic Party (PvdA) and the Socialist Party (SP).

6. http://booking.malmo.se/booking/forening.start.asp, accessed on 17-12-2002.
7. Several visits were made to the premises of the associations and very rarely were women observed to take part in everyday associational life. The exception were the Iranian associations in which women played a more active role, although they still did not figure as much as the men on the association board. The Turkish associations were dominated by men almost to the extent that one would be tempted to label the associations as a forum for Turkish men rather than Turkish speakers in general.

## 2  Historical Overview: Patterns of Immigration, Immigration and Citizenship Policies

8. Naturalisation for foreigners with at least 15 years' residence and for those of the second and third generation aged between 16 and 25 with at least 8 years' residence (Geddes, 2003).
9. In the final agreement on the post-colonial relationship between the Netherlands and its former colony, it was decided that all persons who became Surinamese citizens on independence day had the right upon arrival in the Netherlands to apply for Dutch citizenship as long as they had not chosen to become Dutch citizens as a minor. This final agreement was called *Toescheidingsovereenkomst*.
10. The Dutch Antilles population consists of the three main categories of 'white', 'mulatto' and 'black' alongside migrants from Surinam, Colombia, Venezuela, immigrants from the British and Dutch Windward Islands as well as Portugese from Madeira and the Azores.
11. This definition is not entirely unproblematic. First, it implies that a member of a recognised ethnic minority can eventually be 'de-ethnisised' if he or she improves socio-economically. Second, given the Dutch definition of an immigrant (born abroad or with at least one parent born abroad), this suggests that ethnic minorities can eventually cease to exist over time even though their somatic and cultural characteristics and their socio-economic position may still be the same (Entzinger, 1985).
12. The Moluccan situation was extremely complex to solve. Part of the Moluccan force served in the Dutch Colonial Army in the Dutch Indies (KNIL) and certain parts of the Moluccan Islands declared themselves independent from the Netherlands and Indonesia. This further complicated the demobilisation of those Moluccan soldiers who were stationed elsewhere in the former Dutch East-Indies. They could not be brought back as Moluccans since this would mean that the Dutch government interfered in the conflict between the Moluccans and the new Indonesian state. They could not be demobilised in for example Java, Kalimantan, Sumatra or any of the islands as they presented a danger to the newly built Indonesian state. Instead, they were transported to the Netherlands and upon arrival demobilised and subsequently became stateless citizens, since they at the time (and to a certain extent still today) continue to uphold an ideal of an independent Moluccan state (see further Smeets and Veenman, 2000).
13. Although a key player in the area its advice is not always followed (compare the impact of, for instance, the WRR reports from 1979 and 1989). See also Lin Pang (2002).
14. Other so-called ethnic groups had their own umbrella organisations on the national and local level. Today, these organisations have been dissolved and

replaced by FORUM as a centre for knowledge on the multicultural society. It includes all interested target groups of the integration of minorities policies.

15. This view altered in the late 1990s after several parliamentary debates and pressure from the Saami population. On 1 December 1999 five groups were recognised as entitled to ethnic minority status these included Saamis, the Swedish-Finns (however, not Finnish immigrants), Tornedal-Finns, Roma and Jews.

16. However, what the authors' omit in the account of the Jewish success story is that the choice of career could be a response to the anti-Jewish sentiments and discrimination experienced on the labour market, that is, setting up a private business as a way of countering exclusion.

17. 'Very broadly speaking, at this level people are able to follow straightforward spoken explanations and hold a conversation on a familiar topic' (Home office webpage, 2004).

## 3 The Role of Institutions in Shaping the Opportunities and Constraints on Actors' Behaviour

18. Clemens, for instance, defines institutions as 'basic rules of the game or principles of order that characterise a particular society at a particular time' (1998: 110).

19. 'There's an incubation period, they register and then a judgement is made, if the association corresponds to the aims of the board, and then they get registered as a children and youth association. After that they have to wait a year until they can get funding and that's because we want some continuity in the association. They have to exist for a year, they have to have annual meetings, there has to be some order in the work they do, some sort of stable foundation' (Director of Malmö Board of Recreation A, 2001).

20. 'It's a difficult problem because there are also these sub-councils here and they have their own subsidising policy and as a self-organisation you have to know where to go, if you have an activity which is area specific, you have to go to the sub-council, if the activities concern the whole of Rotterdam then you got to go to the city council; they spend a lot of time writing proposals and asking for money, searching where you to go for the money and that takes a lot of time' (SAMS A, 2001).

21. For a list of interviewees by name and political organisation, see Bibliography.

22. Mauricio Rojas is now a member of the Liberal Party (Folkpartiet).

23. The term refers to a group or an individual with domicile, entitled to most rights given to fully naturalised citizens.

24. 'The Turkish community is so diverse so trying to unify them on any question is very difficult, every Turk has his own direction, you have the Islamic Turks, the secularised Turks, the Grey Wolves, the Kurds' (Socialdemocrat B, 2001).

25. The Scania Party can be briefly described as a populist party with xenophobic ideas (see Peterson *et al.*, 1998, for a more thorough discussion on the party and its ideas). The appearance of the Scania Party was followed up by a local referendum in the municipality of Sjöbo (a neighbour to Malmö), in which the voters were asked whether they wanted the municipality to arrange settlement for a group of refugees. The outcome was negative, despite positive encouragement from the national parties, and no refugees were placed in Sjöbo (Hammar, 1991).

26. 'I don't think we ever discussed what our stand or attitude towards them should be, I mean we never said that we should boycott them but then again we never said that we should invite them either, so I don't think that they played any

significant part in the election campaign' (Left Party B, 2001).

27. 'Any form of co-operation with an immigrant party is totally uninteresting for the Conservatives and I don't believe in that idea and I don't think it will be a success' (Conservative Party A, 2001).

28. 'They didn't even have to knock on the door, it was just walk right in ... what they wanted to carry out was exactly what we wanted to do' (Green Party B, 2001).

# 4  Identity, Citizenship and Identification

29. Note, however, that these two variants are not uncontested. For instance van Steenburgen (1994) lists the following developments, or additions to the term: neo-republican, cultural, active, race and gender neutral, global, European and ecological citizenship.

30. However, due to insufficient questionnaire material received from the Turkish speaking group, the main emphasis will be on the Iranian and Chilean samples.

31. The change in migrant composition created a certain tension between the 'old' and the 'new' Chileans as the following quote shows: '[w]hat Pinochet did in the early 1980s was to open up the prisons and let everyone go. So you got all sorts of people leaving the country, everything from killers to political prisoners, and some criminals came here to Sweden unfortunately. But the first ones who came here were highly educated and managed to fit in society smoothly, but then these criminals gave us a bad name' (Male, mid-50s, 2001).

32. Compare Adolino's (1998) study on Asian and Afro-Caribbean organisational patterns in the United Kingdom.

33. The Surinamese ethnic group is diverse and reflects their colonial history. Apart from the indigenous inhabitants, the Carib Indians, all residents in Surinam are of foreign origin. Three groups dominate the demographic make-up; the first to arrive were the African slaves who were to become what is today the ethnic group of Creole-Surinamese and constituted in 1991 around 31 per cent of the population. After emancipation from slavery in 1863, Hindustani labourers were contracted from the former British colony of India and they constitute the dominant ethnic group (37 per cent). Alongside these two major groups a number of smaller ethnic groups are included in the term Surinamese, these include Javanese (descendants from Muslim indentured labourers from Indonesia), Maroons (descendants from slaves who fled the plantations prior to the abolition of slavery), Amerindian, Chinese and White Dutch (Brinkerhoof and Jacob, 1994).

34. Although it should be noted that it has become increasingly more difficult to obtain dual nationality in the Netherlands, especially since the latter half of 1990s when an emphasis was placed on renouncing one's previous nationality.

35. In comparison one-eighth of these groups also stated that they would like more individuals of non-Dutch origin in their area compared to 5 per cent of the Turks.

36. Again, it should be emphasised that the small sample size makes it difficult to draw any firm conclusions about the meaning of this ratio.

37. All correlation coefficients were calculated using the formula outlined by Clarke and Cooke (1983). The object of the correlation analysis is to measure the strength of the relationship between political participation, as the dependent variable, and identification, the independent variable, for each of the national migrant groups. First, the deviation of all individual 'satisfaction'; 'likelihood'; 'intensity'; and 'interest' scores from the mean of all 'satisfaction'; 'likelihood';

'intensity'; and 'interest' scores were established. The deviation from the mean of all individual 'total level of identification' scores was then calculated. Second, the sum of products of all deviations made the basis for the correlation coefficient. The *product–moment* correlation coefficient, $r$, will have a value between $-1$ to $+1$. A negative correlation will be closer to $-1$, when there is no correlation $r$ will take a value close to 0 and when there is a strong correlation $r$ will take a value near to $+1$.

## 5 Civil Society, Migrant Organisations and Political Parties

38. Other interpretations include civil society as the place where citizens learn the democratic habits of participation and toleration (republican); civil society as a mechanism in order to offer and deliver social services without trapping citizens in welfare dependency (market libertarians); civil society as the road to a broader and deeper democracy (post-Marxist) (Hefner, 1998).
39. Keane (1988) adds that any non-market, non-state organisation such as churches, professional associations and even political parties are also components of the modern civil society.
40. According to the database on migrants organisations developed by the Institute for Migration and Ethnic Studies at the University of Amsterdam, Rotterdam had 70 Moroccan, 136 Surinamese and 80 Turkish organisations that were registered with the local authorities in 2001.
41. 'In general, as long as it's for youth, women and elderly people they get money ... I think it's the same everywhere, but each sub-council has its own theme so they have different amounts of money for different activities, it also depends on which parties that are in the sub-councils' (Advisor of Social and Economic Affairs A, 2001).
42. 'You have to give them a detailed report on what type of activities you want to do and they will then decide if that's to be subsidised, so we don't get money first and then do the activities, it's the other way around' (Turkish Male, mid-40s, 2001).
43. 'When you have a meeting with them, they always want to know about everything that goes on, they don't give you any spare time to do things. I know that big brother is watching us and I know that they want to know what's going on here' (Creole-Male, late-40s, 2002).
44. Compare the following quotes: 'We don't have special actions directed at any groups, we don't go to the Mosques or to the Turkish or Moroccan pool halls and say "Vote for the VVD" ' (VVD A, 2001); 'We can't reach all 160 different cultures and some parties had already monopolised some of the minority groups so we had to carve out our own political niche.' (Christian Democrat B, 2002); 'We haven't approached any groups in that way, we approach them as individuals or they approach us, and they have their own background related to their ethnic background but that doesn't mean that they are on the same social or economic level' (D66 A, 2001).
45. 'There is no ethnic cleavage in the union and there's no special union for migrants either, there's one big union and that's where they go to solve their problems' (FNV A, 2001); 'If you want to do that, you first have to distinguish who is Swedish and who is an immigrant so you can say whether it's justified or not, but having that division you can easily get into difficult situations' (LO A, 2001); 'There's a difficulty involved in this type of argument because first we have to define what an immigrant is and our regulations don't make it any easier

either ... the union would probably say that it's not a trade union issue because they don't dare to deal with that type of question' (SIF A, 2001).

46. 'If they make certain claims that we consider to be legitimate ones, then it usually comes up on the political agenda. ... democracy on that level is very accessible, you can come to the city council, you can come to the commission meetings and it works, we listen to them, but critically of course' (Green Party A, 2001); 'We are open to discussion with any group that approaches us, but we always start these discussions from the standards that we have in the party, if they have the arguments and we agree, sure, if it complies with our party programme and what we believe in' (Christian Democrat A, 2001); 'We pay attention to whatever people have to say to us because they are voters but if they want to make claims relating to ethnicity or culture, then that's very difficult within our party because we don't want it to become too fractionalised' (Socialdemocrat E, 2002).

# Bibliography

Abell, J.P., Havelaar, A.E. and Dankoor, M.M., *The Documentation and Evaluation of Anti-Discrimination Training Activities in the Netherlands* (International Migration Papers 16, Geneva: ILO, 1997).

Adolino, J.R., *Ethnic Minorities, Electoral Politics and Political Integration in Britain* (London: Pinter, 1998).

Ahmadi Lewin, F., 'The divergent attitudes of Iranian immigrant men and women towards integration into the Swedish society', *International Migration*, 39:3 (2001), pp. 121–35.

Ahrne, G., 'Civil Society and uncivil organizations', in Alexander, J.C. (ed.) *Real Civil Societies: Dilemmas of Institutionalization* (London: Sage, 1998), pp. 84–96.

Almond, G.A., 'Comparative political systems', *Journal of Politics*, 18 (1956), pp. 391–409.

Ålund, A. and Schierup, C-U., *Paradoxes of Multiculturalism* (Avebury: Aldershot, 1991).

Amersfoort, van J.M.M., *Immigration and the Formation of Minority Groups. The Dutch Experience 1945–1975* (Alphen aan den Rijn: Samson, 1982).

Anderiesse, R.M., Bol, P., Oudijik and Bons, C.P., *Migration and Major Cities Policy in Rotterdam* (Paper presented at the Second International Metropolis Conference, Copenhagen, 25–27 September, 1997).

Anderson, B., *Imagined Communities: Reflections on the Origin and Spread of Nationalism* (London: Verso, 1983).

Andersson, R., *Svenskglesa Bostadsområden*. Invandrare och Minoriteter (Socialstyrelsen: Social Rapport, 2001).

Andeweg, R.B., 'Centrifugal forces and collective decision-making: the case of the Dutch cabinet', *European Journal of Political Research*, 16 (1988), pp. 125–51.

Andeweg, R.B. and Irwin, G.A., *Dutch Government and Politics* (Basingstoke: MacMillan Press Ltd, 1993).

Andrews, W.G. and Hoffman, S., *The Impact of the Fifth Republic on France* (New York: State University of New York Press, 1981).

Anheier, H.K., *The Third Sector in Europe*. Civil Society Working paper 12 (Centre for Civil Society: London School of Economics, 2002).

Arendt, H., *On Revolution* (Harmondsworth: Penguin, 1973).

BBC, 'Immigrants "should try to feel British" ', taken from http://news.bbc.co.uk/1/hi/uk_politics/1699847.stm (09-12-2001), accessed 28-03-2005.

Bäck, H. and Soininen, M., 'Electoral participation among immigrants in Sweden: integration, culture and participation', *New Community*, 20:1 (1993), pp. 111–30.

Bade, K., *Das Manifest der 60. Deutschland und die Einwanderung* (Munich, 1994).

Bagley, C., *The Dutch Plural Society: a Comparative Study in Race Relations* (London: Oxford University Press, 1973).

Balibar, E., 'Es gibt keinen Stat: racism and politics in Europe today', *New Left Review*, 186 (1991), pp. 5–19.

Ballis Lal, B., 'Symbolic interaction theories', *American Behavioural Scientist*, 38:3 (1995), pp. 421–41.

Banton, M., *Racial Minorities* (London: Fontana, 1972).

Barats-Malbrel, C., 'The politicization of belonging: post-war legal developments in the administrative identities of non-nationals in France', in Geddes, A. and

Favell, A. (eds) *The Politics of Belonging: Migrants and Minorities in Contemporary Europe* (Aldershot: Ashgate, 1999), pp. 76–93.

Bartels, D., 'Can the train ever be stopped again? Developments in the Moluccan community in the Netherlands before and after the hijackings', *Indonesia,* 41 (1986), pp. 23–46.

Bartolini, S. and Mair, P., *Identity, Competition, and Electoral Availability: the Stabilisation of European Electorates, 1885–1985* (Cambridge: Cambridge University Press, 1990).

Bauböck, R., *Transnational Citizenship: Membership and Rights in International Migration* (Aldershot: Edward Elgar, 1994).

Bennulf, M. and Hedberg, P., 'Utanför demokratin. Om det minskande valdeltagandets sociala och politiska rötter', *Valdeltagande i förändring* (SOU 1999:132, 1999), pp. 75–135.

Berger, M. and Vermeulen, F., *New Policy for an Old Problem? The Integration of Migrants in Amsterdam and the role of Ethnic Organizations in this Process.* Paper presented for the workshop *NGOs in the Face of Immigrant and Refugee Reception and Settlement Dynamics* (6th International Metropolis Conference in Rotterdam, 2001).

Berger, M., Galonska, C. and Koopmans, R., *Not a Zero-Sum Game: Ethnic Communities and Political Integration of Migrants in Berlin.* Paper presented at Workshop on Political Participation of Immigrants and their Descendents in Post-War Western Europe (ECPR Joint Session, Turin, Italy, 22–27 March 2002).

Berntson, L., 'The state and parliamentarism in Sweden', in Fry, J.A. (ed.) *Limits of the Welfare State: Critical Views on Post-War Sweden* (Aldershot: Gower, 1983), pp. 10–25.

Birch, A., *Naturalisation and National Integration* (London: Unwin Hyman, 1989).

Bloom, W., *Personal Identity, National Identity and International Relations* (Cambridge: Cambridge University Press, 1990).

Bobo, L. and Gilliam, F.D. Jr, 'Sociopolitical participation, and black empowerment', *American Political Science Review,* 84:2 (1990), pp. 377–93.

Borevi, K., *The Welfare State in a Multicultural Society* (Uppsala: Acta Universitatis Upsaliensis, 2002).

Bouchard, G. and Chandler, W., *The Politics of Inclusion and Exclusion: Immigration and Citizenship Issues in Three Democracies* taken from http://web.uvic.ca/ecsac/toronto/papers/on/line/pdf/8D-gbouchard-wchandler.pdf, accessed on 20-01-2005.

Breton, R., 'Institutional completeness of ethnic communities and the personal relations of immigrants', *American Journal of Sociology,* 70:2 (1964), 193–205.

Bretschneider, P., *Iranian Immigrant Perception of Childhood and Parenthood: the Impact of Indigenous Pedagogy on Risk Management and Traffic Safety Education* (Uppsala: Uppsala Research Report in Cultural Anthropology, No. 16, 2001).

Brinkerhoff, M.B. and Jacob, J.C., 'Racial, ethnic and religious social distance in Surinam – an exploration of the "strategic alliance hypotheses" in a Caribbean community', *Ethnic and Racial Studies,* 17:4 (1994), pp. 636–61.

British Census, Office for National Statistics (2001).

Broeder, P. and Extra, G., 'Language', in Vermeulen, H. (ed.) *Immigrant Policy for a Multicultural Society: A Comparative Study of Integration, Language and Religious Policy in Five Western European Countries* (Brussels: Migration Policy Group, 1997), pp. 57–101.

Brubaker, R., *Citizenship and Nationhood in France and Germany* (Cambridge, MA: Harvard University Press, 1992).

Bruff, I., 'The Netherlands, and the challenge of Lijst Pim Fortuyn and the Third Way', *Politics,* 23:3 (2003), pp. 156–63.

Budge, I. and Farlie, D., *Voting and Competition* (London: Wiley, 1983).

Budge, I., 'Great Britain and Ireland: Variations on dominant party government', in Colomer, J.M. (ed.) *Political Institutions in Europe* (London, Routledge, 1996), pp. 18–62.

Burkhart, H. and Robertson, R., 'Identity and authority: a problem analysis of processes of identification and authorization', in Burkhart, H. and Robertson, R. (eds) *Identity and Authority: Explorations in the Theory of Society* (Blackwell: Oxford, 1980), pp. 1–40.

Calvert, R., 'The rational choice theory of social institutions: cooperation, coordination and communication', in Banks, J. and Hanushek, E. (eds) *Modern Political Economy: Old Topics, New Directions* (Cambridge, MA: Cambridge University Press, 1995), pp. 216–28.

Castles, S., 'How nation-states respond to immigration and ethnic diversity', *New Community*, 21:3 (1995), pp. 293–308.

Castles, S. and Davidson, A., *Citizenship and Migration: Globalization and the Politics of Belonging* (London: MacMillan Press, 2000).

Castles, S. and Kosack, G., 'From aliens to citizens; redefining the status of immigrants in Europe: how the trade unions try to control and integrate immigrant workers in the German Federal Republic', *Race*, 15:4 (1974), pp. 497–514.

Castles, S. and Miller, M., *The Age of Migration* (Basingstoke: Palgrave, MacMillan, 2003).

CBS, *Statistical yearbook of the Netherlands* (The Hague: CBS, 1998).

Cesarani, D., 'Citizenship and Nationality in Britain', in Cesarani, D. and Fulbrook, M. (eds) *Citizenship, Nationality and Migration in Europe* (London: Routledge, 1996), pp. 57–74.

Christoffersson, U., 'Storbrittannien', in Lindahl, R. (ed.) *Utländska Politiska System* (Lund: Dialogos, 1991), pp. 27–56.

Clarke, G.M. and Cooke, D., *A Basic Course in Statistics* (London: Arnold, 1983).

Clemens, E., 'To move mountains: Collective action and the possibility of institutional change', in Guigni, M., McAdam, D. and Tilly, C. (eds) *From Contention to Democracy* (Lanham, MD: Rowman and Littlefield, 1998), pp. 109–125.

Cohen, J.L. and Arato, A., *Civil Society and Political Theory* (Cambridge, MA: MIT Press, 1995).

Cole, A., *French Politics and Society* (Hemel Hempstead: Prentice Hall, 1998).

Collier, D. and Mahon Jr, J.E., 'Conceptual "stretching" revisited: adapting categories in comparative analysis', *American Political Science Review*, 87 (1993), pp. 845–55.

Conradt, D.P., *The German Polity* (New York: Addison-Wesley Longman, 2001).

Cordero-Guzmán, H., 'Immigrant aid societies and organizations', in Ciment, J. (ed.) *Encyclopedia of American Immigration* (Armonk M.E: Sharpe, 2001), pp. 334–40.

COS, *Centrum voor onderzoek en statistiek*, taken from www.cos.nl/html/cijfers/demgeg_cijfers.html (accessed on 12-05-2003).

CRE, *Commission for Racial Equality*, taken from http://www.cre.gov.uk/about/about.html (accessed 03-11-2004).

Daalder, H., 'Changing procedures and changing strategies in Dutch coalition building', *Legislative Studies Quarterly*, 11 (1986), pp. 506–31.

Dahl, R.A., 'The behavioural approach in political science: epitaph for a monument to a successful protest', *American Political Science Review*, 55:4 (1961a), pp. 763–72.

Dahl, R.B., *Who Governs? Democracy and Power in an American City* (Yale University Press: New Haven, 1961b).

Dahlstedt, M., *Politiskt Medborgarskap, Integration och Mångkulturell Demokrati, Segregation* (Umeå Universitet: PfMI, 1998).

Dalstra, K., 'The south Moluccan minority in the Netherlands', *Contemporary Crisis*, 2:7 (1983), pp. 195–208.

Dalton, R.J., 'A divided electorate?', in Smith, G. Paterson, W.E. and Padgett, S. (eds) *Developments in German Politics 2* (Basingstoke: MacMillan, 1996), pp. 35–54.

Darvishour, M., 'Intensified gender conflicts within Iranian families in Sweden', *Nordic Journal of Women's Studies*, 7:1 (1999), pp. 20–33.

Dearlove, J. and Saunders, P., *Introduction to British Politics* (Cambridge: Polity Press, 2000).

De Graaf, H., Penninx, R. and Stoové, E., ' "Minorities" policies, social services and ethnic organizations in the Netherlands', in Jenkins, S. (ed.) *Ethnic associations and the Welfare State: Services to Immigrants in Five Countries* (New York: University of Columbia Press, 1988), pp. 203–38.

De Rahm, G., 'Naturalisation: the politics of citizenship acquisition', in Layton-Henry, Z. (ed.) *The Political Rights of Migrant Workers in Western Europe* (London: Sage, 1990), pp. 158–86.

Diermeier, D. and Krehbiel, K., *Institutionalism as a Methodology* (Research Paper Series: Stanford University, 2001).

Doise, M., Deschamps, J.C. and Meyer, C., 'The accentuation of intra-group similarities', in Tajfel, H. (ed.) *Differentiation between Social Groups* (London: Academic Press, 1978), pp. 159–71.

Doomernik, J., *The effectiveness of integration policies towards immigrants and their descendents in France, Germany and The Netherlands* (Geneva: International Labour Organisation, 1998).

Dryzek, J.S., 'Political inclusion and the dynamics of democratization', *American Political Science Review*, 1 (1996), pp. 475–87.

Dunleavy, P. and O'Leary, B., *Theories of the State: the Politics of Liberal Democracy* (Basingstoke: Macmillan, 1987).

Du Preez, P., *The Politics of Identity: Ideology and the Human Image* (New York: St. Martin's Press, 1980).

Duyvendak, J.W. and Koopmans, R., 'Protest in een pacificatiedemocratie. Nieuwe sociale bewegingen in het Nederlandse politieke systeem', in Dyvendak, J.W. (ed.) *Tussen Verbeelding en Macht: 25 Jaar Nieuwe Sociale Bewegingen in Nederland* (Amsterdam: SUA, 1992), pp. 39–58.

Easton, D., *The Analysis of Political Structure* (New York: Routledge, 1990).

Eckstein, H., 'A perspective on comparative politics, past and present', in Eckstein, H. and Apter, D.E. (eds) *Comparative Politics: A Reader* (New York: Free Press, 1963), pp. 3–32.

Eggertson, T., *Economic Behaviour and Institutions* (Cambridge, MA: Cambridge University Press, 1990).

Elder, N., 'Corporatism in Sweden', in Cox, A. and O'Sullivan, N. (eds) *The Corporate State: Corporatism and the State Tradition in Western Europe* (Cambridge: Cambridge University Press, 1988), pp. 153–70.

Elder, N.C.M., Thomas, A.H. and Arter, D., *The Consensual Democracies?: The Government and Politics of the Scandinavian Countries* (Oxford: Blackwell, 1988).

Entzinger, H., 'The Netherlands', in Hammar, T. (ed.) *European Immigration Policy: A Comparative Study* (Cambridge: Cambridge University Press, 1985), pp. 50–89.

Entzinger, H., 'The rise and fall of multiculturalism: the case of the Netherlands' in Joppke, C. and Morawska, E. (eds) *Toward Assimilation and Citizenship: Immigrants in Liberal Nation-States* (Basingstoke: MacMillan, 2003), pp. 59–87.

Entzioni, A., *The Spirit of Community* (New York: Simon and Schuster, 1993).

Esser, H. and Korte, H., 'The policy of the Federal Republic of Germany' in Hammar, T. (ed.) *European Immigration Policy: A Comparative Analysis* (Cambridge: Cambridge University Press, 1985), pp. 165–205.

Evans, J.M., *Immigration Law* (London: Sweet and Maxwell, 1983).

Evans, P., 'Immigration: British-style', *Transition,* 40 (1971), pp. 42–7.

Faist, T., 'How to define a foreigner: the symbolic politics of immigration in German partisan discourse', *West European Politics,* 17:2 (1994), pp. 50–71.

Faulks, K., *Citizenship in Modern Britain* (Edinburgh: Edinburgh University Press, 1998).

Favell, A., *Philosophies of Integration: Immigration and the Idea of Citizenship in France and Britain* (London: Macmillan/New York: St. Martin's Press, 1998).

Federal Ministry of the Interior, www.bmi.bund.de, accessed on 03-02-2005.

Federal Statistical Office Germany, www.destatis.de, accessed on 24-02-2005.

Feldman, D., 'There was an Englishman, an Irishman and a Jew ... immigrants and minorities in Britain', *The Historical Journal,* 26:1 (1983), pp. 185–99.

Fennema, M. and Tillie, J., 'Political participation and political trust in Amsterdam's civic communities and ethnic networks', *Journal of Ethnic and Migration Studies,* 35:4 (1999), pp. 703–26.

Fennema, M. and Tillie, J., 'Civic community, political participation and political trust of ethnic groups', *Connections* 24:1 (2001), pp. 26–41.

Fennema, M. and Tillie, J., 'The Paradox of Multicultural Democracy'. Paper presented for Workshop 7: *Rescuing Democracy: The Lure of the Associative Elixir,* (ECPR Joint session of Workshops, Turin, March, 2002).

Fine, R., 'Civil society theory, enlightenment and critique', in Fine, R. and Shirin, R. (eds) *Civil Society: Democratic Perspectives* (London: Frank Cass, 1997), pp. 7–29.

Fitzgerald, M., 'Immigration and race relations: political aspects – No. 15', *New Community,* 13 (1986), pp. 265–71.

Frears, J., *Parties and Voters in France* (New York: St. Martin's Press, 1991).

Fred, M.A., *Managing Culture Contact: the Organization of Swedish Immigration Policy* (Liber Förlag: Stockholm, 1983).

Freyne-Lindgren, M. and Pettersson, H., *Utanför demokratin? Del 7, Politiskt deltagande i Örebro kommun* (Integrations 2000:20, Integrationsverkets Rapportserie, 2000).

Friborg, C., 'M-profilering eller verklig omorientering?' (*Dagens Nyheter,* 01-09-1999).

Friedman, J., *Cultural Identity and Global Process* (London: Sage, 1994).

Fulbrook, M., 'Germany for the Germans? Citizenship and nationality in a divided nation', in Cesarani, D. and Fulbrook, M. (eds) *Citizenship, Nationality and Migration in Europe* (London: Routledge, 1996), pp. 88–106.

Gainer, B., *The Alien Invasion: The Origins of the Aliens Act of 1905* (London: Heinemann, 1972).

Geddes, A., *The Politics of Migration and Immigration in Europe* (London: Sage, 2003).

Gidlund, J-E., 'Demos och makten i den politiska demokratin', in Sannerstedt, A. and Jerneck, M. (eds) *Den moderna demokratins problem* (Lund: Studentlitteratur, 1994), pp. 187–214.

Gilroy, P., *Between Camps: Race, Identity and Nationalism at the End of the Colour Line* (London: Allen Lane, 2000).

Giugni, M. and Passy, F., 'Migrant mobilisation between political institutions and citizenship regimes: a comparison between France and Switzerland', *European Journal of Political Research,* 43 (1) (2004), pp. 51–82.

Gladdish, K., *Governing from the Centre: Politics and Policy-Making in the Netherlands* (London: Hurst and Co, 1991).

Glaeßner, G-J., 'Government and political order', in Smith, G., Paterson, W.E. and Padgett, S. (eds) *Development in German Politics 2* (Basingstoke: MacMillan, 1996), pp. 14–33.

Goffman. E., *Asylums: Essays on the Social Situation of Mental Patients and Other Inmates* (London: Pelican, 1961).

Goodin, R. and Klingemann, H., 'Political science: the discipline', in Goodin, R. and Klingemann, H. (eds) *A New Handbook for Political Science* (Oxford: Oxford University Press, 1996), pp. 3–49.

Goodman, N., *Fact, Fiction and Forecast* (Indianapolis: Bobbs-Merril, 1965).

Gordon, P., *Policing Immigration: Britain's Internal Controls* (London: Pluto, 1985).

Goudsblom, J., *Dutch Society* (New York: Random House, 1967).

Governmental Bill, 1968:142, *Angående riktlinjer för utlänningspolitiken m.m.*

Governmental Bill, 1975:26, *Regeringens proposition om riktlinjer for invandrar- och minoritetspolitiken m.m.*

Governmental Bill, 1985/86:98, *Om Invandrarpolitiken*.

Governmental Bill, 1997/1998:16, *Sverige, Framtiden och Mångfalden: från invandrarpolitik till integrationspolitik*.

Governmental Directive 1998:50, 'Kommittedirektiv: Tilläggsdirektiv till 1997 års medborgarkskapskommitte' (*Kommittedirektiv 1998: Årsbok*: Ministry of Justice), pp. 328–30.

Governmental Proposition 2001/02:129, *Integrationspolitik för 2000-talet*.

Gray, J., *Post Liberalism: Studies in Political Thought* (London: Routledge, 1993).

Green, S., *The Politics of Exclusion: Institutions and Immigration Policy in Contemporary Germany* (Manchester University Press, 2004).

Grillo, R., *Pluralism and the Politics of Difference: State, Culture and Ethnicity in Comparative Perspective* (Oxford: Clarendon Press, 1998).

Guiot, J.M., 'Attribution and identity construction: some comments', *American Sociological Review*, 42 (1977), pp. 692–704.

Habermas, J., 'Citizenship and national identity: some reflections on the future of Europe', in Beiner, R. (ed.) *Theorizing Citizenship* (Albany: State University of New York Press, 1995), pp. 255–81.

Hakim, C., *Preference Theory: Work-Lifestyle Choices in the 21st Century* (Oxford: Oxford University Press, 2000).

Hall, P., *Governing the Economy: The Politics of State Intervention in Britain and France* (Cambridge: Polity, 1986).

Hall, P. and Taylor, R., 'Political science and the three new institutionalisms'. MPIFG Discussion Paper 96/6: Max-Planck-Institute, taken from www.mpi-fg-koeln.mpg.de/pu/mpifg_dp/dp96-6.pdf (accessed on 08-09-2003).

Hall, S., 'Cultural identity and diaspora', in Williams, P. and Chrisman, L. (eds) *Colonial Discourse and Post-Colonial Theory: A Reader* (Hemel Hempstead: Harvester Wheatsheaf, 1994).

Hammar, T., 'Sweden', in Hammar, T. (ed.) *European Immigration Policy: A Comparative Study* (Cambridge: Cambridge University Press, 1985), pp. 16–49.

Hammar, T., *Democracy and the Nation State: Aliens, Denizens and Citizens in a World of International Migration* (Ashgate: Aldershot, 1990).

Hammar, T., ' "Cradle of freedom on earth": refugee immigration and ethnic pluralism', in Lane, J-E. (ed.) *Understanding the Swedish Model* (London: Frank Cass, 1991), pp. 182–97.

Hampshire, J., *Citizenship and Belonging: Immigration and the Politics of Demographic Governance in Post-war Britain* (Basingstoke: Palgrave MacMillan, 2005).

Hannan, M.T. and Freeman, J., *Organizational Ecology* (Cambridge, MA: Harvard University Press, 1989).

Hansen, R., 'The dog that didn't bark: dual nationality in the United Kingdom', in Hansen, R. and Weil, P. (eds) *Dual Nationality, Social Rights and Federal Citizenship in the U.S. and Europe: The Reinvention of Citizenship* (New York: Berghan Books, 2002), pp. 179–91.

Hansen, R., 'Citizenship and integration in Europe', in Joppke, C. and Morawska, E. (eds) *Toward Assimilation and Citizenship: Immigrants in Liberal Nation-States* (Basingstoke: Palgrave, 2003), pp. 87–109.

Heater, D., *What is Citizenship?* (Cambridge: Polity Press, 1999).

Heclo, H. and Madsen, H., *Policy and Politics in Sweden* (Philadelphia, PA: Temple University Press, 1987).

Heelsum, van A., 'Political participation and civic community of ethnic minorities in four cities in the Netherlands', *Politics,* 25 (1) (2005), pp. 19–31.

Hefner, R.W., 'Civil society and democracy', *Civnet's Journal for Civil Society,* 2 (3) (1998) taken from www.civnet.org/journal/issue7/journal.htm (accessed on 14-07-2003).

Held, D., *Models of Democracy* (Cambridge: Polity Press, 1987).

Held, D., *Democracy and the Global Order: From the Modern State to Cosmopolitan Governance* (Cambridge: Polity Press, 1995).

Hicks, A., 'National collective action and economic performance: a review article', *International Studies Quarterly,* 32 (1988), pp. 131–53.

Hjerm, M., 'National identity: a comparison of Sweden, Germany and Australia', *Journal of Ethnic and Migration Studies,* 24:3 (1998), pp. 451–69.

Hobbes, T., *Leviathan* (London: Dent, 1973).

Hohensinner, G., Synek, M. and Öberg, S., *Hur vi tar emot Flyktingar och Asylsökande: en Komparativ Studie av Mottagandets Praktik i Sverige och Österrike* (Uppsala: Institutet för framtidsstudier och Kulturgeografiska Institutionen, 1993).

Hollifield, J., 'Immigration and the politics of rights: the French case in a comparative perspective', in Bommes, M. and Geddes, A. (eds) *Immigration and Welfare: Challenging the Borders of the Welfare State* (London: Routledge, 2000), pp. 109–33.

Home Office webpage, taken from http://www.ind.homeoffice.gov.uk/ind/en/ home/news/archive/2004/august0/new_language_requirement.html (accessed on 02-09-2004).

Hosseini-Kaladjahl, H., *Iranians in Sweden: Economic, Cultural and Social Integration* (Stockholm: Almqvist and Wiksell International, 1997).

Hulst, van H., 'A continuing construction of crisis. Antilleans, especially Curaçaoans, in the Netherlands', in Vermeulen, H. and Peninx, R. (eds) *Immigrant Integration: The Dutch Case* (Amsterdam: Het Spinhuis, 2000), pp. 93–123.

IGC, *Overview of Asylum Applications as Reported by Participating States.* Geneva: IGC (Intergovernmental Consultations on Asylum and Migration Policies in Europe, North America and Australia, 1995).

Imhoff, E., van Schoorl, J., van der Erf, R. and van der Gang, N., *Regionale Prognose Bevolking van Turkse, Marokkaanse, Surinaamse of Antilliaanse Afkomst, 1992–2000.* (Den Haag: NIDI, 1994).

Immergut, E.M., 'The normative roots of the new institutionalism: historical institutionalism and comparative policy studies', in Benz, B. and Seibel, W. (eds) *Theorieentwicklung in der Politikwissenschaft – eine Zwischenbilanz* (Baden-Baden: Nomos Verlagsgesellschaft, 1997), pp. 325–55.

Ireland, P., 'Reaping what they sow: institutions and immigrant political participation in Western Europe', in Koopmans, R. and Statham, P. (eds) *Challenging Immigration and Ethnic Relations Politics* (Oxford: Oxford University Press, 2000), pp. 233–82.

Jackson, J.A., *The Irish in Britain* (London: Routledge, 1963).

Jacobs, B.D., *Racism in Britain* (London: Christopher Helm, 1988).

Janoski, T., *Citizenship and Civil Society: A Framework of Rights and Obligations in Liberal, Traditional, and Social Democratic Regimes* (Cambridge: Cambridge University Press, 1998).

Järtelius, A., *Bortastaden: Kommunalt invandrarmottagande i Malmö 1966–1997* (Malmö: Malmö Stad, 1998).

Jenkins, C.J. and Klandermans, B., 'The politics of social protest', in Jenkins, C.J. and Klandermans, B. (eds) *The Politics of Social Protest: Comparative Perspectives on States and Social Movements* (London: UCL Press, 1995), pp. 3–14.

Jepperson, R.L., 'Institutions, institutional effects and institutionalism', in DiMaggio, P.J. and Powell, W.W. (eds) *The New Institutionalism in Organizational Analysis* (Chicago: Chicago University Press, 1991), pp. 143–64.

Johnson, R.W., *The Long March of the French Left* (London: MacMillan, 1981).

Joppke, C. and Morawska, E., 'Integrating immigrants in liberal nation-states: policies and practices', in Joppke, C. and Morawska, E. (eds) *Toward Assimilation and Citizenship: Immigrants in Liberal Nation-States* (Basingstoke: MacMillan, 2003), pp. 1–37.

Kamrava, M., *Understanding Comparative Politics: A Framework for Analysis* (London: Routledge, 1996).

Karatani, R., *Defining British Citizenship: Empire, Commonwealth and Modern Britain* (London: Frank Cass, 2003).

Katzenstein, P., *Policy and Politics in West Germany: The Growth of a Semi-Sovereign State* (Philadelphia, PA: Temple University Press, 1987).

Keane, J., 'Introduction' in Keane, J. (ed.) *Civil Society and the State: New European Perspectives* (London: Verso, 1988), pp. 1–33.

Keohane, R.O., *Institutional Institutions and State Power: Essays in International Relations* (Boulder, CO: Westview Press, 1989).

Kitschelt, H.P., 'Opportunity structures and political protest: anti-nuclear movements in four democracies', *British Journal of Political Science*, 16:1 (1986), pp. 57–85.

Kitschelt, H.P. and McGann, A.J., *The Radical Right in Western Europe: A Comparative Analysis* (Ann Arbor: University of Michigan Press, 1995).

Kjellberg, A., 'Svensk fackföreningsrörelse ur internationellt perspektiv', in Olsson, L. and Hult, C. (eds) *Arbetets Historia* (Lund: Arbetshistoriska Seminariet, 1988), pp. 85–97.

Klandermans, B., 'The formation and mobilisation of consensus', in Klandermans, B. Kriesi, H. and Tarrow, S. (eds) *From Structure to Action: Social Movement Participation across Cultures* (New York: JAI Press, 1988), pp. 173–96.

Klandermans, B. and Oegama, D., 'Potentials, networks, motivations and barriers: steps towards participation in social movements', *American Sociological Review*, 52 (1987), pp. 519–31.

Klingemann, H.D., 'Measuring ideological conceptualisation', in Barnes, S.H. and Kaase, M. (eds) *Political Action* (Beverly Hills, CA: Sage Publications, 1979), pp. 215–54.

Köchler, H., 'The concept of the nation and the question of nationalism: the traditional "nation state" versus a multicultural "community state" ', in Dunne, M. and Bonazzi, T. (eds) *Citizenship and Rights in Multicultural Societies* (Keele: Keele University Press, 1995), pp. 43–53.

Koopmans, R., 'Good intentions sometimes make bad policy: a comparison of Dutch and German integration policies', in Giugni, M. and Passy, F. (eds) *Political Altruism: Solidarity Movements in International Perspective* (Lanham, MD: Rowman and Littlefield, 2001), pp. 111–32.

Koopmans, R., 'Migrant mobilisation and political opportunities: variation among German cities and a comparison with the United Kingdom and the Netherlands', *Journal of Ethnic and Migration Studies*, 30:3 (2004), pp. 449–70.

Koopmans, R. and Statham, P., 'Challenging the liberal nation-state? Postnationalism, multiculturalism, and the collective claims making of migrants and ethnic minorities in Britain and Germany', *The American Journal of Sociology*, 105:3 (1999), pp. 652–96.

Koopmans, R. and Statham, P., 'Migration and ethnic relations as a field of political contention: an opportunity structure approach', in Koopmans, R. and Statham, P. (eds) *Challenging Immigration and Ethnic Relations Politics: Comparative European Perspectives* (Oxford: Oxford University Press, 2000), pp. 13–57.

Koopmans, R. and Statham, P., 'How national citizenship shapes transnationalism: migrant and minority claims-making in Germany, Great Britain and the Netherlands', in Joppke, C. and Morawska, E. (eds) *Toward Assimilation and Citizenship: Immigrants in Liberal Nation-States* (Basingstoke: Palgrave, 2003), pp. 195–239.

Koopmans, R., Statham, P., Guigni, M. and Passy, P., *Contested Citizenship. Immigration and Cultural Diversity in Europe* (Minneapolis, MN: University of Minnesota Press, 2005).

Koser, K., 'Social networks and the asylum cycle: the case of Iranians in the Netherlands', *International Migration Review*, 31:3 (1997), pp. 591–611.

Kruyt, A. and Niessen, J., 'Integration', in Vermeulen, H. (ed.) *Immigrant Policy for a Multicultural Society: A Comparative Study of Integration, Language and Religious Policy in Five Western European Countries* (Brussels: Migration Policy Group, 1997), pp. 15–57.

Kymlicka, W., *Multicultural Citizenship* (Oxford: Oxford University Press, 1995).

Lacey, C., *Hightown Grammar: The School as a Social System* (Manchester: Manchester University Press, 1970).

Lane, J-E. and Ersson, S., *The New Institutional Politics: Performance and Outcomes* (London: Routledge, 2000).

Laver, M. and Schofield, N., *Multi-party Government* (Oxford: Oxford University Press, 1990).

Layton-Henry, Z., *The Politics of Race in Britain* (London: George Allen and Unwin, 1984).

Lees, C., ' "Dark matter": institutional constraints and the failure of party-based Euroscepticism in Germany', *Political Studies*, 50:2 (2002), pp. 244–67.

Lehmbruch, G., 'Introduction: neo-corporatism in comparative perspective', in Lehmbruch, G. and Schmitter, P.C. (eds) *Patterns of Corporatist Policy Making* (London: Sage, 1982), pp. 1–29.

Levy, D., 'Coming home? Ethnic Germans and the transformation of national identity in the Federal Republic of Germany', in Geddes, A. and Favell, A. (eds) *The Politics of Belonging: Migrants and Minorities in Contemporary Europe* (Aldershot: Ashgate, 1999), pp. 93–108.

Lewin, L., *Ideology and Strategy* (Cambridge: Cambridge University Press, 1988).

Lewis, J., 'Reviewing the relationship between the voluntary sector and the state in Britain in the 1990s', *International Journal of Voluntary and Nonprofit Organizations*, 10:3 (1999), pp. 255–70.

Lijphart, A., *The Politics of Accommodation: Pluralism and Democracy in the Netherlands* (Berkeley: California University Press, 1975).

Lijphart, A., *Democracy in Plural Societies: A Comparative Exploration* (New Haven, CT: Yale University Press, 1977).

Lijphart, A., *Democracies: Patterns of Majoritarian and Consensus Government in Twenty-One Countries* (New Haven, CT: Yale University Press, 1984).

Lindahl, R., 'Förbundsrepubliken Tyskland', in Lindahl, R (ed.) *Utländska Politiska System* (Lund: Dialogos, 1991), pp. 127–77.

Lindqvist, B., *Drömmar och Vardag i Exil*. *Om Chilenska Flyktingars Kulturella Strategier* (Stockholm: Carlsson, 1991).

Lin Pang, C., *The Netherlands: adaptation and integration. The debate about integration – immigrants and cultural diversities in Europe: the case of the Netherlands*, taken from www.emz.berlin.de/projekte_E/pj32_1pdf/netherlands.pdf (accessed on 9-02-2004).

Lippmann, W., *The Public Philosophy* (New York: Mentor Books, 1956).

Löfgren, O., 'The nationalization of culture', *Ethnologia Europaea, Journal of European Ethnology*, 29:1 (1989), pp. 5–24.

Lorwin, V.R., 'Segmented pluralism: ideological cleavages and political cohesion in the smaller European democracies', *Comparative Politics*, 3:2 (1971), pp. 141–75.

Lowi, T.J., 'American business, public policy, case studies and political theory', *World Politics*, 16:4 (1964), pp. 677–715.

Lowndes, V., 'Rescuing Aunt Sally: taking institutional theory seriously in urban politics', *Urban Studies*, 38:11 (2001), pp. 1953–71.

Lucardie, P., 'Fragments from the pillars: small parties in the Netherlands', in Muller-Rommel, F. and Pridham, G. (eds) *Small Parties in Western Europe – Comparative and National Perspectives* (London: Sage, 1991), pp. 115–34.

Lundberg, S., *Flyktingskap: Latinamerikaner i Exil i Sverige och Västeuropa* (Lund: Arkiv, 1989).

Lundquist, L., *Förvaltning, Stat och Samhälle* (Studentlitteratur: Lund, 1992).

Lyon, W., 'Defining ethnicity: another way of being British', in Modood, T. and Werbner, P. (eds) *The Politics of Multiculturalism in the New Europe* (London: Zed Books Ltd, 1998), pp. 186–207.

MacDonald, I. and Blake, N., *MacDonald's Immigration Law and Practice* (London: Butterworths, 1995).

McAdam, D., *Political Process and the Development of Black Insurgency, 1930–1970* (Chicago: University of Chicago Press, 1982).

McAdam, D., 'Conceptual origins, current problems, future directions', in McAdam, D. McCarthy, J.D. and Zald, M.Z. (eds) *Comparative Perspectives on Social Movements: Political Opportunities, Mobilising Structures, and Cultural Framings* (Cambridge, MA: Cambridge University Press, 1996), pp. 23–41.

McCarthy, J.D. and Zald, M.N., 'Resource mobilization and social movements: a partial theory', *American Journal of Sociology*, 82:6 (1977), pp. 1212–41.

McGovern, J.R., *Anatomy of a Lynching: The Killing of Claude Neal* (Baton Rouge: Louisiana State University Press, 1982).

McLeod, M., Owen, D. and Khamis, C., *Black and minority ethnic voluntary and community organisations: Their role and future development in England and Wales* (York: Joseph Roundtree Foundation, 2001).

Malmö Local Council, taken from http://booking.malmo.se/booking/forening.start.asp (accessed on 17-12-2002).

Malmö Local Council, taken from www.malmo.se/reg/mandat (accessed on 24-06-2003).

Malmö Statistics Office, taken from www.malmo.se (accessed, 27-01-2002).

March, J.G. and Olsen, J.P., 'The new institutionalism: organizational factors in political life', *The American Political Science Review*, 78:738 (1984), pp. 734–49.

March, J.G. and Olsen, J.P., *Rediscovering Institutions* (New York: Free Press, 1994).

Marshall, B., *Europe in Change: The New Germany and Migration in Europe* (Manchester University Press, 2000).

Marshall, T.H., *Citizenship and Social Class* (Cambridge University Press: London, 1950).

Martin, P.L., 'Germany: reluctant land of immigration', in Cornelius, W.A., Martin, P.L. and Hollifield, J.F. (eds) *Controlling Immigration: A Global Perspective* (Stanford, CA: Stanford University Press, 1994), pp. 193–225.

Melbourn, A., *Byråkratins Ansikten: Rolluppfattningar hos Svenska Högre Tjänstemän* (Stockholm: Liber förlag, 1979).

Mény, Y., 'France', in Colomer, J.M. (ed.) *Political Institutions in Europe* (London: Routledge, 1996).

Mény, Y. and Knapp, A., *Government and Politics in Western Europe; Britain, France, Italy and Germany* (Oxford: Oxford University Press, 1998).

Micheletti, M., *Civil Society and State Relations in Sweden* (Avebury: Aldershot, 1995).

Migration Information (2005a), taken from http://www.migrationinformation.org/ GlobalData/countrydata/data.cfm, accessed, 23-02-2005.

Migration Information (2005b), taken from http://www.migrationinformation.org/ Profiles/display.cfm?ID=266, accessed on 23-02-2005.

Migrationsverket, taken from www.migrationsverket.se (accessed on 19-08-2001).

Miles, R., *Racism and Migrant Labour* (London: Routledge and Kegan Paul, 1982).

Miles, R., 'Racism: the evolution of the debate about a concept changing times', in Thränhardt, D. (ed.) *Europe: A New Immigration Continent. Policies and Politics in a Comparative Perspective* (Munster: LIT, 1996), pp. 88–117.

Miles, R. and Phizacklea, A., *White Man's Country* (London: Pluto, 1984).

Mill, J.S., *On Liberty and Representative Government* (London: J.M. Dent, 1976).

Miller, D., *On Citizenship* (Oxford: Oxford University Press, 1995).

Miller, D., *Citizenship and National Identity* (Cambridge: Polity Press, 2000).

*Minderhedenbeleid in een gewijzigde situatie* (Rotterdam: Gemeente Rotterdam, 1985).

Modood, T., 'Anti-essentialism, multiculturalism and the "recognition" of religious groups', in Kymlicka, W. and Norman, W. (eds) *Citizenship in Diverse Societies* (Oxford: Oxford University Press, 2000), pp. 175–99.

Moloktos Liederman, L. 'Religious diversity in schools: the Muslim headscarf controversy and beyond' *Social Compass*, 47 (2000), pp. 367–81.

Mouffe, C., 'Democratic politics and the question of identity', in Rajchman, J. (ed.) *The Identity in Question* (London: Routledge, 1995), pp. 33–47.

Municio, I., 'Hemspråksreformen – gräsrotsbyråkrater, makt och genomförande', in Lithman, Y. (ed.) *Nybyggarna i Sverige: Invandring och Andra Generationen* (Helsingborg: Carlssons, 1987), pp. 224–71.

Muus, P.J. and Gerritsma, E., *Migration, Immigrants and Policy in the Netherlands: Recent Trends and Developments SOPEMI Netherlands* (Utrecht: ERCOMER, 2000).

Narud, H.M., *Voters, Parties and Governments: Electoral Competition, Policy Distances and Government Formation in Multi-Party Systems* (Oslo: Institute for Social Research, 1996).

National Statistics, http://www.statistics.gov.uk/cci/nugget.asp?id=764 (accessed, 18-10-2004).

Nelson, B. and Kavolis, V., 'The civilisation-analytical approach to comparative studies', *Comparative Civilizations Bulletin*, 5 (1973), pp. 13–14.

Nesdale, D. and Mak, A.S., 'Immigrant acculturation attitudes and host country identification', *Journal of Community and Applied Social Psychology*, 10 (2000), pp. 483–95.

Newton, K., 'Social capital and democracy in modern Europe', in van Deth, J.W., Maraffi, M., Newton, K. and Whiteley, P. (eds) *Social Capital and European Democracy* (London: Routledge, 1999), pp. 3–24.

Nicolaas, H. and Sprangers, A., *Migration Motives of Non-Dutch Immigrants in the Netherlands*. Paper for the UN/ECE Work Session on Migration Statistics, taken from www.unece.org/stats/documents/2001/05/migration/2.add.16.e.pdf (accessed on 03-09-2003).

Niekerk, van M., 'Paradoxes in paradise. Integration and social mobility of the Surinamese in the Netherlands', in Vermeulen, H. and Peninx, R. (eds) *Immigrant Integration: The Dutch Case* (Amsterdam: Het Spinhuis, 2000), pp. 64–93.

Nollert, M., 'Neocorporatism and political protest in Western Democracies: a cross-national analysis', in Jenkins, C.J. and Klandermans, B. (eds) *The Politics of Social Protest: Comparative Perspectives on States and Social Movements* (London: UCL Press, 1995), pp. 138–67.

Norval, A.J., 'Social ambiguity and the crisis of apartheid', in Laclau, E. (ed.) *The Making of Political Identities* (London: Verso, 1994), pp. 115–38.

*Nota Migranten in Rotterdam* (Rotterdam: Gemeente Rotterdam, 1978).

Nozick, R., *Anarchy, State and Utopia* (Oxford: Blackwell, 1974).

Oberschall, A., *Social Conflict and Social Movements* (Englewood Hills: Prentice Hall, 1973).

Odmalm. P., 'Civil society and migrant organisations in Sweden', *Journal of Ethnic and Migration Studies*, 30:3 (2004a), pp. 471–89.

Odmalm. P., 'Invandrarföreningar som intressekanaler – möjligheter och hinder på lokal nivå', in Bengtsson, B. (ed.) *Föreningsliv, Makt och Integration* (Fritzes Offentliga Publikationer: Stockholm, 2004b), pp. 99–129.

Odmalm, P. and Lees, C., 'Getting ethnic questions on the agenda: party formation as a strategy for social movements', *Social* Movements Studies: *Journal of Social, Cultural and Political Protest*, forthcoming.

OECD, *Acquisition of nationality in selected OEDCD countries*, taken from http://www.oecd.org/dataoecd/24/5/2956518.xls, accessed on 23-02-2005.

Official Website of the Office of the French Prime Minister and Government, taken from http://www.archives.premier-ministre.gouv.fr/jospin_version3/en/ie4/contenu/29905.htm, accessed on 24-01-05.

Oliver, D. and Heater, D., *The Foundations of Citizenship* (Hemel Hempstead: Harwester Wheatsheaf, 1994).

Olsen, J.P., *Statsstyre og institusjonsutformning* (Oslo: Universitetsforlaget, 1988).

Olsen, M., 'Social and political participation of Blacks', *American Sociological Review*, 35:4 (1970), pp. 682–96.

Oommen, T.K., *Citizenship, Nationality and Ethnicity: Reconciling Competing Identities* (Oxford: Polity Press, 1997).

Östergaard-Nielsen, E.K., *Turkish and Kurdish Transnational Political Mobilisation in Germany and the Netherlands* (Paper presented at Conference on Migration and Development, Princeton University, 4–6 May 2000).

Penninx, R. Schoorl, J. and Praag, van C., *The Impact of International Migration on Receiving Countries: The Case of the Netherlands* (The Hague: NIDI, 1994).

Penninx, R., 'Immigration, minorities policy and multiculturalism in Dutch society since 1960', in Westin, C. (ed.) *The Challenge of Diversity: Integration and Pluralism, in Societies of Immigration* (Aldershot: Avebury, 1996), pp. 187–207.

Peters, B.G., *Institutions Theory in Political Theory: The 'New' Institutionalism* (London: Pinter, 1999).

Petersson, O., *Swedish Government and Politics* (Stockholm: CD Fritzes AB, 1994).

Petersson, O., Westholm, A., and Blomberg, G., *Medborgarnas Makt* (Helsingborg: Carlssons, 1989).

248    *Bibliography*

Peterson, T., Stigendal, M., and Fryklund, B., *Skånepartiet: Om Folkligt Missnöje i Malmö* (Lund: Arkiv Förlag, 1998).

Platform Buitenlanders Rijnmond (PBR), taken from www.migrantenkoepelpbr.nl, (accessed on 13-07-2003).

Pontusson, J., *Swedish Social Democracy and British Labour: Essays on the Nature and Conditions of Social Democratic Hegemony*. Western Societies Papers No. 19 (Ithaca, NY: Cornell University, 1988).

Powell, W.W., and DiMaggio, P., 'Introduction', in Powell, W.W. and DiMaggio, P. (eds) *The New Institutionalism in Organizational Analysis* (Chicago: Chicago University Press, 1991), pp. 1–38.

Pred, A., *Even in Sweden: Racisms, Racialized Spaces, and the Popular Geographical Imagination* (Berkeley, CA: University of California Press, 2000).

Prior, D., Stewart, J. and Walsh, K., *Citizenship: Rights, Community and Participation* (London: Pitman Publishing, 1995).

Putnam, R., Leonardi, R. and Nenetti, R.Y., *Making Democracy Work: Civic Traditions in Modern Italy* (Princeton, N.J: Princeton University Press, 1993).

Putten, van J., 'Policy styles in the Netherlands: negotiation and conflict', in Richardson, J. (ed.) *Policy Styles in Western Europe* (London: George Allen and Unwin, 1982), pp. 168–97.

Rath, J., *Minorisering: de sociale constructie van 'etnische minderheden'* (Amsterdam: Het Spinnhuis, 1991).

Rath, J., Penninx, R., Groenendijk, K. and Meyer, A., *Western Europe and its Islam: The Netherlands, Belgium and Great Britain React to an Emerging Religious Community* (Amsterdam: Het Spinhuis, 2001).

Regeringskansliet, *Sweden in 2000 – A Country of Migration: Past, Present and Future* (Stockholm: Ministry for Foreign Affairs, 2000).

Reich, S., 'The four faces of institutionalism: public policy and a pluralistic perspective', *Governance*, 13:4 (2000), pp. 501–22.

Rex, J., Tomlinson, S. and Hearnden, D., *Colonial Immigrants in a British City: a Class Analysis* (London: Routledge, 1979).

Rex, J. and Drury, B., *Ethnic Mobilisation in a Multi-cultural Europe* (Aldershot: Ashgate, 1994).

Riesenberg, P., *Citizenship in the Western Tradition: Plato to Rousseau* (Chapel Hill: University of North Carolina Press, 1992).

Riker, W.H., 'Implications from the disequilibrium of majority rule for the study of institutions', *American Political Science Review*, 74 (1980), pp. 27–43.

Ring, H., 'Refugees in Sweden: inclusion and exclusion in the welfare state', in Miles, R. and Thränbart, D. (eds) *Migration and European Integration: The Dynamics of Inclusion and Exclusion* (London: Pinter, 1995), pp. 159–76.

Robertson, D.A., *Theory of Party Competition* (London: Wiley, 1976).

Rockman, B.A., 'The new institutionalism and the old institutionalism', in Dodd, L.C. and Jillson, C. (eds) *New Perspectives on American Politics* (Washington, DC: Congressional Quarterly Press, 1994), pp. 143–62.

Rogers, A., Tillie, J. and Vertovec, S., 'Introduction: multicultural policies and modes of citizenship in European cities', in Rogers, A. and Tillie, J. (eds) *Multicultural Polices and Modes of Citizenship in European Cities* (Aldershot: Avebury, 2001), pp. 1–13.

Rojas, M., *Förnyelse och Medborgarmakt: Moderat Politik mot Social Segregation och Utanförskap* (Arbetsgrupp mot social segregation och utanförskap, Rapport till partistämman, 1999).

Rothstein, B., 'Political institutions: an overview', in Goodin, R.E. and Klingemann, H.D. (eds) A *New Handbook for Political Science* (Oxford: Oxford University Press, 1996), pp. 133–66.

Rotterdam Local Council, taken from www.stadhuis.rotterdam.nl (accessed on 24-01-2003).

Rueschmeyer, D., Stephens, E.H. and Stephens, J.D., *Capitalist Development and Democracy* (Cambridge: Polity Press, 1992).

Ruin, O., *Att Komma Överens och Tänka Efter Före: Politisk Stil och 1970–talets Svenska Samhällsutveckling* (Stockholms Universitet: Statsvetenksapliga Institutionen, 1981).

Ruin, O., 'Sweden in the 1970s: policy-making becomes more difficult', in Richardson, J. (ed.) *Policy Styles in Western Europe* (London: George Allen and Unwin, 1982), pp. 141–68.

Samers, M., 'Invisible capitalism: political economy and the regulation of undocumented immigration in France', *Economy and Society*, 32:4 (2003), pp. 555–83.

Sartori, G., 'Concept misinformation in comparative politics', *American Political Science Review*, 64 (1970), pp. 1033–53.

Saunders, P. and Klau, F., *The Role of the Public Sector: Causes and Consequences of the Growth of Government* (Paris: Organisation for Economic Co-operation and Development, 1985).

Schain, M., 'Minorities and immigrant incorporation in France: the State and the dynamics of multiculturalism', in Joppke, C. and Lukes, S. (eds) *Multicultural Questions* (Oxford: Oxford University Press, 1999), pp. 199–223.

Schick, A., 'Governments versus budget deficits', in Weaver, K.R. and Rockman, B.A. (eds) *Do Institutions Matter?: Government Capabilities in the United States and Abroad* (Washington, DC: The Brookings Institution, 1993), pp. 187–235.

Schmidt, M.G., 'Germany: the grand coalition state', in Colomer, J.M. (ed.) *Political Institutions in Europe* (London: Routledge, 1996).

Schmitter, P.C., 'Still the century of corporatism?', in Schmitter, P.C. and Lehmbruch, G. (eds) *Trend Towards Corporatist Intermediation* (Beverly Hills, CA: Sage, 1979), pp. 259–81.

Schmitter, P.C., 'Interest intermediation and regime governability in contemporary Western Europe and North America', in Berger, S. (ed.) *Organizing Interests in Western Europe* (Cambridge: Cambridge University Press, 1981), pp. 287–327.

Schnapper, D., Krief, P. and Peignard, E., *French Immigration and Integration Policy*, EFFNATIS Working Paper 30 (2003), taken from http://www.uni-bamberg.de/projekte/effnatis/Paper30_EHESS.pdf, accessed on 25-01-2005.

Schopflin, G., *Nations, Identity, Power: the New Politics of Europe* (London: Hurst, 2000).

Schrover, M., *Immigrant Organisations in the Netherlands: Then and Now*. Paper presented for the workshop 'Paths of Integration: Similarities and Differences in the Settlement' (IMIS Osnabrueck, 19–21 June 2003).

Schumpeter, J., *Capitalism, Socialism and Democracy* (London: Allen and Unwin, 1943).

SFS 2000:216, *Förordning (2000:216) om statsbidrag till organisationer som främjar integration* (Swedish Department of Justice: Stockholm, 2000).

Shepsle, K.A. and Bonchek, M.S., *Analyzing Politics: Rationality, Behaviour and Institutions* (New York: Norton and Company, 1997).

Sherman, A., *Island Refuge: Britain and Refugees from the Third Reich* (London: Karia Press, 1973).

Siaroff, A., 'Corporatism in 24 industrial democracies: meaning and measurement', *European Journal of Political Research*, 36 (1999), pp. 175–205.

Skinner, Q., *The Foundations of Modern Political Thought* (Cambridge: Cambridge University Press, 1978).

Skocpol, T., *Protecting Soldiers and Mothers: The Political Origins of Social Policy in the United States* (Cambridge: Cambridge University Press, 1992).

Skowronek, S., *Building a New American State: The Expansion of National Administrative Capacities 1877–1920* (Cambridge: Cambridge University Press, 1982).

Smeets, H. and Veenman, J., 'Three generations of Moluccans in the Netherlands', in Vermeulen, H. and Penninx, R. (eds) *Immigrant Integration: The Dutch Case* (Amsterdam: Het Spinhuis, 2000), pp. 36–64.

Smith, A., *The Ethnic Origins of Nationalism* (Oxford: Basil Blackwell, 1986).

Smith, G., 'In search of small parties: problems of definition, classification and significance', in Muller-Rommel, F. and Pridham, G. (eds) *Small Parties in Western Europe: Comparative and National Perspectives* (London: Sage, 1991), pp. 23–41.

Soininen, M., 'The "Swedish Model" as an institutional framework for immigrant membership rights', *Journal of Ethnic and Migration Studies*, 25:4 (1999), pp. 685–702.

Solomos, J. and Schuster, L., 'Citizenship, multiculturalism, and the politics of identity: contemporary dilemmas and policy agendas', in Koopmans, R. and Statham, P. (eds) *Challenging Immigration and Ethnic Relations Politics: Comparative European Perspectives* (Oxford: Oxford University Press, 2000), pp. 74–95.

Solomos, J., *Race and Racism in Britain* (Basingstoke: Palgrave MacMillan, 2003).

SOU 1974:69. *Invandrarutredningens betänkande Invandrarna och Minoriteterna* (Stockholm: Fakta Info Direkt).

SOU 1984:58. *Invandrar- och minoritetspolitiken: slutbetänkande av Invandrarpolitiska kommittén* (Stockholm: Fakta Info Direkt).

SOU 1996:55. *Sverige, Framtiden och Mångfalden: slutbetänkande av Invandrarpolitiska kommittén* (Stockholm: Fakta Info Direkt).

SOU 1999:34. *Svenskt Medborgarskap: slutbetänkande av 1997 ars medborgarskapskommitté* (Stockholm: Fakta Info Direkt).

Soysal, Y.N., *Limits of Citizenship: Migrants and Postnational Membership in Europe* (Chicago: University of Chicago Press, 1994).

Spencer, I., *British Immigration since 1939: the Making of Multi-Racial Britain* (London: Routledge, 1997).

Statistiska Centralbyrån (SCB), taken from www.malmo.se (accessed on 25-03-2002).

Statistiska Centralbyrån (SCB), taken from www.scb.se (accessed on 23-02-2005).

Stolcke, V., 'New rhetorics of exclusion in Europe', *International Social Science Journal*, 51:159 (1999), pp. 25–35.

Steenburgen, van B., 'The condition of citizenship: an introduction', in Steenburgen, van B. (ed.) *The Condition of Citizenship* (London: Sage, 1994), pp. 1–10.

Steiner, J., *European Democracies* (New York: Longman, 1998).

Steinmo, S. and Thelen, K., 'Historical institutionalism in comparative politics', in Steinmo, S., Thelen, K. and Longsreth, F. (eds) *Structuring Politics: Historical Institutionalism in Comparative Analysis* (Cambridge: Cambridge University Press, 1992), pp. 1–32.

Stepan, A., *Arguing Comparative Politics* (Oxford: Oxford University Press, 2001).

Stone, J., 'Race, ethnicity, and the Weberian legacy', *American Behaviourial Scientist*, 38:3 (1995), pp. 391–406.

Swedish Institute, *Fact Sheet on Sweden*, taken from www.si.se/docs/infosweden/engelska/fs63.pdf (accessed on 10-07-2001).

Swedish National Board for Health and Welfare, *Levnadsförhållanden hos fyra invandrargrupper födda i Chile, Iran, Polen och Turkiet* (Stockholm: Norstedts, 1998).

Swedish Immigration Policy (SIP), Official document from the Ministry of Labour (1983).

Swedner, H., *Invandrare i Malmö: Forskningsrapport från invandrarutredningen* (Stockholm: Ministry of Interior, 1973).

Taggart, P., *Populism* (Buckingham: Open University Press: Concepts in the Social Sciences, 2000).

Taggart, P., *2004 European Parliament Election Briefing No.14: The European Parliament Election in the United Kingdom 2004*, taken from http://www.sussex.ac.uk/sei/ 1-4-2-2.html (accessed, 11-11-2004).

Tajfel, H., *Differentiation Between Social Groups: Studies in the Social Psychology of Intergroup Relations* (London: Sage, 1978).

Tarrow, S., *Power in Movement: Social Movements, Collective Action and Politics* (Cambridge: Cambridge University Press, 1994).

Tarrow, S., 'States and opportunities', in McAdam, D., McCarthy, J.D. and Zald, M.N. (eds) *Comparative Perspectives on Social Movements: Political Opportunities, Mobilizing Structures, and Cultural Framings* (Cambridge, MA: Cambridge University Press, 1996), pp. 41–61.

Tarrow, S., *Power in Movement: Social Movements and Contentious Politics* (Cambridge: Cambridge University Press, 1998).

Taylor, C., 'The politics of recognition', in Gutmann, A. (ed.) *Multiculturalism: Examining the Politics of Recognition* (Princeton, N.J: Princeton University Press, 1994), pp. 25–75.

Tema Modersmål, taken from www.modersmalsskolutveckling.se/projekt (accessed on 19-06-2003).

Theen, R.H.W. and Wilson, F.L., *Comparative Politics: An Introduction to Seven Countries* (Upper Saddle River, N.J: Prentice Hall, 2001).

Thielemann, E., 'Between interests and norms: explaining burden-sharing in the European Union', *Journal of Refugee Studies*, 16 (2003), pp. 253–73.

Thränhardt, D., 'Germany's Immigration Policies and Politics', in Brochmann, G. and Hammar, T. (eds) *Mechanisms of Immigration Control: A Comparative Analysis of European Regulation Policies* (Oxford: Berg, 1999), pp. 29–58.

Thränhardt, D., 'Conflict, consensus, and policy outcomes: immigration and integration in Germany and the Netherlands', in Koopmans, R. and Statham, P., *Challenging Immigration and Ethnic Relations Politics: Comparative European Perspectives* (Oxford: Oxford University Press, 2000), pp. 162–86.

Tillie, J., *De Etnische Stem; Opkomst en Stemgedrag van Migranten tijdens Gemeenteraadsverkiezingen, 1986–1998* (Utrecht: Forum, 2000).

Tilly, C., *From Mobilization to Revolution* (New York: Random House, 1978).

Tocqueville, A. de, *Democracy in America*. Edited by Bowen, F. and Bradley, P., (New York: Knopf, 1972).

*Treaty concerning the Accession of the Kingdom of Denmark, Ireland, the Kingdom of Norway and the United Kingdom of Great Britain and Northern Ireland to the EEC and the European Atom Energy Community (with Final Act) Decision of the Council of the European Community Concerning the Accession of Said States to the European Coal and Steel Community*, Cmnd. 4862-I, HMSO, 22 January 1972.

Tsebelis, G., *Nested Games: Rational Choice in Comparative Politics* (Berkeley: University of California Press, 1990).

Turner, J., 'Social comparison and social identity: some prospects for intergroup behaviour', *European Journal of Social Psychology*, 5 (1975), pp. 5–34.

Twine, F., *Citizenship and Social Rights: The Interdependence of Self and Society* (London: SAGE Publications, 1994).

252    Bibliography

Uddhammar, E., *Partierna och den Stora Staten: En Analys av Statsteorier och Svensk Politik under 1900-talet* (Stockholm: City University Press, 1993).
Ugelvik Larsen, S. and Ugelvik, I.L., 'Scandinavia', in Eatwell, R. (ed.) *European Political Cultures: Conflict or Convergence?* (New York: Routledge, 1997), pp. 210–33.
Vasta, E., 'The politics of community', in Vasta, E. (ed.) *Citizenship, Community and Democracy* (Basingstoke: Macmillan and St. Martin's Press, 2000), pp. 107–27.
Verba, S., and Nie, N.H., *Participation in America* (New York: Harper and Row, 1972).
Vermeulen, F., *Why Do Migrant Organisations Exist? – A Theoretical Approach to the Formation and Development of Migrant Organisation.* Paper presented at the workshop 'Migrant Organisations I' for Network Ethnicity and Migration (European Social Science History Conference, The Hague, 27 February 2002).
Vermeulen, F., *The Immigrant Organising Process: The Emergence and Persistance of Turkish Immigrant Organisations in Amsterdam and Berlin and Surinamese Organisations in Amsterdam, 1960–2000* (Amsterdam: IMES, 2005).
Vermeulen, H. and Penninx, R., 'Introduction', in Vermeulen, H. and Penninx, R. (eds) *Immigrant Integration: The Dutch Case,* (Amsterdam: Het Spinhuis, 2000), pp. 1–36.
Vogel, J. and Hjerm, M., '90-tals Krisen Slog Hårt Mot Flyktingar', *Välfärdsbulletinen* (2002).
Wahlbäck, K., 'Frankrike', in Lindahl, R. (ed.), *Utländska Politiska System* (Lund: Dialogos, 1991), pp. 56–88.
Waldron, J., 'Cultural identity and civic responsibility', in Kymlicka, W. and Norman, W. (eds) *Citizenship in Diverse Societies* (Oxford: Oxford University Press, 2000), pp. 155–75.
Wallin, G., 'Towards the integrated and fragmented state: the mixed role of local government', in Lane, J-E. (ed.) *Understanding the Swedish Model* (London: Frank Cass, 1991), pp. 96–122.
Walzer, M., 'The concept of civil society', in Walzer, M. (ed.) *Toward a Global Civil Society* (Oxford: Berghan Books, 1998), pp. 7–29.
Weaver, K.R. and Rockman, B.A., 'Assessing the effects of institutions', in Weaver, K.R. and Rockman, B.A. (eds) *Do Institutions Matter?: Government Capabilities in the United States and Abroad* (Washington, DC: The Brookings Institution, 1993), pp. 1–40.
Weber, M., *Economy and Society* (New York: Bedminster, 1968).
Weil, P., 'Nationalities and citizenships: the lessons of the French experience for Germany and Europe', in Cesarani, D. and Fulbrook, M. (eds) *Citizenship, Nationality and Migration in Europe* (London: Routledge, 1996), pp. 74–87.
Weingast, B.R., 'Political institutions: rational choice perspectives', in Goodin, R.E. and Klingemann, H.D. (eds) *A New Handbook of Political Science* (Oxford: Oxford University Press, 1996), pp. 167–90.
Westin, C., 'Equality, freedom of choice and partnership: multicultural policy in Sweden', in Baubӧck, R., Heller, A. and Zolberg, A.R. (eds) *The Challenge of Diversity: Integration and Pluralism in Societies of Immigration* (Aldershot: Avebury, 1996), pp. 207–27.
Westin, C., interviewed in Andersen, J., Rydahl, M. and Salehi K.E., *Personer med Invandrarbakgrunds Engagemang i den Svenska Politiken: Bildandet av Partiet, Regnbågen i Malmö* (Malmö: IMER, 1998).
Westin, C. and Dingu-Kyrklund, E., *Reducing Immigration and Reviewing Integration The Swedish Rimet Report for 1995: An Account of the Current Facts, Figures and Legislation Concerning Multiculturalism in Sweden* (Stockholm: CEIFO, 1996).
Whitehead, L., 'Bowling in the Bronx: the uncivil interstices between civil and political society', in Fine, R. and Shirin, R. (eds) *Civil Society: Democratic Perspectives* (London: Frank Cass, 1997), pp. 94–115.

Widgren, J., *Svensk Invandringspolitik – En faktabok* (Lund: Liber förlag, 1982).

Wieviorka, M., *La France Raciste* (Paris: Fayard, 1992).

Wieviorka, M., 'Contextualizing French multiculturalism and racism', *Theory, Culture and Society* 17:1 (2000), pp. 157–62.

Williamson, P.J., *Corporatism in Perspective: An Introductory Guide to Corporatist Theory* (London: Sage, 1989).

Withol de Wenden, C., 'The French debate: legal and political instruments to promote integration', in Fassman, H. and Münz, R. (eds) *European Migration in the Late Twentieth Century: Historical Patterns, Actual Trends, and Social Implications* (Aldershot: Edward Elgar, 1994), pp. 67–81.

WRR, *Etnische minderheden* (Den Haag: Staatsuitgeverij, 1979).

WRR, *Allochtonenbeleid* (Den Haag: Sdu Uitgeverij, 1989).

Wusten, van der H. and Roessingh, M., 'Belgium and the Netherlands', in Eatwell, R. (ed.) *European Political Cultures: Conflict or Convergence?* (New York: Routledge, 1997), pp. 32–50.

Young, I.M., *Justice and the Politics of Difference* (Princeton, N.J: Princeton University Press, 1990).

Zizek, S., 'Identity and its vicissitudes; Hegel's "logic of essence" as a theory of ideology', in Laclau, E. (ed.) *The Making of Political Identities* (London: Verso, 1994), pp. 40–76.

Zolberg, A.R., 'Modes of incorporation: toward a comparative framework', in Steenburgen, van B. (ed.) *The Condition of Citizenship* (London: Sage, 1994), pp. 139–55.

## Interviews

### Elite

*Malmö and Rotterdam*

Christian Democrat A (Christen-Democratisch Appèl), male, interview conducted 19-04-2001, Rotterdam.

Christian Democrat B (Christen-Democratisch Appèl), male, interview conducted 06-05-2002, Rotterdam.

Christian Democrat (Kristdemokraterna), male, interview conducted 07-02-2001, Malmö.

Conservative Party A (Moderaterna), male, interview conducted 15-02-2001, Malmö.

Conservative Party B (Moderaterna), female, interview conducted 08-02-2001, Malmö.

D66 A (Democraten 66), male, interview conducted 19-04-2001, Rotterdam.

Manager of Ethnic Relations A (Etniska Relationer), female, interview conducted 09-03-2001, Malmö.

Ex-Rainbow Party A, male, interview conducted 19-07-2000, Malmö.

Ex-Rainbow Party B, male, interview conducted 09-08-2000, Malmö.

FNV A (Federatie Nederlandse Vakbeweging (Dutch Federation of Trade Unions), male, interview conducted 02-05-2001, Rotterdam.

Green party A (Groen Links), male, interview conducted 23-04-2001, Rotterdam.

Green Party B (Miljöpartiet), female, interview conducted 06-02-2001, Malmö.

Left Party A (Vänsterpartiet), female, interview conducted 26-02-2001, Malmö.

Left Party B (Vänsterpartiet), female, interview conducted 26-02-2001, Malmö.

Liberal Democrat A (Folkpartiet), male, interview conducted 14-02-2001, Malmö.

LO A (Landsorganisationen (Confederation of Trade Unions), male, interview conducted 07-02-2001.

Director of Malmö Board of Recreation A, male, interview conducted 06-03-2001, Malmö. NGO Co-ordinator A, female, interview conducted 06-03-2001.
SAMS A (Stedelijke Adviescommissie Multiculturele Stad (Advisory Organ for the Local Council), male, interview conducted 23-04-2001, Rotterdam. NGO, Co-ordinator A, female, interview conducted 06-03-2001.
SIF A (Svenska Industritjänstemannaförbundet (Union for Professional Employees representative), male, interview conducted 28-02-2001.
Advisor of Social and Economic Affairs A, male, interview conducted 02-05-2001, Rotterdam.
Socialdemocrat A (Socialdemokratiska Arbetarpartiet), male, interview conducted 05-02-2001, Malmö.
Socialdemocrat B (Partij van de Arbeid), male, interview conducted 24–04–2001, Rotterdam.
Socialdemocrat C (Socialdemokratiska Arbetarpartiet) and FAI (Association for migrants active in unions) representative, female, interview conducted 13-02-2001, Malmö.
Socialdemocrat D (Socialdemokratiska Arbetarpartiet), male, interview conducted 02-09-2001, Malmö.
Socialdemocrat E (Partij van de Arbeid), female, interview conducted 06-05-2002, Rotterdam.
Socialdemocrat F (Partij van de Arbeid), male, interview conducted 06-05-2002, Rotterdam.
Socialist Party A (Socialistische Partij), male, interview conducted 19-04-2001, Rotterdam.
Socialist Party B (Socialistische Partij), male, interview conducted 23-04-2001, Rotterdam.
VVD A (Volkspartij voor Vrijheid en Democratie), male, interview conducted 25-04-2001.

## Non-elite in Malmö

### Chileans

Male, mid-50s, interview conducted 06-02-2001.
Female, early-30s, interview conducted 13-03-2001.
Male, early-30s, interview conducted 13-03-2001.
Male, late-30s, interview conducted 28-09-2001.

### Iranians

Iranian-Swedish Association representative, male, mid-40s, interview conducted 03-02-2001.
Male, early-30s, interview conducted 04-03-2001.
Female, mid-30s, interview conducted 12-03-2001.
Male, late-20s, Iranian Solidarity Association representative, interview conducted 11-09-2001.

### Turkish

Male, late-30s, Turkish association representative, interview conducted 13-02-2001.
Male, mid-50s, ex-member of the Turkish Association, interview conducted, 06-09-2001.

## Non-elite in Rotterdam

*Iranians*

Male, late-50s, IRC representative, interview conducted 07-05-2001.

Female, late-30s, IRC representative, interview conducted 27-05-2002.

*Surinamese*

Hindustani Male, late-30s, KROSBE representative, interview conducted 23-04-2001.

Hindustani Male, mid-50s, interview conducted 23-04-2001.

Creole Male, late-40s, Wimasanga representative, interview conducted 15-05-2002.

*Turkish*

Male, mid-40s, HADD representative, interview conducted 07-05-2001.

# Index